THE HIDDEN
JOB MARKET

THE HIDDEN JOB MARKET

A System to Beat the System

by TOM JACKSON
and DAVIDYNE MAYLEAS

NYT

Quadrangle / The New York Times Book Co.

Library of Congress Cataloging in Publication Data

Jackson, Tom.
    The hidden job market.

    1. Vocational guidance.   2. Labor supply.
3. Success.   I. Mayleas, Davidyne, joint author.
II. Title.
HF5381.J36   650'.14   74-24284
ISBN 0-8129-0602-0

This book is lovingly
dedicated to my family:

Mother
Pete
Louise
Dick
Bunkie

—TWJ

This work is dedicated to my husband, William Mayleas, who first taught me what it meant to do the work you want to do.

—DM

CONTENTS

Part Four · MORE TOOLS

A SYSTEM TO BEAT THE SYSTEM

This book is for men and women dealing with today's economy—the employed and the unemployed. It is based on the interaction of three major principles—game rules as we call them—that when properly applied can help you beat the American job system. The heart of our system rests on the existence of the *hidden job market*. Eighty-five to 90 percent of the jobs available on any given day exist in the *hidden job market*, not in the classified ads or the employment agency listings or in placement offices. This book arms you with strategies for locating that market. The system, which is the product of many thousands of hours of research and testing, takes you even further. It shows you how to be your own best job counselor; it shows you not only how to locate jobs you want, but once you do, it instructs you in methods and techniques for presenting yourself in the most favorable light to a prospective employer and for landing a job.

The system has value even for those not actively seeking a new position now. It gives an insider's view of how the job market actually functions; shows how to translate your skills and interests into work which is personally satisfying as well as economically rewarding; and how to do this in hard times as well as in good times. It also gives you a personal course of action to advance your future career growth.

The Hidden Job Market is a series of games—tactical games—which require your participation. In effect, *you* are writing this book with us, and so the system which we create together is, as you will see once you begin the book, customized to meet your needs. The games and exercises will work for you. They were originally developed under a federal contract which had the objective of uncovering new ways for people to deal with their lives in work terms. Since then, the ideas and techniques have been expanded and tested with thousands of people and have proven successful, no matter how high the unemployment rate has been.

When you understand our new system you will have a totally fresh view of how to choose your job objectives, and even more, how to achieve them.

Part One

EXPLORATION

RULES OF THE GAME

Rule One: Get in Touch With
the *Hidden Job Market*

The System: For years most people have felt that the jobs that exist for them are those which are shown in today's classified section or in employment agency listings. When they have wanted to change jobs or investigate new opportunities for themselves they have joined with thousands of others, calling the same telephone numbers, sending resumes to the same box numbers, sitting in the same waiting rooms.

The New System: It now is recognized that on any given day, only 10 to 15 percent of the available job openings are listed in the newspapers or with agencies. There is another vastly larger reservoir of jobs and opportunities available for consideration. These are the thousands of positions which are in the process of being created, or revised, or which you can create within a company if you know how. These jobs are available but have not yet, or may never, flow through the corporate pipeline into the public job market. These openings are in the *hidden job market*. In Part Two of this book—Strategies—we will show you how to locate the *hidden job market* where 85 to 90 percent of the job openings actually exist. When you know how to get in touch with the *hidden job market* you will have a private, major advantage over the competition for the rest of your working life. You will never then have to rely on someone else to tell you what's available. You will be able to control your own career growth.

Rule Two: It Is Not the Best Qualified People
Who Get the Jobs but Those Who Are
the Best Qualified at Job Getting

The System: For years everyone has believed that if you were the best qualified for a particular job, you would get it. You simply sent in a resume, sat back, and waited for the employer to invite you in and make an offer. Sometimes the employer did, more often he didn't. If he didn't, you assumed someone more qualified than you had shown up.

The New System: Any manager or personnel interviewer will tell you that there are a multitude of job applicants who submit resumes and take interviews that give the potential employer no indication that they are admirably qualified for a particular job. That's why those who *do* get the job offers are actually the applicants who make the best overall self-presentation, who know how to relate their resumes and interviews to the needs of the prospective employer. *These people have made job seeking itself into a skill. They get the jobs.*

We have interviewed hundreds of successful job getters, as well as employment counselors, placement officials, and supervisors, and distilled for you, from their observations, the elements involved in a successful self-selling presentation. In Parts Two and Three of this book we deal with how you analyze your most rewarding job prospects, develop the necessary techniques for writing resumes, taking interviews, and much more, to help you develop for yourself the crucial job-getting skills.

Rule Three: Be Prepared to Have Two or Three Careers in Your Lifetime

The System: Time was when people took a job they were trained for or followed their father's occupational path, and expected to stay in that job area, that industry, for life. It meant stability. That's not the way it is today.

The New System: Because of the accelerating economic, social, political, and technological changes which the world is now experiencing, it is highly likely that the specific job area that you are working in, or seeking now, will become obsolete before you are ready for retirement. Whole industries and the jobs associated with them can change or disappear within a few years.

You will need to be able to have two, or more, entirely different careers in your lifetime as you adapt to this ever-changing work world. How to make these necessary adaptations is part of our system. We will show you how to analyze your skills and interests, and how to relate them to the constantly changing work world in a way that keeps you abreast of the demand cycle.

THE WORK PLEASURE OPTION

Once you understand that you must be prepared to have several careers in a lifetime, and that to do this you need to have a fuller understanding of your skills and interests, an important idea emerges: *Finding what you like to do, what gives you "Work Pleasure," is your best job security.* If you do what you like to do, if you enjoy your work, you will do it that much better. You will put more into it. If you do a better job, you will render more value to an employer—you will be worth more. And if you are worth more, you will get more. Work Pleasure equates with Work Survival.

That is why Part One of this book concerns itself, not with strategies for dealing with the external job market, but with games and techniques for making a journey of self-discovery into yourself as a total human being, not as a Job Title—accountant, salesman, purchasing agent. *The total you* covers a variety of skills and interests, many of which you may not even realize exist. This complex of skills and interests will, when fully appreciated, give you considerably more opportunity for choice in the world of work, and provide you with one of the most valuable survival skills you can have in our ever-shifting economy. With this skill developed, you will not again be afraid of being "furloughed."

Moreover, once you know what gives you work pleasure, and recognize how this pleasure relates to work skills, you take a giant step into the *hidden job market*. You arrive there knowing what you are looking for, not floundering around, groping for "any job."

Given the employment situation as it is today, we fully realize that if you are unemployed you may in panic want to go straight to Parts Two, Three, and Four to learn the tactics and strategies for dealing with the job market. You may want to ignore entirely the self-exploration of Part One. Before you do that think twice. Think three times. Don't do it. The extra hours put in on Part One will give you a much clearer picture of who you are in relation to the world of work— where you want to go, how you want to feel during the 10,000 days of your life that you will probably be working. This self-insight can only increase your efficiency in job changing.

Not only will your motivation be increased by the prospect of finding work that you like, rather than any job for a paycheck, but the clearer picture you obtain of your own interests and skills will enable you to make a much stronger self-presentation to a prospective employer when the time comes.

WARNING

Now that we have told you the Game Rules, and indicated how this book will make it possible for you to deal more profitably with the job market, we must add a warning. If you ignore it, you neutralize most of the value the book can have for you. It is this: This book, unlike any other book you have ever read, is *unfinished, half-written*. It is half-written because we could *not* finish it without you. *You* are its co-author. The book is about *you* and no one else in the world. For the sake of your own success, and a happier, more pleasurable survival in the world of work, you must obey this crucial warning. It is the glue that binds you and us together for your future success.

YOU MUST WRITE IN THIS BOOK WHEREVER WE INDICATE THAT YOU SHOULD WRITE, AND, IF NECESSARY, OVERLAP INTO MARGINS AND SPILL OVER THE PAGE. Use this book, write in it, participate in the exercises, play the games, do the outside work as well as the introspective work, *follow the rules*. When you do, you will be fully versed in the system that beats the system. The *hidden job market* will then be at your disposal.

1

WORK ITSELF

When you head down to work Monday morning, in your car, on your bike, on the bus, subway, or on foot, how do you feel about the coming work week? Check the statements below that you have come to associate with "going to work."

_____ Numb
_____ Nervous
_____ I like my work better than weekends
_____ Sick—the economy worries me
_____ Scared—I'm out of work
_____ Anxious—I'm looking for my first job
_____ It's eight A.M. I'm a night person
_____ I wish I'd gone to college
_____ Fifty-fifty, it's not all bad
_____ I should be making more money
_____ It's a pleasure
_____ I like the people I work with
_____ Charged up
_____ I'm afraid of another layoff
_____ Is this why I went to college?
_____ The bills have to be paid
_____ Stale
_____ Fulfilled

_____ I love my work
_____ I need a change
_____ No complaints
_____ It's drudgery
_____ There must be more to life
_____ I feel like a whore
_____ I feel like a cog
_____ I wish it were Friday
_____ Successful
_____ Rotten
_____ Bored
_____ Powerful
_____ Trapped
_____ I hate it
_____ My job is my life
_____ My job's convenient
_____ A chimp could do what I do
_____ I make good money
_____ My boss gets the credit
_____ Great
_____ Challenged
_____ Help!
_____ You heard of Black Monday?

Add any feelings you have about work which have not been listed:

_____	_____
_____	_____
_____	_____

These remarks are excerpts from numerous interviews with people who do various kinds of work: teacher, pilot, hairdresser, production supervisor, policeman, social worker, salesman, bank vice-president, physical therapist, copy chief, chemist, librarian, market researcher, pediatrician, cost analyst, model, visiting nurse, psychoanalyst, brand manager, student advisor, secretary, commercial announcer, photographer, and many more.

We asked these people the same question we just put to you, "How do you feel about the coming work week?" And we quickly got the message that what may have sounded like a simple question, was not so simple after all. After the hemming and hawing, when the answers finally came, further interviewing showed that they were often still not the real answers. This did not surprise us.

Years of job counseling had convinced us that many people frequently confuse their feelings about *work* with their feelings about their *job*. The two are not identical, and we were testing this theory of confused references in preparation for writing this book.

Also, as we expected, the most enthusiastic responses were often the cliche, shorthand answers people give when they are suspicious, guarded, or defensive about revealing their feelings. Allan M., a middle-level executive in a drug chain, said "I wouldn't do it if I didn't like it." In-depth interviewing revealed that the statement had very little to do with the actual "work" of his work week. What he really enjoyed about his job were the trips in the company plane, a schedule that permitted him a lot of free time out of the office and, of course, the salary.

As for the responses that were direct, dynamite blasts of negativity at the "work week," such as "Rotten" or "I hate it," here too, frequently people didn't know what they were hating. For example, the statement, "I wish it were Friday," was translated by Harold M., a market researcher, after much back and forth questions and answers, into "My boss is a bastard!" Harold M.'s boss, though certainly important and possibly unpleasant, is a peripheral aspect of Harold M.'s job. His actual "work" is market research which he so relishes he often voluntarily works at home on weekends. He wished it were Friday so he could get away from his boss, not his work.

JOB AND WORK

But Harold M. is typical. Most people, when answering the question, usually spoke about their *job*, and its good or bad impact on them. Their *work*, whatever it was, was simply a necessary evil, or once in a while, a surprising pleasure. It took probing and prodding to lead them, as we hope to lead you, on a personal voyage of discovery; an excursion conducted as it were by Sigmund Freud, John Kenneth Galbraith, and George Meany. It begins with a journey inward to find the pleasure seeker in you, and concludes with your return to the world of jobs—in today's work era—which will now never be the same for you. On your initial stop you'll see, perhaps for the first time, the difference between job and work.

Some realists know it without prompting. But they are in the minority. Leona B. is such a woman. When we asked her how she felt about the coming work week, she said with no reserve, "Lousy! It's drudgery. I'm sick to death of purchase orders." Leona B. has been a purchasing agent for a paper company for eleven years, and she was genuinely fed up to the teeth with her work. Some aspects of the job—congenial co-workers, convenient location, and status—made up for much of the pain, but the net result was still a state of mental anesthesia that made her despise the work which paid her rent.

In the same vein was Robinson Clark, a secretary in a public relations firm. He observed, "I love my job. The people are great. I like the office. But secretarial work is a crashing bore."

The catch in the question "How do you feel about the coming work week?" is the meaning of the key word "work." When responding, people automatically equated the word work with the word job. It is the same kind of set thinking that equates money with happiness, sex with love, or a TV announcer's open smile with sincerity.

But work and job have vastly different meanings. The *job* is the *total situation* within which a human being does his or her *work*. Webster's definition of "work," originating in the nineteenth century and subscribed to by millions of people who own dictionaries and go to work, is "the exertion of physical or mental energy toward some purpose or end; the matter on which one is employed . . ." or, to paraphrase Webster, *work is what you are hired to do for those who hire you.*

However, there is a fresher, freer, more humanistic meaning of *work itself.* Erich Fromm, the eminent psychiatrist, has pointed out that satisfying work and love are a person's healthiest outlets for creative life and the prime source of all his pleasure energy.

Repressing the need for personally satisfying work invites trouble. Your most vital self will not sit still for a snubbing. It can't be stored away in mothballs in a back closet of your personality. Continuing medical studies have shown the damage people do themselves by staying in unsuitable jobs. One day you may be handed a grab bag of ailments ranging from shingles, to high blood pressure, to diabetes. For your own sake then, take a deep breath and let it out slowly, give yourself a new chance. Open your mind to the possibility that the work that you do can be work that will use the best of you and give the best to you—employ your aptitudes, talents, and interests as they long to be employed. So that the primary value of your job will be the pleasure it gives you—the *work pleasure*. When the returns are in, you will have discovered how this same work that gives you pleasure will earn you a living, too. You can be paid for doing what you like to do. Does it sound vaguely sinful? It isn't.

All this attention to *work itself* is not intended to bypass the dignity of the job. Think of work as the core of the job, as the nucleus is the core of a living cell. But *work itself* is certainly not all there is to a job. Or even all that matters. All manner of comfortable advantages or disquieting drawbacks of a job can matter very much. These we refer to as *job benefits*.

Job benefits are:

• *The money you make:* enough or not (including pension plans, profit sharing, insurance, options, etc.)

• *The status you have:* office location, job title, etc. Job status can also effect your private life status and private life-style.

• *Job style:* The hours, vacation time, expense account, convenience (or inconvenience) of the job location, the pleasantness or unpleasantness of the climate where the job is located, indoor or outdoor work, amiability of co-workers; in short, a whole mix of tangibles and intangibles can make or ruin a job for you.

• *Job security:* This is your feeling that your job will continue for as long as you wish to keep it and that you will not be "cut back," "retrenched," or just plain "fired."

Job security undoubtedly is the most powerful force keeping people locked into positions which do not give them pleasure. Generally, job security is a mirage. Changing economy, new product developments, mergers, management shakeups, acts of God, and a hundred other things, can put most workers out on the street as fast as it takes to type a pink slip. Your best security is to keep constantly in touch with your skills and interests, and with the ways they relate to the changing world in terms which will give you pleasure.

WORK PLEASURE AND JOB BENEFITS

Perhaps you wonder why it is important to draw this thick line between the ideas of *work pleasure* and *job benefits*. Not only is this separation necessary, it is absolutely crucial. As you play the games in this book, you will see that the health of your job life rests squarely on your ability to differentiate between work pleasure and job benefits. As you are about to see, the psychological and economic payoffs of these two job values are as different as speech and music.

Psychological differences: Work pleasure is something you give yourself. It is not given to you in a pay envelope.

Job benefits are made up of enticements someone gives you in order to make you stay. However, they can be taken away when you are no longer wanted.

Economic differences: Work pleasure can lead to the development of a high skill and interest in the work. A skill, whatever it is, is a negotiable asset. The more you develop it, the better your bargaining position and your job security.

Job benefits cannot be marketed. A job title of vice president, a corner office, or an expense account will mean nothing to a potential employer unless he is convinced that you received them because you could do the *work itself* of your previous job, or of the job you're applying for.

Do you now see why we separated the two major values of a job? These are not casual distinctions. How you approach these values (work pleasure and job benefits) can seriously influence your job life.

Look at what has been happening to someone else, Eileen Graham, for example. Ms. Graham is copy chief of the advertising department of the home office of a mass-merchandising chain. What she has to say about her job illustrates somewhat grimly the difference between work pleasure and employment satisfaction.

A lot of people say it's drudgery to go to the office every day. I don't look at it that way. I don't say I love my work, but then I don't hate it either. Why hate it? It's something you have to do. Maybe it doesn't have the excitement it used to have. But what does?

I started working for the company when I was eighteen—a kid in clerical. I went to night school and studied advertising. Eventually they transferred me into this department. I'm not on time clock anymore. I moved up; I'm copy chief. That's my title. With five people reporting to me. We create newspaper ads and radio commercials for the stores in our chain. Hundreds of them.

When I first came into this department I had high hopes. I thought I would make great advertising. Be an ad genius. I guess that's been my greatest frustration—I never did it. They promoted me, that's all. I never can get my ideas across to my supervisor, the advertising manager. When I do—it's a freak. He has five years on me.

Sometimes I get very discouraged. I think—wouldn't it be wonderful to be in a position where I could make great ads. I'd like that. I was always a doer.

I never did understand people who complained about their work and then did nothing about it. Now I understand. I'm in that boat. Because where would I go? With a small company I wouldn't have as much job security. And I know people here. I get benefits: vacation, seniority, profit sharing. My family has complete medical coverage. I need these benefits.

I figure I can wait out my boss. I've seen other hot shots in my 18 years here. Maybe the next one will be better. They'd never give a woman that job. Funny, I'm only 38 years old and some days I feel like 58.

Think about Ms. Graham's remarks. They have the ring of what a tough-minded poet once called "quiet desperation." Today she has no work pleasure. In fact her *work itself* is an unadmitted embarrassment. Today, the job benefits and satisfactions—the title, profit sharing, vacation time, etc.—constitute the entire value of her job. In clinging to these satisfactions she finds herself marooned in "frustration." At 38 she feels 58.

But is she marooned? Are there no options? Are all the doors closed? We do not think so. We think that a woman with Ms. Graham's advertising skills and experience can never be grounded unless she chooses to be. Of course if thinking makes it so, and she thinks it is so—then it is so. But for the open mind there are open doors.

Using the techniques described in this book, in the Job Family Game, the Sourcing Game, the Interview Game, to name a few, Eileen Graham could come up with enough job offers to keep her awake nights deciding which job to take. These jobs would give her work pleasure as well as appreciating her current employment satisfactions. And what a profit that would be—creativity and challenge as she has not experienced in years. The price she fears she will pay is loss of her pension plan, seniority, and her profit sharing. Still, if she worked it all out with an accountant it would probably cost her less than $5,000 (the present unvested portion of her future pension)—a low price to pay to get paroled from 20 more years of drudgery.

Work pleasure and job benefits are important. You should be able to recognize each of them as it applies to you, in order to find the most satisfying employment. The exercise below will help you know what you want, and will provide the first step toward finding both work pleasure and job benefits. Think of a position you would like to hold, and look at the following list of specific activities and job aspects in terms of that position. First, cross out those statements which do not apply to you. For the remaining statements, check either the Work Pleasure or Job Benefits column (or both, if applicable) to reflect how you view each aspect of the job.

Statement	YOUR JOB ANALYSIS	
	Work Pleasure	Job Benefits
Chance for advancement		
Having responsibilities		
Having corner office		
Having a long vacation		
Being a team worker		
Opportunity for achievement		
Supervising people		
Having an expense account		
Doing detail work		
Doing independent thinking		
Making policy decisions		
Being supervised well		
Having a secretary		
Carrying out policy decisions		
Meeting people		
Self-expression		
Plush offices		
Working with machines		
Flexible hours		
Hiring status		

	Your Job Analysis	
Statement	Work Pleasure	Job Benefits
Becoming proficient at something		
Chance to become partner or officer		
Profit sharing		
Lack of pressure		
Intellectual challenge		
Chance to be financially independent		
Convenient job location		
Congenial co-workers		
Use of company car		
Company travel		
Having authority		
Retirement benefits		
A title		
Creative expression		
Having an assistant		

We hope that as you responded, you did not have any nagging concerns about giving the right or the wrong answers. There are no right or wrong answers. The point of this game—as of all games in this book—is to tell you something about yourself. If most of your answers referred to work pleasure, future games will help you focus more clearly on these areas, and how to expand them; if job benefits governed most of your answers, this book will help you discover the natural sources of work pleasure.

A man named Hal Davis, who works in a hothouse on Long Island, is a good man for you to know. Hal knows a lot about work pleasure. When we asked him our opening question, "How do you feel about the coming work week?" he said, "Fine. Why not?" As it turned out, on depth interviewing, he was as true as his words. On both levels of his job—work pleasure, and almost all job benefits—Hal was well set up.

Hal's *work* was his primary pleasure. He said, "I like growing plants and working with living things. I like the way they smell. Just looking at them makes me feel good. . . ." "I like taking care of them." "Plants are a lot more beautiful than people. And they don't sass you."

Hal's job benefits were a mixed bag. He said things like, "I get up at 5 A.M. But I like it so it's okay. . . ." "I don't like waiting on customers but I have to. It's part of the job. . . ." "I hate business suits and I don't have to wear them. . . . I don't make as much money as I would if I worked in the city, but I like it here . . . my boss is an OK guy."

Hal Davis is doing well. Are you? No, we are not suggesting that you go to work in a hothouse in order to find work pleasure. You might hate it. You may prefer people to plants. And when it comes to growing things you have a brown thumb. But still, do you know as much as he does intuitively about work pleasure—about what you like to do?

Now that you're thinking about it, you may be asking yourself what pleasure can I get out of work? The next step in thinking this out is to take a good look at the kinds of pleasure you get out of life. You don't have to stop living when you work, do you?

If you enjoy what you do for a living, you are bound to do it better—thus creating greater economic value. As a result, work pleasure can lead to job survival. In the next chapter we're going to let you take a closer look at your own personal pleasures, and begin to see how you can translate them into work pleasure.

2

WORK PLEASURE
The Hedonist Work Ethic

Well, what's your pleasure? What do you like to do—do so willingly, so eagerly, that you'll do it without pay? Of course, we agree it sounds like pure fantasy to contemplate being paid for doing something you enjoy. But fantasy can become reality and the pursuit of work pleasure is also the road to job survival.

Review the 77 statements listed below. All are pleasure-logged notions, pastimes, hobbies, diversions, amusements, relaxations, play. If some of them look to you suspiciously like work in the traditional sense, you are right. They are somebody's *salaried work* as well as being that somebody's pleasure.

Don't try to think of this list in terms of work possibilities. For that you need a key which we will give you over the next few games. For now, just play the What I Like to Do Game. On the following list, check each activity that could give you at least a quiver of pleasure if you had the time to pursue it. Add to the list any pleasure-giving activities that we left out. If a statement comes close, but does not match up with your own private interests, rewrite it:

What I Like to Do

_____ I like collecting music boxes

_____ I like planting trees

_____ I like racing cars

_____ I like meeting new people

_____ I like fishing

_____ I like planting flowers and bushes

_____ I like caring for animals

_____ I like feeding birds

_____ I like playing tennis

_____ I like working with machinery

_____ I like making jewelry

_____ I like giving parties

_____ I like driving a car

_____ I like collecting things

_____ I like caring for old people

_____ I like being with teenagers

_____ I like counseling families

_____ I like teaching

(16)

_____ I like giving advice
_____ I like making cabinets
_____ I like being funny at parties
_____ I like looking at art and art objects
_____ I like working at night
_____ I like raising money for a worthy cause
_____ I like designing things like packages
_____ I like sex
_____ I like arranging furniture and decorating houses
_____ I like doing things outdoors
_____ I like doing physical labor
_____ I like living in a small town
_____ I like living in a big city
_____ I like preparing a gourmet meal
_____ I like solving theoretical problems in biology
_____ I like solving practical problems with numbers
_____ I like building structures
_____ I like making a good bargain
_____ I like negotiating a contract
_____ I like navigating a sailboat
_____ I like interviewing people
_____ I like supervising people
_____ I like being supervised by someone I respect
_____ I like sewing clothes
_____ I like designing clothes
_____ I like solving people's problems
_____ I like solving organizational problems

_____ I like working alone
_____ I like listening to music
_____ I like going to the theater
_____ I like to sing
_____ I like to act
_____ I like to gamble
_____ I like to race—cars, boats, dogs
_____ I like to run a house
_____ I like to be an assistant to someone important
_____ I like to do research in chemistry
_____ I like to do research in history
_____ I like to analyze research reports
_____ I like to repair furniture
_____ I like to be my own boss
_____ I like to teach people
_____ I like to attend meetings
_____ I like to sell
_____ I like to persuade people to agree with me
_____ I like to do nursing
_____ I like to take care of children
_____ I like to cut down trees
_____ I like tinkering with machinery
_____ I like doing routine, orderly tasks
_____ I like settling arguments
_____ I like helping people
_____ I like collecting coins
_____ I like camping outdoors
_____ I like free-falling
_____ I like collecting pre-1930 phonograph records
_____ I like reading palms, tea leaves, and Tarot cards
_____ I like collecting antique cars
_____ I like deep sea diving

We must have left out other activities, so add any that please you.

_____ I like_____   _____ I like _____
_____ I like_____   _____ I like _____
_____ I like_____   _____ I like _____

How many did you check? _____ We bet you probably could have gone for several more pages and dozens more "I likes."

This exercise is meant to demonstrate several very important ideas: We want you to start seeing yourself in pleasure terms—to relish the surprisingly high number of interests that turn you on. Incorporate those very important words *I like* into all phases of your job thinking. Take them with you throughout the remaining chapters of this book, and out into the world as you search for work pleasure.

There are literally thousands of people getting paid for each of these "I likes"—why not you?

This chapter is subtitled The Hedonist Work Ethic. What is *hedonism?* It is an ancient and honorable Greek doctrine that celebrated pleasure as the highest good. So successful has this philosophy been that it has been handed down from century to century. It has been confirmed, sustained, and ratified by succeeding generations of human minds and human inclinations at one time or another in all the countries of western civilization. It is a philosophy that has rarely been out of fashion. Has no one told you about it? Thank our puritan heritage.

Puritanism was an extremely moral, English-born religious cult that stigmatized pleasure as the greatest evil. Unfortunately for pleasure seekers, the Puritans arrived in America well before the hedonists. The Puritans disappeared as a political entity after the seventeenth century. But to this day, their attitudes and ethics continue to linger over those of us who show any natural hankering after pleasure.

In the last half of the twentieth century the idea of "doing your own thing" emerged from the American unconscious. Historically speaking it was the coming of age of the American version of hedonism. This new idea of pleasure expressed itself in a series of culture shocks. Our society began talking, arguing, writing, and breaking through in many areas of human activity where the stamp of our puritanism had once been indelibly etched. The hedonist in each of us began questioning, thinking, wondering, reassuring each other, and asserting our natures in ways that saluted pleasure rather than puritanism. The following is a brief, incomplete, but illustrative list of the type of shifts that have begun to cause cracks in the puritan hold on our personality.

Sex. We now speak and write of the joy of sex for both men and women. It is an accepted aspect of human life, participated in by the young, the older, and these days even the very old. Sex has come out from behind the barn.

Marriage. The institutionalized now-and-forever, unexamined marriage is passing. Today marriage is open to new arrangements in terms of the needs, rights, and feelings of both partners. Divorce statistics rise, and so do remarriage figures, as we grope our way to more self-expressive matings.

Motherhood. Women no longer must prove their womanhood by having children. They are demanding, and achieving, the engagement of their brains and talents.

Children. Children, who until recently were nonpeople, are currently recognized as members of the human race. At the same time, there is a new sense of the "rights of parents." A negotiation between equals is taking place.

Fashion. Both men and women are no longer subject to standardized ways of dressing in order to prove either their sex, or their respectability. There are more options in fashion than ever before and more people taking these options.

War. Men want to live and enjoy life, not die for meaningless slogans. "When Johnny Comes Marching Home Again," as a theme, has been replaced by its final line of frightful insight—"Johnny We Hardly Knew You."

Environment. As we realize that we are part of the earth and that to ravage the earth is to ravage ourselves, the quality of the landscape becomes as important as the quality of the car we buy to drive through the landscape.

Life-style alternatives. Many people are discovering that there is no longer a point to "keeping up with the Joneses." There are no Joneses. The wise choice then is to live the life-style that gives you, not the mythical Joneses, the greatest pleasure.

Despite all of these emerging changes in various regions of human interplay, the role of *work* has retained for most people the deep dye of its original puritanism. Even now, puritan job attitudes are as formidable a foe of work pleasure as they once were of sex pleasure. To the Puritan, man by nature was wholly sinful, a rounder and scalawag, who could be saved only by severe and unrelenting self-discipline. With the object of achieving this salvation, hard work was considered a religious duty; and the more unpleasant, the more self-improvement for the spirit. Quite unknowingly, you yourself may be a staunch work puritan, who thanks to good behavior is granted a parole from your puritan heritage after five, or on weekends, on vacation, or when goofing off.

But all that is changing and you're going to change it for you. You know now that a career should be a combination of work pleasure and job benefits. Go back to page 7 and reconsider the opening list of statements. This time when you respond, do it in relation to how you feel about your *work*—not the job benefits. Do your answers still apply? If not, make changes.

Choose the single, most meaningful statement checked and elaborate on it. Translate it into what you *really* mean. In the space given, write a statement that explains why you feel the way you do about your work in 50 words or less. Remember, be honest. The book has a built-in lie detector technique.

My most meaningful statement was _____
_____
_____

I feel that way because _____
_____
_____
_____

Reread what you wrote. On balance, are you getting enough *pleasure,* not just job benefits, out of your work? Don't fake—it's a key question. It's important because it touches on a vital issue—how you spend the largest chunk of your time allotted on earth.

YOUR 10,000 DAYS—LIVE THEM AS A HEDONIST OR A PURITAN

You are not immortal. You will not live forever. Yet probably no one has ever clued you in to the fact that the average 9 to 5 job occupies 10,000 days of your most productive, pleasure-potential years. Otherwise stated, the amount of time you spend on a job—10,000 days—is more than is often spent in marriage, in family life in school, or any other organized human activity. Now that we've said it, you may be nodding your head. Please don't forget it. It's really easier if you stare back at that round number. Stare. Yes, 10,000 days. With so much precious lifetime at stake, you have no right to do work in which you are expected to ignore your feelings, your thoughts, and your pleasures. If you persist in accepting such work, you must ask yourself "Why?"

If, now that you think about it, you sense that you are not getting enough pleasure from your remaining work days, list in the space below the things that get in the way:

_____
_____

_____

_____

_____

_____

If you wrote comments such as

I have a job now that I hate, but I don't know how to find one that's more fun.

OR

I don't like what I do as much as some of the interests I checked, but I don't know if I could do any of those things well enough to get paid for it.

OR

I think I know now what I like to do, but I don't have a clue as to how to get work doing it.

OR

I'm afraid. Suppose I can't do what I like to do?

OR

In today's job market I'm lucky to have anything.

Or . . . , or. . . . Think again. And let us repeat our message—work pleasure is the real key to survival. You are not *that* locked in.

Whatever your reasons, helping you overcome these obstacles is one aim of this book. Just keep turning the pages and doing the games and exercises. Eventually, you will be giving yourself the answers.

Right now, look back at the What I Like to Do Game on page 16. Review all the interests that you checked. From this group, pick the ten most important and list them below.

1. _____
2. _____
3. _____
4. _____
5. _____
6. _____
7. _____
8. _____
9. _____
10. _____

Now you know something worth knowing about yourself—your ten most important interests. Given the right orientation, these interests can grow and expand into job possibilities to which you never gave a thought. Then, with the skills and experience you now have, new ones you will develop, and the techniques we'll show you, you will soon be off—on the track of work pleasure you never realized was possible.

Right now, there are about 87 million jobs in this country. Every year a minimum of 15 percent of these jobs turn over—that is, 13 million USA job changes a year. Even without turnover, jobs don't stay still. Jobs change, shift, and disappear. New kinds of jobs replace old ones as fast as pop tunes replace each other. Even with the unemployment rate up, one million *new* jobs are added to the economy annually. In such a job world, the only reason not to find yourself a creative job match, is lack of the right kind of thinking and organized effort on your own behalf. Your dream job could have been vacated yesterday at 3 P.M. and is waiting around for you to find it. Or perhaps it exists in the mind of an employer somewhere who doesn't realize how much he needs you because you haven't found him to tell him. What we're really saying is, the right jobs are there for your own brand of pleasure—you have to find them. But we are a little ahead of ourselves; before we can show you how to find those jobs, we have to make certain you have found yourself.

KNOW YOURSELF

To practice the hedonist work ethic, to give up work puritanism, you have to know yourself. Your total self—your mind and body pleasures, both separate and combined. We use the term "mind" here to describe the more purely intellectual pleasures of thinking, learning studying, etc. We use the term "body" to describe physical pleasures that relate to our bodies essentially—dancing, sports, manual labor, etc., and the sensual pleasures such as eating, listening to music, looking at beautiful objects, etc. Then there are those pleasures, by far the widest category of all, that emphasize both aspects of our self—mind and body. This group includes interpersonal pleasures, communication pleasures, creative pleasures, aesthetic pleasures, and mechanical pleasures.

Given these categories, start thinking, wishing, daydreaming, remembering what gives you pleasure. Recall the taste of pleasure. Pleasure is different from "interest." As we define it, an interest is intrinsically attractive to you, but the pursuit of it always is active, and usually fairly structured. The pleasures we speak of now are more amorphous, unstructured, spontaneous, peripheral. These pleasures may be active or they may be passive. They do not necessarily involve "doing" though they may. Think of these pleasures without any reference to the work you do now, or would like to do. Let your mind fantasize and free-float as you fill in the lines below. Remember, pleasure can make sense or nonsense, have a purpose, or be purposeless. But whatever gives you pleasure is revealing in describing who you are to yourself.

Your Pleasure Profile—Part I

In this section you will find eight types of mind-body pleasures listed. In each category, list what gives you pleasure. As you will note, within each category is a quote from someone else's response to this particular kind of pleasure. Don't worry if what you say in one category overlaps others.

1. Physical Pleasures

Examples: exercising, sport, performing (i.e., dancing, singing), hiking, running, working with hands, home repair, building things, boating, contact sports, etc.

Tony Bellow: I don't much like home repair work or any of that stuff. I like sports. I'm a very good athlete. Well-coordinated.

_____

_____

_____

_____

_____

2. Sensual Pleasures

Examples: eating, smelling, seeing, hearing, tactile experiences, and sexuality.

Jeanne Eagles: I love colors. I can see a dress color in my head, and I have to match shoes; well I don't need a swatch or anything. I know the right color match instantly.

_____

_____

_____

_____

_____

3. Intellectual Pleasures

Examples: reading, studying, researching, analyzing, organizing, problem solving, decision making, planning, etc.

Agnes Hill: I like researching projects and analyzing subjects but I must say I don't like the responsibility of making the decision. That would keep me up nights.

_____

_____

_____

_____

_____

4. Creative and Aesthetic Pleasures

Examples: painting, composing, writing, designing, acting, craft arts, collecting art and art objects, sewing, cooking, etc.

Robert Coomb: I never did like the arts of the home like cooking and sewing. But I love decorating and working with fabrics and furniture. I spend hours thinking about room layouts.

_____

_____

_____

_____

_____

5. Interpersonal Pleasures

Examples: meeting people, talking to people, learning about people, understanding people, helping people, teaching people, participating in team work, supervising team work, participating in competition, all ego pleasures like winning, etc.

Eugene Frame: I enjoy face to face talking to one or a few people I know. I do not like talking in large groups or to strangers in public.

_____

_____

_____

_____

_____

6. Communication Pleasures

Examples: contacting people, persuading people, arguing with people, negotiating or bargaining, explaining ideas, etc.

Allan Mann: I prefer to have other people do the bargaining for me. I think I tend to be too agreeable and always want to keep peace. I do this with my wife all the time.

_____
_____
_____
_____
_____

7. Mechanical Pleasures

Examples: operating office machines, operating heavy equipment, driving a car, fixing mechanical things, etc.

John Jacoby: I like tinkering with mechanical toys. I can fix anything. I have more fun than kids do.

_____
_____
_____
_____
_____

8. Temperament Conditions

Examples: like calm situations, like pressure, optimistic, pessimistic, risk taker, cautious, fast temper, slow fuse, enjoy challenge, enjoy conformity, like change, like routine, etc.

Herbert Aarons: I like to know where everything is. Even my shoe horn. I find unexpected change very upsetting.

_____
_____
_____
_____
_____

Your Pleasure Profile—Part II

Take as much time as necessary to give accurate answers to the following questions.

1. Who would you like to be if you weren't yourself? _____
_____

2. If you were working a three-day work week, what would you do with the remaining four days? _____
_____

3. List the three places and climates you find most enjoyable. _____
_____
_____
_____

4. What do your closest friends like most about you? _____
_____

5. What do you like most about yourself? _____
_____

6. What is your most secret pleasure? _____
_____

7. What are your favorite tools? _____
_____

8. What kind of person do you find most attractive? _____
_____

9. When you meet people for the first time, what would you like them to think about you? _____
_____
_____
_____

10. Looking back over the past five years, list three events or occasions, in which you were personally involved, that gave you the most pleasure. _____
_____
_____
_____
_____

Now go back and reconsider your list of ten interests on page 21; do they still hold? Look again, at your Pleasure Profile (Parts I and II). Does it stand up on a second reading? Is it you? If something troubles you, change it. Remember, as you go through this book, you will be constantly revising your answers, as you learn more about work pleasure, and more about your relation to it.

Try to summarize, in 50 words or less, what you think you've learned about yourself in terms of what pleases you, or fills your basic pleasure needs. You are now on your way to self-awareness, leading to work pleasure.

Personal Pleasure Summary

_____
_____
_____
_____
_____

In the opening pages of this book we asked you to tell yourself some of the feelings you have about going to work. These feelings represented the "bottom line" of your job attitude, the product of the positive and negative aspects of your work. In this chapter you glimpsed what kinds of activities interest you, and which experiences give you pleasure. In the next chapter we show you how to begin to free yourself from the tyranny of job titles.

3

HOW ARE YOU,
WHAT DO YOU DO?

DON'T BELIEVE THESE ADS

RESEARCH WRITER   fee paid $16,000

MA + 2 yrs qualitative experience including ability to deal effectively w/others. Sm bkgrnd industry studies req. Fast growing Co. Good benefits. Call Mr. Matthews 784-3218.

EXEC SECY   fee paid $9,100

Assistant to one of NYC's nicest exec. Make your own decisions during crisis. Play support role also. Typg, steno, & good people skills. Prudential Bldg. Call Miss Barrow CE8-2904.

DIETICIAN

To manage entire school lunch program of Monroe Woodbury School District. Central Valley, New York. Beginning June 1976. Experience desirable. Salary range $9,600 to $14,000 depending on experience. (10½ month position) Contact Mrs. Grimaldi 928-2221 extension 453.

Except for the most standard jobs, the language of many job ads is hazy and imprecise. *Job titles* often describe only one or two aspects of the job; sometimes the aspects described are the least important ones in terms of what you do and what's in it for you. Job descriptions read like a telegram taken down by a tired clerk and delivered to the wrong address. They overlook many important details pertaining to the activities of the job, and include much irrelevant information.

None of this misinformation is deliberate. We all do it all the time. Someone asks you, "What do you do?" and you answer, "I'm a teacher," "I'm a bookkeeper," "I'm an advertising writer," "I'm a production chief," "I'm a fashion coordinator." All these job titles do exist and they provide a very rough categorization of the job—but that's all. Much is hidden which may be more crucial to holding the job, and functioning in it successfully, than the teaching or the book-keeping or the fashion coordinator title. For example, that the fashion coordinator puts together the appropriate jewelry and accessories that go on the models in the window of the Fifth Avenue store where she works is the coordinating aspect of the job. But what makes her successful is that she gets the most difficult, irascible buyers to cooperate with her. She has to have a high level of people skills.

Consider the three classified employment ads at the beginning of this game. We'll start with the research writer ad. Can you tell what this job really requires from reading the ad? Come along with us on our investigation at the office of the man who inserted this listing, and see what we turned up.

Question: At the opening of the ad you list first a masters degree and two years experience. Are these essential requirements?

Mr. Matthews: When you get right down to it—maybe not, I guess. There's nothing magic about a masters, or even the two years experience really. But we received so many responses the last time we ran the ad, I decided to be more particular this time to cut down the interviewing load.

Question: What's really required then?

Mr. Matthews: Good clear writing of a particular type—writing that can deal with technical data, statistics, figures, conclusions—and make a complicated subject come across clearly and understandably.

Question: What's the subject matter?

Mr. Matthews: It varies. The company does a variety of research projects for industry. Mostly the work is done in the area of utilization of materials, testing for various characteristics of materials, such as metal crystallization, stress, corrosion—that sort of thing.

Question: How are these reports prepared by the writer?

Mr. Matthews: There's always a Project Engineer responsible for each project—he accumulates all the data, comes up with the conclusions, organizes the elements of the report; then meets with the writer for a day or two, going over the information. Then the writer puts together a rough draft which the engineer reviews to make sure it is accurate, and the writer does a finished version which is approved by the engineer and by one of the partners of the firm.

Question: So what you really need is a writer that can work with technical terms and data and make it understandable. If such a person got to see you—but didn't have an MA would you consider him?

Mr. Matthews: I think I would, as a matter of fact, our best writer has a BS in engineering and no prior job experience—he's straight out of school. But he really knows how to get the ideas across and that solves the problem. He's completely upgraded the quality of the reports.

Conclusion for You

As you can see, job titles and descriptions often hide as much as they reveal and they can be misleading, and paralyzing, preventing you from making any effort toward the job. But if something about the ad catches you, and you can overcome your hesitation and decide to make a try, some investigation might reveal that the work problem to be solved in the job—in this case preparing interesting reports, with the technical data furnished by a true technician, could be done by many people with combinations of skills not indicated in the advertisement. In this case for instance, an engineer who can write could do the job. So could an ad writer with some industrial advertising background. A statistician who could write clear English might also be appropriate, as might someone with a technical library background, who is accustomed to handling a heavy load of data and writing reports. If you were interested in this job, you would try to see a sample of the kind of writing which is now being satisfactorily done. If you could then demonstrate with your own sample that you could do the writing as well or better, you would undoubtedly be seriously considered for the job, whether you have the required background or not.

The Exec Secy job is an example of a "say-nothing" ad. What does executive secretary mean? Ten different things in ten different companies. When we explored the requirements for this job, we found out how meaningless the description of the job was.

Question: How much typing is there in this job?

Ms. Barrow: Not more than an hour a day. If that. There's a typing pool which gets out most of the heavy work on mag-tape typewriters. But the typing must be neat and accurate.

Question: And the stenography?

Ms. Barrow: Very little.

Question: Would speed writing do?

Ms. Barrow: I don't see why not.

Question: Is it essential that this person have experience as an executive secretary?

Ms. Barrow: I'd say so.

Question: Why?

Ms. Barrow: Well, so they'd be familiar with general office procedures, and be able to work well with people, and have general office skills.

Question: Suppose someone could demonstrate that they had these abilities but had never worked specifically for an executive, would you consider them?

Ms. Barrow: Perhaps. As long as they were organized, and could show me that they could work on their own, and take responsibility, making sure that everything got done in the boss's absence.

Question: I see. Is that what you mean by a "support role"?

Ms. Barrow: Yes. This is the secretary for a VP of sales. He's constantly on the move, so his secretary must help run the office when he's gone—see that reports are compiled, that materials are mailed out, sales meetings set up, and so on.

Question: It's really an assistant's sort of job, even more than secretarial.

Ms. Barrow: I guess you could say that.

Question: Are there reasonable opportunities for advancement?

Ms. Barrow: Oh my, yes! Our company's in the cosmetics business and puts on demonstrations of products all over the country, which are run by traveling field managers. This job is a natural stepping stone for someone in a secretarial—or if you want to call it secretarial assistance—position. That's if they're interested in traveling and can handle the operations I've described. As a matter of fact, the woman who is being replaced was promoted into a field manager position after less than a year as executive secretary.

Question: What's the salary for a field manager?

Ms. Barrow: Starts at $12,000 plus expenses.

Conclusion for You

Obviously what was left out of this ad was more important than what was put in. Here we have a job which actually requires very few

specific skills. What is wanted is a general knowledge of office procedures, energy, the willingness to take responsibility, and an ability to
type neatly and accurately. With ambition, the right person could use
this job for a real career thrust.

The dietician ad attracted our eye for a number of reasons. First,
the salary range was quite broad—$9,600 to $14,000—indicating that
the company hadn't quite made up its mind about what was wanted.
Second, it looked like a fine area for career advancement, with the expanding interest in food and nutrition.
We talked with Ms. Grimaldi, to get her analysis of the job, and
here are some excerpts from our interview.

      Question: How many lunches are involved in this program?
Ms. Grimaldi: There are 5,000 students in the five schools that
make up the district. Each of these schools has its
own building and food manager who coordinates the
recipes and the preparation of the meals.
      Question: These five food managers report to the dietician?
Ms. Grimaldi: Yes.
      Question: Does the dietician prepare the menus and recipes for
each day's meal?
Ms. Grimaldi: Not really. The menus are fairly standard and the
food managers make their suggestions each month of
things that they would like to change or add or sub-
tract. The basic lunches are the same, but we're interested in varying them as much as possible within
the budget.
      Question: If the dietician doesn't plan all the menus then a for-
mal detailed knowledge of formal dietetics is not essential?
Ms. Grimaldi: No—but the person should know the basics of good
nutrition. Have at least some background in that.
Maybe college courses. The most important aspect of
the job is to be able to coordinate all of the purchasing and delivery of the various supplies that are
needed, and as I said, stay within the budget. Also
this person would deal with the state and federal
agencies which provide support to our lunch program.
      Question: So, an ability to get along with people plus basic
management skills are more important here than
dietician training?
Ms. Grimaldi: Yes, management skills are very important. Maybe
more so than anything.

Question: Why is there such a wide range in the salary? Would the duties be different for someone who came in at $10,000 vs. someone you hired at $13 or $14,000?

Ms. Grimaldi: No. The duties would be the same. It's just that a person with more experience would probably do a better job more quickly than one with less.

Question: Well, would the new person have any support in learning about the job after they were hired?

Ms. Grimaldi: Oh yes. They would spend two to three weeks with the outgoing dietician, and would have lots of support from the food managers if they ran into any problems.

Question: Well, with so much support, do you think a bright, capable, enthusiastic person with good management skills and some food background might not do so well as someone with years of experience in this particular field?

Ms. Grimaldi: I guess that's true. I never thought of it that way.

Conclusion for You

Here you have a job that is actually mistitled. It's called "dietician" but it really isn't. It requires no formal dietetic training, just an understanding of nutrition and an ability to coordinate a variety of purchasing activities, as well as manage five people who already know their jobs. It's a job with far wider appeal than the ad indicates and someone with a flair for cost cutting, management, and a simple nutritional background could probably get the job and hold it successfully.

The purpose of this investigation of job titles and job descriptions is to show you that outside the authentic assembly line work, most jobs have a high number of variables that are hard to reduce to a small number of words, in fact, each could probably take a small book.

Prove it to yourself.

In the following lines write a classified advertisement that might be written to hire someone for *your* present or most recent position, or for a position that you are seeking. Start with the job title and then provide a 25 word description.

_____

_____

_____

_____

_____

_____

How much of the actual flavor of your job did you get into the ad? It's not easy to capture it all in a few words, is it?

Job titles are shorthand labels we pick up through lazy thinking. We learned their use as children and it stayed with us. "What do you want to be when you grow up?" someone asks a child. The child answers, "a fireman," or "a lawyer," or "an astronaut," or "a nurse," etc. But these answers are only labels; and as is true for labels, they usually contain very little information about the product. In this connection it is interesting to note that at least 75 percent of the freshmen law class one year at Georgetown University had never been inside a law office. They never had discussed the day-to-day practice of law with a practicing attorney—the working conditions, the problems to be solved, the rewards other than money, etc. Many of the students had made the decision to become lawyers, simply because they'd heard about it and it sounded interesting, or a distant relative was a lawyer and they were intrigued by the salary and status.

When you meet George Neel at a party, and you say, "How are you, what do you do?" George will say,

> Neel's the name. George Neel. I'm a bookkeeper in a large firm. You ask me do I like my work? Sure. There's one great thing about bookkeeping. You can always get a job. Look at the classified section—hundreds of ads on bookkeepers. In fact there are even employment agencies that just specialize in bookkeeping so I can take my pick. This is the fourth bookkeeping job I've had since I graduated 12 years ago from Roosevelt College. I took this one because the salary's higher and it's closer to home. But the work's identical. A bookkeeper's a bookkeeper.
>
> Actually, when I think about it, I never had a bookkeeping job that I really liked. Not when I look back on it. While I'm at it, I don't mind so much. But when I look back—at some of the crap I've had to put up with, like changing the trial balances for the sixth time because management doesn't know what they're doing, I boil.
>
> What do I like to do? Here I'll show you. I write letters to the editors. See these clippings. I publish about three letters a month, I'm a very good letter writer. And chess. I played chess since I was 10. I've won a lot of tournaments. No national stuff. But I do win.
>
> And I guess I like deep sea fishing best of all. Every two years for the last ten years or so I manage to get enough money together and I go off on a two-week vacation trip and fish. Last year was the best of all. When I got to San Diego I met a guy at the marina who had his own boat and he invited me out for six days. We did nothing but fish for six days. We picked our own

spots and stayed as late as we felt like and didn't get hasseled by a lot of amateurs who get seasick when it gets rocky.

No, I've never thought of doing anything but bookkeeping. What else could I do? I've never seen any employment ads for chess players. Or letter writers. Or for deep sea fishermen.

. . . Leave Detroit? Why would I do that? Well, I guess I could live in San Diego. They must have bookkeepers there and it's good fishing. I never thought of that before. I guess I kind of connected my life to Detroit. Say, do you think that the magazine *Fishing Gazette* needs a bookkeeper? If I'm going to be stuck as a bookkeeper I might as well do it in a field I like. Ha! Ha! I bet I could even probably help out on one of those fishing boats once in a while. Can't you just see that? Ha! Say . . . I wonder if it's really possible.

Dear Reader: What about the bookkeeper in you? Would he be happier on a fishing boat?

4

YOU, THE PLAYER

This is a book about you, and your relation to work. Think of us as detectives pointing to a trail of clues for you to follow to help you identify that elusive part of you—the Work Hedonist.

The Work Hedonist in you is an uneasy fugitive. There are fears and deeply entrenched cliches which keep your job holding you in a buttoned-down puritan straitjacket. You have already noted what a poor map of the territory job titles and job descriptions can be. You have also discerned that the notion of "security" may only be a self-imposed hoax and that the best way to survive in the job market is to find work you like and are good at. It is not a moment too soon to re-establish yourself in the equation of you and your work, to recognize finally and forever that *your job world revolves around you.* You are the center, not the satellite.

Implicit in the idea of work is that it *solves a problem,* an economic one, a political one, a scientific one, a problem in some area of human activity that benefits society. In the truest, deepest sense it is our human problem-solving skills—yours and everyone else's—that makes the world of work go around. In essence, it is your ability to solve problems that represents your major work value to society. The great hedonist trick then is to plug your problem-solving skills, specifically those that give you pleasure, into those work situations where they can be best used and expressed—in offices, shops, labs, libraries, schools, farms, houses, banks, restaurants—wherever connections can be found. The lucky people who know and recognize their pleasure-giving skills are in a better position to find outlets for the skills than are those men and women who know only dimly what they can do, and even less what they like to do.

The following excerpts from interviews provide examples of people who use their problem-solving skills to give them work pleasure, and get paid for doing what they like to do.

1. *Irene Bass*

PROBLEM-SOLVING SKILL

I know how to make people young again. I know all about nutrition and exercise. If a woman does what I tell her to do, she leaves me looking years younger than when she walked in. It gives me a good feeling looking at this new person I practically made.

APPLICATION

I manage a reducing salon, and have lectured at a number of modeling schools. I'm thinking of writing a book. I'll never have trouble doing what I want to do so long as people are still concerned about their looks.

2. *Steve Dunn*

PROBLEM-SOLVING SKILL

I have a real sense of the mystery of cell life. I would rather work in a well equipped laboratory than eat. I'd rather puzzle over the whys and wherefores of gram negative bacteria than sleep.

APPLICATION

It took me several years to realize that teaching wasn't my bag. I finally accepted myself, and now I'm a research biologist for NIH. I love it, and it would take a lot of pressure to change. Oh, I could change employers, that would be all right, but I'd always find a job back in a lab somewhere.

3. *Anatole Plisser*

PROBLEM-SOLVING SKILL

My hands know many things I never taught them. When my fingers finish resetting a broken chair leg you cannot see anything. Nothing. If you look very close you just think that thin line is 200 years old also. I've worked with my hands since I was very young. It makes me feel peaceful.

APPLICATION

I work three days a week for an antique store 10 miles from my home. I've worked for many antique stores throughout Connecticut. That's OK, there's always more work than I need. I work three days for them, and three days for myself. My wife I see on Sundays.

4. Tony Porter

PROBLEM-SOLVING SKILL

I'm a born salesman. Even before college I was peddling magazine subscriptions. I like to deal with people face to face, get to
know them briefly—anticipate their hesitations and objections.
Show them how the product will help them, and close the sale.
I'm a great closer. I believe in myself and in the products which
I sell. I love the fact that I can be mobile. The transactions are
short, and I am really on my own. My biggest enemy is paperwork—and I avoid it.

APPLICATION

I'm now a computer salesman—and the complexity and size of it
fascinates me. I've built my earnings into over $40,000 in recent
years. But I'm not married to this industry. I could sell toy trains
if need be.

At this point we hope that you have begun to recognize and accept
the following new truths:

• You have been working or will be working many years of your
life.

• Your psychic health depends upon work pleasure—finding a job
which is satisfying and which utilizes your preferred skills and interests.

• Work pleasure is also your best guarantee of work survival. All
job studies indicate that work that utilizes the worker's preferred
skills and interests is more likely to be well done.

• You are a worker who is a problem solver, not a job title or
description.

• You are a problem solver looking for problems that give you a
bang! to solve. Bang! is what we said—work pleasure.

Accomplishments

The next question is, how do you know what kind of problems give
you pleasure? The fact is you know. Think about the accomplishments you were most proud of in the last 5 years. Think about the
word "accomplishment." Doesn't it imply solving a problem in a way
that gave you pleasure? It means that and more. To solve these problems you must have had certain skills. What were they? It's important
to know. But before we guide you on your own private tour of your
skills, look at what Debbie Benson told us about the four accomplishments she was most proud of. Debbie's job is developing package
designs for a display firm. Her accomplishments:

● "I'm divorced. I raised a son and daughter singlehandedly and did a super job."

● "I bought an old, run-down barn and turned it into a summer house for me and the kids. Did the whole restoration job myself with the help of the kids and Jack, a local handyman. In winter I rent it out and it brings in extra money."

● "I won a POPAI award for a new design for a display shipper.

● "I started out seven years ago as a staff assistant at $150. per week, and now I make $20,000 per year."

Next, Debbie analyzed her accomplishments—how she did what she did. Note the list of skills that went into barn restoration alone. It will show you, as it showed Debbie, that she had problem-solving skills that she had not given credit to, and that ultimately made the achievement possible.

Accomplishment: Barn Restoration

● "I'm a pretty good persuader when I want to be. I convinced the bank to give me a mortgage. They thought the barn was too much of a risk. They even thought I was a risk. How could I fix up a barn when I couldn't hold a marriage together. But I persuaded them."

● "I'm a natural handywoman. I can fix anything."

● "I'm not a licensed electrician but I got a book and learned wiring and plumbing and such."

● "I have an instinct for real estate. I knew that I could probably rent the barn in the winter once it was finished. My barn is near a university town, so there are always winter people looking for places."

From Debbie's analysis of her problem-solving skills that went into the barn restoration, it is clear that she has many work skills, in addition to package design.

● She is persuasive, which is always a useful human skill.

● She has an instinct for real estate investment.

● She has a handywoman's ability and what looks like a "feel" for all the requirements of house restoration.

● She is a hard worker, who is not scared by physical labor.

An analysis of *all* of Debbie's accomplishments showed a very broad diversity of skills—including many quite unrelated to her job. In fact, just a surface review of her abilities suggests that the housing and real estate industries might have a place for her.

Your Accomplishments

Now you. Make a list of 4 accomplishments in the last 5 years, that, when all was said and done, made you feel pleased with yourself. The accomplishments need not be earth shattering. Look at your private life as well as any work experience.

Accomplishments

1. _____
_____

2. _____
_____

3. _____
_____

4. _____
_____

On the following forms, list the problem-solving skills you think made each accomplishment possible.

1. ACCOMPLISHMENT: _____
_____
PROBLEM-SOLVING SKILLS: _____
_____
_____
_____
_____

2. ACCOMPLISHMENT: _____
_____
PROBLEM-SOLVING SKILLS: _____
_____
_____
_____
_____

3. ACCOMPLISHMENT: _____
_____
PROBLEM-SOLVING SKILLS: _____
_____
_____
_____
_____

4. ACCOMPLISHMENT: _____
_____
PROBLEM-SOLVING SKILLS: _____
_____

_____
_____
_____

You have more problem-solving skills than you thought. Now make a list of the ten skills that recur most often in achieving your accomplishments.

Recurring Skills

1. _____
2. _____
3. _____
4. _____
5. _____
6. _____
7. _____
8. _____
9. _____
10. _____

What about problem-solving skills that you have, that haven't yet shown up in particular accomplishments? Still, they are there for everyday use if you need them. Think about it. Can you tune a guitar? Make a pretty good omelette? Drive a truck? Use a calculator? Speak Spanish? Teach people? List the skills that are first rate, as well as those that are good, though they won't set the world on fire. Don't be shy, pat yourself on the back for whatever you can do that might be called a problem-solving skill.

Additional Skills

1. _____
   _____
2. _____
   _____
3. _____
   _____
4. _____
   _____
5. _____
   _____
6. _____
   _____
7. _____
   _____

THE SKILL/INTEREST CROSS INDEX

Now you know more about your problem-solving skills. What do they tell you? The chart below will help you find out. Along the vertical axis, fill in the "What I Like to Do" interests you listed on page 16. Along the horizontal axis list the ten problem-solving skills listed under Recurring Skills and Additional Skills. Then put a check mark in each box where an interest relates to a skill.

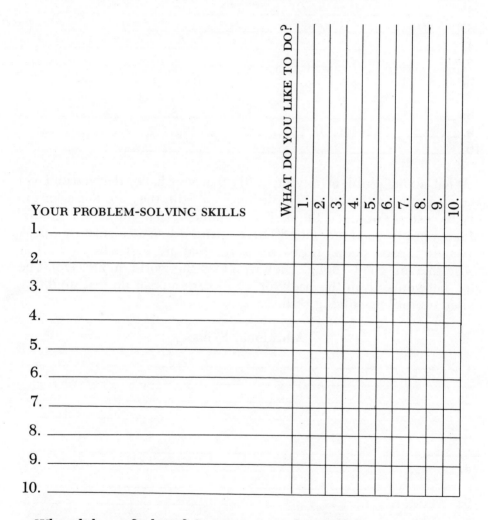

What did you find out? Suppose one of your skills is teaching people? The "I Likes" this skill might relate to are:

I like to act   I like old people
I like children   I like helping people

But not:

I like to raise flowers
I like to play the zither
I like making toys

All interests and all skills do not mesh. But if none of your interests and skills overlap, you couldn't have thought them through. Most often, where you have a genuine interest you also have related skills. And where you have a skill, it has to lead to an interest. If there is no overlap in all your interests and skills, go back and rethink both categories.

How to Evaluate Your Skill/Interest Cross Index

Wherever a cluster of skills appears in an "I like" column, it indicates a high potential for your controlling a source of work pleasure. If you find that some of your ten "I like" interests are not supported by skills, sit back and take a long, sober look at the interest. Ask yourself if this "I like" is interest—real interests are usually supported by some problem-solving skills. Of course, you may discover that the skill is there, but just didn't get on your list. If so, and if it is an important skill, go ahead and add it.

For example, "I like raising money for worthy causes" might be an interest not supported by any type of fund-raising skill or experience. You then have three alternative approaches:

1. The interest is "unreal."

2. You may have overlooked some quite real problem-solving skills that you possess and that would relate to the interest. For example, you may not have actually raised money for anything, but you know how to do research and how to write interesting letters. This means you would know how to research for the appropriate mailing lists for your worthy cause, and to write persuasive letters to prospective patrons.

3. If after digging, you still find you have no skill in a particular interest, or only the barest skill, than consider the intensity of the pleasure you derive from the interest. When the intensity of pleasure is high, it will compensate you for time spent taking courses, reading texts, going to lectures, and otherwise "boning up" and developing problem-solving skills in your interest.

Take the case of Ellie Feurgeson, a speech therapist, who was bored with phonetics. Ellie had other skills besides a good ear and an aptitude for teaching diction. She liked to bake cakes and pies on weekends. In fact, she had such a gift for cake baking that her friends constantly offered to pay her to make baked desserts for their parties. When baking showed up on her "I like" list, Ellie thought about it, wondering how to improve her skill and give it commercial value. She knew nothing about the baking business. However, through the techniques described later in the book (pp. 248 to 252), she found out about a six-week commercial baking course. In the course she learned about bread and rolls and volume baking. Her enthusiasm helped her pick up a great deal of knowledge in a very short time, and to carry her directly into the baking business. Today she is an assistant baker in a moderate-size bakery that supplies a number of the better restaurants around San Francisco.

So much for interests. What about skills you have that do not relate to any interest you have listed?

If a skill, or several skills, that you have is not related to any interest, it probably is not going to connect you to jobs with much work pleasure and may not be useful to you unless connected to other interests and skills in a secondary way.

For the moment, forget your problem-solving skills and just think about today's social and economic problems. They represent work problems—jobs that need to be done. Let your mind wander, expand your thinking, free associate, think big, think small, think up and down and around—invent ten opportunities for problem-solving jobs which may or may not exist, but which would give you pleasure to solve and would also have a social and economic benefit. Here are two we just invented:

1. Gourmet tidbits service to liven up the menu on company cafeterias, at nongourmet prices.

2. Designing a management consulting service providing a full range of services inexpensively to very small businesses.

Now you—invent five problem-solving jobs which would interest you.

1. _____

_____

2. _____

_____

3. _____

_____

4. _____

_____

5. _____

_____

5

THE SILENT EXPLOSION

List ten jobs that existed at least 20 years ago and still exist today.

Our List

1. Bank teller
2. Salesman
3. Carpenter
4. Teacher
5. Lawyer
6. Tailor
7. Sailor
8. Accountant
9. Grocer
10. Jeweler

Your List

1. _____
2. _____
3. _____
4. _____
5. _____
6. _____
7. _____
8. _____
9. _____
10. _____

List ten jobs that did *not* exist 20 years ago.

Our List

1. Inland oyster farming
2. Children's TV producer
3. Nuclear power plant designer
4. Medical paraprofessional
5. Energy efficiency expert
6. Heart transplant surgeon
7. Computer typesetter
8. Feminist magazine editor
9. Oral contraceptive packager
10. Satellite communication engineer

Your List

1. _____
2. _____
3. _____
4. _____
5. _____
6. _____
7. _____
8. _____
9. _____
10. _____

There have been changes made. In the last 20 years we have added 28 million new jobs to our work force. Many of those jobs in indus-

tries that didn't exist, or were infants in 1955, and more jobs are opening every day, at the rate of one million new jobs a year. Should a
recession or a business shift wipe out your job or even your industry,
you have the luck to be living in a changing society in which there
are many brand new work areas to explore that may be right for you
that didn't exist before. Probably you take this growth so much for
granted you have not realized that it is like a *silent explosion*. It is an
opportunity explosion if you know how to take advantage of it.

This silent explosion is the *job explosion*. In 1955 there were 58
million jobs. In 1975 there were 85 million. As we said, we're continuing to add jobs at the rate of more than one million each year—an
encouraging development for those seeking work pleasure. The variety of jobs has multiplied far beyond the wildest expectations of even
two generations ago. Many of them did not exist even 20 years ago,
and some might be quite appealing to you. Some jobs are travel jobs.
Some are desk jobs that are concerned with statements—balance
sheets, political statements, legal statements. There are jobs that
require talking to animals, or talking to plants, or talking to computers. In some jobs, people work with music; in others, with food, or
God, or gold, or sex, or seaweed. There is an infinite variety of jobs in
the market today—in offices, store windows, fields, studios, factories,
barns, bars, or underwater. Some jobs are created to solve problems
that never existed before.

This process goes on whether the economy is expanding or contracting. With every social, political, and industrial shift, old-
fashioned, irrelevant job titles get phased out, and new problem-solving opportunities appear, with new job titles and requirements. Consider the recent happenings in only a sample of fields such as,

Education	Computers
Communications	Religion
Transportation	Television
Photography	Food
Energy	Retailing
Ecology and environment	Advertising
Leisure life	Machinery
Medicine	Accounting
Optics	Fishing
Finance	Crime detection
Electronics	Metallurgy

Just a limited view of these developing fields can boggle the mind
with the numbers of opportunities involved. Use your imagination—think what just a few innovations can mean.

Education: New automated teaching aids, requiring people to develop, promote, sell and service same.

Communication: TV monitoring screens, i.e., closed circuit TV satellite reporting, video phones and perhaps even high speed mail.

Transportation: Computerized vehicles—new mass transit systems, space shuttles, calling for those who know how to operate computers and understand traffic flows.

Photography: Instant films and holography—people to perfect, promote, advertise, and market them.

Personal care: Hair transplants requiring hair stylists and cosmeticians to work with the medical profession.

Optics: The soft lens requiring doctors, technicians, and quasi-authorities for promotion and marketing.

Leisure life: The metal racquet, the all-weather court, artificial snow—these innovations lead to a variety of jobs for sports enthusiasts and others.

Finance: The cashless society—requiring people to deal with its functioning as well as its promotion, legislation, and control.

This is the mere tip of the iceberg. Innovations which bring into being new kinds of jobs with ultimately new kinds of work pleasure are being created constantly. Technological shifts, as well as social, political, and economic ones, have ignited the job explosion. For you it means that contemporary society has literally millions of new problem-solving needs which make it possible for the thoughtful and dedicated pleasure seeker to find work pleasure as well as job benefits.

Maybe your current job doesn't inspire you, or is contracting. Then how do you feel about occupational therapy? Communication? Food? Library work? Marketing? Boating? All these fields have had and will continue to have dramatic growth curves. The purpose of this broad-angle view of the job world is to focus your attention on the fact that all job situations including your own or one you may want are in constant flux. Approached perceptively, persuasively, and with your eye out for the main chance, this continual job fermentation can mean new kinds of jobs and ipso facto a whole new world of pleasurable work choice and paycheck for you.

Let's take a look at you and the job explosion.

YOU AND THE JOB EXPLOSION

1. What field are you in now, or what field do you plan to enter? ___
_____

2. In your view, what are the most likely future areas of growth and decline in this field?
Growth: _____
_____
_____

Decline: _____
_____
_____

3. What job within the field you picked do you think would offer the greatest growth potential? _____
_____
_____

4. What specialized skills or training would you need to keep up with the areas of greatest growth, and how could you get them? _____
_____
_____
_____

5. List three organizations in your field which you feel are among the most progressive and intelligent in planning for the future. (Include your place of employment if it qualifies.)
1. _____
2. _____
3. _____

6. What outside events (technological, social, political, economic, etc.) could most likely have a serious negative effect on your specific job area in the next 5–10 years? _____
_____
_____

7. List three job situations in your field which would be most likely to offer greater future growth and work pleasure.
1. _____
2. _____
3. _____

If you gave serious thought to your answers, you should have a pretty good, if self-made job horoscope to inform you of some of the things that can or will happen in your chosen job field. Do you like what you see in your field? If you don't, the job explosion provides you with a route to other job pleasures. Having examined your inner wishes, it's a comfort to know that the job explosion has made more feasible than ever before a diversity of opportunities, any one of which might satisfy your yearnings for work pleasure.

With the right techniques you will be able to find jobs with the right combination of

- what you work at
- where you work
- how you work
- who you work for or with

to give you your humanly required quota of pleasure from work throughout the thousands of days of your job life.

ONE LIFETIME—FIVE CAREERS

There is another side to the job explosion that makes it not only desirable, but imperative that you face certain of its less comfortable implications. For many of the changes it brings are not optional. It looks as if most people would be well advised to be prepared for many different kinds of work in one lifetime. These may be with the same company, in the same field, or in a new field with entirely different kinds of working situations. Ultimately, the job explosion contributes to the constant changes in the job market, and reflects the ups and downs of industries, social attitudes, political ferment. Consider:

- *Railroads:* Competition of cars, buses, planes, and trucks threw railroads into deep financial trouble for years. Now, with mass transportation zooming toward us, railroads may be the wave of the future.

- *Radio:* In the fifties and sixties the radio industry lost much of its power while everyone sat and watched TV. Today the radio industry is booming and offering many jobs.

- *Wall Street:* Once the target of the get richer-quicker kids it is another place today. Thousands of brokers are selling insurance, or furniture, or doing hair styling. To survive, they had to find second careers.

- *Tennis:* Because of public courts, tennis camps, and other factors, this sport, originally the sport of aristocrats, has become a game for everybody.

Obviously, knowing where the jobs are is a matter of keeping on your toes and keeping up with the continual arrivals and exits of lifestyles, technologies, sociology, politics, etc. Unfortunately, our past cultural and educational training has gone toward encouraging us to become specialists in one field, or at least stay put with one company. This despite the fact that more and more people have found themselves in the agonizing position of having unneeded specialties, or of devoting their lives to companies that one day merge, or are sold, spun off, or otherwise engulfed by our changing society. Even if companies would, they don't have the funding to compensate lifetime employees for job displacement.

However, once you become acclimated to the idea of job alternatives and personal work choice, these times are actually refreshing and liberating. Allow your sense of adventure free passage, and you will find that though industries come and industries go, the optimistic creative spirit in you can go on indefinitely. You are not "locked in" to one kind of work unless you choose to lock yourself in. It all depends on your interest, your motivation, your problem-solving skills, and the work-finding factors and strategies in this book.

As we go through the coming moves you will discover how to identify the possible opportunities you might have once thought impossible, and how to adapt your skills to take advantage of these opportunities. The job explosion can be an opportunity explosion for you.

Job holders are not static. They are changing jobs constantly. There are over 50 thousand job changes every day.

The job that was closed to you 3 P.M. Monday may be open to you at 9 A.M. Friday. Or next Thursday at 5.

Furthermore, in this changing industrial society, you can, if you think it through, create your own job with your own problem-solving skills. Not long ago, there were no pollution engineers, nor were there market-research experts in ethnic markets.

6

WHERE ARE YOU NOW?

Where are you now? What do you now know about yourself that you didn't know when you started this book? Let's check it out. In answering the following questions, if any question reminds you of one you've answered before, *do not go back* to see what you wrote. You may have changed your mind since then. The more you learn about yourself, the wider the view you get of the range of job opportunities for you, and consequently, your answers to the same questions may change. As will your expectations. Start.

1. In your present or most recent job, what values are most meaningful to you?
   ____ Work pleasure
   ____ Job benefits
   ____ Both have equal importance

2. What is the most important work pleasure in your present or most recent job? _____
   _____
   _____

3. What is the most important job benefit of your present or most recent job? _____
   _____
   _____

4. Draw a line to show where you would rate yourself today on a scale from 0 (work puritan) to 100 (work hedonist).
   0 _____ 100

5. Rank the following pleasures in order of their relative importance to you.
   ____ Physical pleasures   ____ Interpersonal pleasures
   ____ Sensual pleasures   ____ Communication pleasures
   ____ Intellectual pleasures ____ Mechanical pleasures
   ____ Creative/aesthetic pleasures ____ Temperament

6. There are 10,000 days in the average person's working career. How many days do you have left to enjoy? _____.

7. Did you identify at all with Ms. Eileen Graham (pp. 11 and 12) the copy chief of the mass-merchandising chain?

   ____Yes

   ____No

   If yes, with which aspect of her job experience did you identify?

   _____

   _____

8. If you didn't identify with Ms. Graham, did you identify with Hal Davis (pp. 14–15), the assistant manager of the hothouse operation?

   If yes, what aspect of his job experience did you identify with?

   _____

9. (Answer only if you have worked at the same organization or job area for at least five years.) What is the major factor keeping you with the same company or job area? _____

   _____

10. How did you get your present (or most recent) job?

    ____ Sent out letters ____ Advertisement ____ Luck

    ____ Employment Agency ____ Placement ____ Other Methods:

    _____

11. Approximately how many full days or equivalent did you spend actively exploring job situations, prior to finding the one you accepted? _____

12. What is the minimum monthly salary on which you could live (assuming you were starting over, without assets or obligations)?

    $_____

13. What are two of your most valuable or marketable problem-solving capacities? _____

    _____

    _____

14. What are your three most pleasurable interests and what percentage of time do you spend on them?

    1. _____ _____ percent

    2. _____ _____ percent

    3. _____ _____ percent

15. Assuming you had to make a change, what new growth field attracts you most in terms of possible jobs in that field? _____

    _____

16. If you had to switch jobs for two years with someone you know, who would you like to be? _____

    _____

17. What is the most pleasure-giving job (not considering salary) that you can imagine or invent for yourself? _____

_____

_____

7

JOB FAMILIES

Now you're ready for the Job Family Game, which will provide you with one of your richest natural resources of job information.

The *job family* is a new concept. It describes a category of work which includes dozens of specific jobs and problem-solving opportunities. Job family is a broad umbrella under which you can position a wide range of opportunities, all of which you *might* be interested in for yourself. For example, a job family, may be an *industry*—movies, plastics, cosmetics, engines, etc. It may provide a *service* such as selling, mental health, transportation, travel, or legal. A job family may refer to an *artistic* activity—painting, performing, singing, graphic design, or writing, or it may be public spirited, and include counseling, social work, teaching, or crime detection. A job family may even be related to *climate or environment*, and deal with forestry, sailing, fishing, or jobs abroad.

The major criterion for a job family is that it be a big enough category to include a great diversity of work situations. Look at only a part of the multiplicity of work situations under the *automotive job family:*

Designing cars
Working in car production
Selling cars
Transporting cars
Driving a cab
Driving a bus
Driving a truck
Driving a racing car
Designing racing cars
Working in a pit
Selling tickets to auto races
Promoting races
Writing about races
Operating a filling station
Selling tires

Repairing trucks
Repairing cars
Running a garage
Running a trucking garage
Managing a fleet of cabs
Managing an automobile company
Writing automobile commercials
Managing a trucking company
Teaching driving
Writing a book about car repair
Giving a course in car repair
Making car parts
Selling car parts

Selling used cars	Operating a fleet of chauffered
Selling antique cars	cars
Writing about antique cars	

But a job family does not have to be as obvious as the automotive. It can be any area of personal interest that is broad enough to include a variety of work opportunities.

The main criterion in selecting a job family is your *interest* in it. It may be an area in which you have a specific proven skill; it may be an area in which you feel you have a chance to grow and learn. Or it may be simply a field which you find intriguing but don't as yet know much about.

For example. *Outdoor work in Florida* is an invented job family that Nat Reynolds believed would give him work pleasure. Nat is a bank teller in Chicago making $175 a week. But most of his pleasures are in the outdoor world. He likes to swim, sail, play tennis, and would rather be outdoors than inside. He likes warm climates. He's looking for a change. He selected outdoor work in Florida to see what would happen. He then took 20 minutes and came up with the following possible work situations in that job family. Not all of these are jobs he would want to hold, but they are possible work situations outdoors:

Work on a Florida estate	Tour guide
Estate management	Manage an outdoor restaurant
Work in a marina	Work as a builder
Crew on a charter boat or yacht	Gardener
Swimming instructor	Signpainter
Sanitation man	House painter
Fisherman	Lifeguard
Traffic cop	Boat repairman
Car-wash operator	Cab driver
Tennis pro	Chauffeur

Now, you play the Job Family Game.

Step 1

Look at our list of 90 sample job families on page 56. This is just the beginning. There are scores more that could be listed. (If you want to make up more of your own to add to the list as you play the game, please do.) Select four categories which appeal to you.

Remember that the main criterion for selection is your *interest* in a given job family. Don't worry about the fact that you may not have too much experience in the job families you picked. Indulge yourself. Dream. Be logical and illogical. Take a chance the way Nat Reynolds did. Spotlight your interests, not just your problem-solving skills and talents.

Once you have selected four job families, put each one at the top of one of the Job Family Inventory forms on pages 60 to 63.

Automotive	Horses
Education	Religion
Television	Botany
Movies	Biology
Grocery	Physics
Packaged foods	Music
Entertainment	Mathematics
Public speaking	Electronics
Publishing	Health
Textile	Nutrition
Interior decoration	Finance
Agriculture	History
Photography	Banking
Gardening	Retailing
Fishing	Fashion
Accounting	Advertising
Office services	Machinery
Investments	Crime detection
Sports	Metalwork
Building services	Government services
Personal services	Economics
Paper	Politics
Travel	Magic
Physical conditioning	Toys
Computers	Aeronautics
Recreation	Weather
Construction	Woodworking
Power	Children's services
Ecology	Personnel
Engines	Communications
Cosmetics	Boating
Real estate	Repair Services
Synthetic fibers	Management Services
Transportation	Sociology
Bookkeeping	Counseling
Secretarial	Marketing
Performing arts	Selling
Camping	Family services

Insurance
Horticulture
Zoology
Fine arts
Museum work
Journalism
Bicycles
Stamp collecting

Mental health
Oceanography
Commercial Arts
Medicine
Interior design
Industrial design
Architecture
Law

Step 2

Under each job family on the Job Family Inventory Form, list every conceivable job title, occupation, work description, or problem-solving opportunity that you can think of. If you don't know the official name for the position just write down the idea.

"The guy who is in charge of designing road signs."

"The person who selects contestants on quiz shows."

"The people who scout out craft items for new catalogs."

These job ideas are not necessarily ones you would want for yourself. List everything you can come up with. The trick is to free-associate and write down as many situations of any kind at any level as you can imagine. Invent jobs you think belong in the family. Remember, you do not have to like or be qualified for every opening on your list. The point is to unleash your imagination, to let it run wild. Free-association works most successfully when you don't hamper it with mental or emotional traffic signals, fences, and road blocks. Just write your list, let one thought lead to another, and see how the list grows. You should have a minimum of 20 work activities under each one of your job families, but shoot for 30, 40, or more. If you can come up with a list from the top of your head, great. But most people like to help themselves with a little research—scouring the classified section of your newspaper for ideas about the job family you're interested in, looking at trade journals in the area, asking the help of librarians, or making a few telephone calls to anyone you know who already works in the job-family area of your interest. All the information you can possibly get about the job possibilities in the family is very helpful.

Following are six Job Family Inventory Forms. The first two are sample lists of work ideas filled out under two job families selected by two people. The next four are for your use.

Sara Thomas' Job Family

JOB FAMILY INVENTORY FORM

(In the spaces below list every job title, position, or problem-solving opportunity you can think of or create. If specific organizations or information sources occur to you, list them too.)

JOB FAMILY: *Transportation (bicycles)*

1. Designing bikes	26.
2. Fixing bikes	27.
3. Selling bikes to stores	28.
4. Teaching bike riding	29.
5. Promoting bike laws	30.
6. Writing about bikes	31.
7. Running bike races	32.
8. Manufacturing bikes	33.
9. Importing bikes	34.
10. Promoting bike trade-ins	35.
11. Opening a bicycle store	36.
12. Designing biking clothes	37.
13. Designing bike accessories	38.
14.	39.
15.	40.
16.	41.
17.	42.
18.	43.
19.	44.
20.	45.
21.	46.
22.	47.
23.	48.
24.	49.
25.	50.

JOB FAMILY INVENTORY FORM

(In the spaces below list every job title, position, or problem-solving opportunity you can think of or create. If specific organizations or information sources occur to you, list them too.)

JOB FAMILY: *Trailers (mobile homes)*

1. Sell used trailers	26.
2. Deliver trailers	27.
3. Custom paint trailers	28.
4. Wash trailers	29.
5. Inspect trailers	30.
6. Design interiors	31.
7. Construct interiors	32.
8. Paint interiors	33.
9. Install equipment	34.
10. Design new equipment	35.
11. Design trailers	36.
12. Trailer rebuilder	37.
13. Operate trailer park	38.
14. Write newsletter	39.
15. Work in the association	40.
16. Repair trailer plumbing	41.
17. Travel books	42.
18. Design small campers	43.
19. Foundations	44.
20. Install intercoms	45.
21. Write articles	46.
22. Licensing and inspection	47.
23. Sell propane	48.
24. Mechanic	49.
25.	50.

JOB FAMILY INVENTORY FORM

(In the spaces below list every job title, position, or problem-solving opportunity you can think of or create. If specific organizations or information sources occur to you, list them too.)

JOB FAMILY: _____

1.	26.
2.	27.
3.	28.
4.	29.
5.	30.
6.	31.
7.	32.
8.	33.
9.	34.
10.	35.
11.	36.
12.	37.
13.	38.
14.	39.
15.	40.
16.	41.
17.	42.
18.	43.
19.	44.
20.	45.
21.	46.
22.	47.
23.	48.
24.	49.
25.	50.

JOB FAMILY INVENTORY FORM

(In the spaces below list every job title, position, or problem-solving opportunity you can think of or create. If specific organizations or information sources occur to you, list them too.)

JOB FAMILY: _____

1.	26.
2.	27.
3.	28.
4.	29.
5.	30.
6.	31.
7.	32.
8.	33.
9.	34.
10.	35.
11.	36.
12.	37.
13.	38.
14.	39.
15.	40.
16.	41.
17.	42.
18.	43.
19.	44.
20.	45.
21.	46.
22.	47.
23.	48.
24.	49.
25.	50.

JOB FAMILY INVENTORY FORM

(In the spaces below list every job title, position, or problem-solving opportunity you can think of or create. If specific organizations or information sources occur to you, list them too.)

JOB FAMILY: _____

1.	26.
2.	27.
3.	28.
4.	29.
5.	30.
6.	31.
7.	32.
8.	33.
9.	34.
10.	35.
11.	36.
12.	37.
13.	38.
14.	39.
15.	40.
16.	41.
17.	42.
18.	43.
19.	44.
20.	45.
21.	46.
22.	47.
23.	48.
24.	49.
25.	50.

JOB FAMILY INVENTORY FORM

(In the spaces below list every job title, position, or problem-solving opportunity you can think of or create. If specific organizations or information sources occur to you, list them too.)

JOB FAMILY: _____

1.	26.
2.	27.
3.	28.
4.	29.
5.	30.
6.	31.
7.	32.
8.	33.
9.	34.
10.	35.
11.	36.
12.	37.
13.	38.
14.	39.
15.	40.
16.	41.
17.	42.
18.	43.
19.	44.
20.	45.
21.	46.
22.	47.
23.	48.
24.	49.
25.	50.

Done? Take one more vital step. From here on you will be in need of what we call your *support system.* Your support system can be your spouse, closest friend, teacher, relative—anyone on whom you can rely to double-check you on certain moves. In the earlier games, when you were dealing with highly personal material, it was your own self-insights that were most crucial. Now as we enter the actual job world, occasionally it will be useful to air your ideas in the company of someone whose judgment you trust. Besides, they will see your inventory from a different standpoint, and may come up with new and productive work situation ideas which you missed.

MAKING THE JOB FAMILY GAME WORK FOR YOU

Now do us a favor. Add up the number of combined work ideas you came up with in all four of your job family categories. Go ahead—total them up: the job descriptions, titles, positions, occupations, problem-solving skills, opportunities, work ideas, everything and anything you listed. How many did you arrive at?

Total job ideas: _____

If you are like most people who have played this game, you should have a total of 80 to 100 job situations and problem-solving opportunities. It took you about an hour, or maybe a little more, to reach this.

If you have closer to 200 items you probably did some research in your job family—looked at trade magazines, went to the library, talked to people in the field. Good for you. You're getting the rhythm. However, if you had difficulty coming up with even 50 work ideas as the combined total of all your four job families, you're headed for trouble. Let's see how we can do better.

Emergency Measures

1. *Let yourself go.* You haven't permitted yourself enough latitude in the job families you've been exploring. Go back and dig in again. Project yourself into each job family and try to see how it functions. Visualize the environment: the offices or the factories, the house, the restaurant, the airport, the studio, the laboratory, or any of the places where each job family is located. Remember to list *all* jobs, even those you wouldn't want for yourself. Next, think about the people in each job family. What do they look like? Talk to them. What are they doing? Who works for whom?

2. *Go to the library.* Look up the field in the card file, and see what it tells you. Check business directories. Ask the librarians for help.

Look up someone who knows the field. If any of your job families are listed in the classified section of the phone book, call a listing. Tell them you're doing a research project (you are) and ask them questions about the field.

3. *Take a short break.* Have a cup of coffee and go for a walk. Come back and put some more energy and creativity into this task. This work is the key to getting the job you want.

4. If after all this extra digging you're still stuck with 50 or less total work activities, for your four job families—that's it. Scrap two of the job families you selected, choose two others, and start again!

When you have at least 75 blanks filled, as a total of your four job family inventory lists, go on to the next game. Now! Keep moving while the motors are humming!

8

YOUR JOB TARGETS

When you completed the four Job Family Inventory Forms, with at least 75 to 100 job ideas, you demonstrated a unique and potent power—the gift of increased choice in the job world. We hope that the Job Family Game was an open minded, spontaneous, and unconstrained stock-taking of all conceivable work situations within the job families you selected. If it was, you now have shown yourself how to develop a personal resource of job information that no employment agency, head hunter, job counselor, or personnel officer—and no astrologer or fortune teller—could give you.

What the Job Family Game did was open the door to a secret side of you. A more detached you, one who could sit back and look at yourself, unthreatened and unfettered by the trauma of job hunting in the daily job world. Freed from these hang-ups and fears, you could approach jobs as you would any other decision or research project. You could more coolly evaluate the work marketplace, think about yourself, note your interests and noninterests, and explore and free-associate as though you were doing it for someone else. What a freedom that is! What we've tried to do is help you externalize this more objective second self, in order to create for yourself a whole new realm of work information, opportunities, and approaches that a more culturally stereotyped approach would never consider. We've seen this happen time and again in our workshops—where job seekers are initially so blocked that when told "List as many job possibilities as you can think of" they are unable to name even a dozen job situations of any kind. Yet once they break through their fears by playing this game, scores and scores of job ideas rise to the surface.

Next comes the *job target* countdown. It's the end product, the payoff for all the game playing, the new thinking and rethinking, the relearning and reorienting you've been doing. Now, you are going to select your own job targets for work pleasure and work survival.

Step 1

Read the listings in your Job Family Inventories with a truly open mind. Review all the work ideas—imagine yourself in each job—see how you respond to each work experience. Do some represent jobs you might want to perform? Which do you absolutely refuse to do? Which would you consider doing under certain circumstances, provided you had the problem-solving skills?

Step 2

In the four Job Family Inventories, circle every work idea you think would give you pleasure (whether you feel capable of doing it or not).

Step 3

From all the work activities you've circled, select the ten that you feel you could perform today if given the opportunity, or those which you would be willing to take out the time and learn to perform. List them:

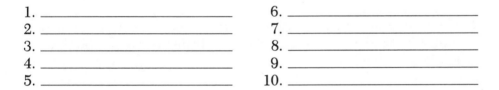

1. _____   6. _____
2. _____   7. _____
3. _____   8. _____
4. _____   9. _____
5. _____   10. _____

Step 4

Out of the ten finalists, select the five that you feel have the most potential for you in today's job world, and that you would be willing to make a serious effort to attain.

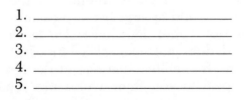

1. _____
2. _____
3. _____
4. _____
5. _____

These are your five job targets.

9

THE LIE DETECTOR

Remember when we told you that this book has a built-in lie detector system? It does. And it's working all the time. Let's see if you've been honest with yourself as you played the games. If you have been, it will be reflected in your answers to these questions about your job targets.

Compare your job targets with the Skill/Interests Cross Index you filled out on page 42.

1. Do all five of your job targets relate to one or more of the "I Like" statements? Yes ____ No ____ If the answer is "no," which job job targets don't relate? _____

_____

_____

2. Do all five of your job targets relate to one or more of your problem-solving skills? Yes ____ No ____ If the answer is "no," which job targets don't relate? _____

_____

_____

If any of your job targets do not relate to any of your "I like" statements, go back to the Pleasure Profile on pages 23 to 27 and see if the job targets relate to this broader interpretation of your pleasures. If so, it probably is a legitimate job target.

Of course, if a job target you've chosen relates to none of your pleasure indicators, there is the chance that you've overlooked a hidden interest or pleasure which is implicit in the job target. This means you may have to add to your list of pleasures.

However, if your job target does not relate to either of your pleasure indicators, and does not conceal a buried pleasure, then you need an explanation. Remember that one of the key criteria of a job target is that it appeal to you from a pleasure standpoint. Perhaps what you did was select job targets which seemed more practicably attainable in the current job market, rather than select those you really would like. This is short-sighted practicality. Review the entire job family containing that job target, or else go and dig for another job family and come up with some work activities more pleasurable to you. If you settle for less, you'll get less.

Job targets that do not relate to *any* of your problem-solving skills are questionable. You do not have to scrap them, but you must realize that in order to reach for the pleasure inherent in that field, you must have or must develop skills to tie into it. What you might uncover in the selection of these job targets, is that without realizing it, you believe you have certain problem-solving skills which you've neglected to list. In that case, go back and list them on pages 41 to 42 for future reference.

In our view, an interest without a skill is happier, and ever more profitable than a skill without an interest—even though the latter may seem more practical in a tight job market. The skill without the interest can trap you in a bleak cul-de-sac, whereas a high interest can be the motivation for developing skills and a full landscape of work pleasure.

If your job targets are not connected to either a pleasure indicator or a problem-solving skill, go back to the beginning and start again. The buzzer just sounded. You've been lying to yourself.

Part Two

STRATEGIES

INSIDE THE
HIDDEN JOB MARKET

Your work, in the first part of the book, taught you what it is you *like* to do, and, at the same time, what you *can* do—your skills and accomplishments. You've been answering a lot of questions about yourself, questions to which only you know the answers. You've been feeling your way to that private, inner person who *can do* and *enjoys doing* certain things, and not others, and is unique in more ways than you may have suspected. Through your participation in Part One, you should have a clearer idea of your pleasures and capabilities, than you had when you began this book. And more concretely, you now have five specific job targets, and you realize you can change careers—have two, three, or more different job lives.

Part Two will give you a behind the scenes look at the machinery of the job market, which you will need in order to penetrate the hidden job market. By answering the questions and performing the required games and exercises, you will learn the methods and techniques for locating the vast reservoir of jobs in the hidden job market.

The techniques and strategies outlined in the following chapters are not theoretical. They are the result of thousands of hours of interviewing and investigating job seekers, employers, and placement consultants. The strategies have been successfully tested by thousands of people participating in job-finding workshops over the past few years. As a result of these workshops, participants were able to find fulfilling, productive work situations in weeks, where previously they may have spent several months searching for any job that would provide a paycheck. In Chapters 10–17 you will follow a proven step-by-step action program which has been designed to accomplish the results you are after: obtaining your job target. As you go through these pages, make them real for yourself—project your true energy and intelligence into these proven steps which will lead you to your job target.

10

JOB PLAN

In Part Two we will present you with an integrated, step-by-step program for finding and getting the job you want. In order to organize the information that results from this program you need a *job plan.*

The job plan is your blueprint. It helps you keep track of your campaign, making for efficient organization of time in the best interest of your objectives. The two factors to consider are:

1. A realistic date by which you should, or must, locate a new position.

2. The number of hours you can invest in your job-finding campaign each week.

Obviously, the less time you have to obtain a job target, the more hours you must put in each week toward reaching it. You will also accelerate your campaign if you are unemployed, and running low on money. On the other hand, if you are employed, but have decided to go after something which will give you more work pleasure, as well as a paycheck, you may plan for a more relaxed campaign consisting of only a few hours each week. In deciding how to allocate your time, there are two limits to keep in mind. First, the job campaign is very personal work, in many instances so demanding emotionally and psychologically, that it is generally advisable if you are unemployed, to limit yourself to a maximum of four or five hours a day, and five a week. Use the rest of the time to relax, pursue other tasks, and generally keep your morale high. If you do put in your four or five hours consistently, Monday to Friday, you have no reason to feel guilty, since you are probably doing as much as can be done, and much more than 80 percent of the job seekers do.

Second, when you have a job and no direct pressure to change other than your own feelings, it doesn't pay to do anything less than four or five hours each week. Less than this will not permit you to build up the right kind of momentum to get things done efficiently.

In both cases the hours you plan to put in should be at prescheduled times to which you adhere as though they were a real work assignment.

How long will your job campaign take?

Although there is no single answer to the question, on the average, a well-run campaign seems to take between a minimum of 100 and a maximum of 200 hours. There are people who have obtained their job targets with only 50 hours of effort. But it is not unusual for others to run well over the 200 hour budget. A key indicator of a well-run job campaign is that the job seekers receive at least three job offers before making a choice.

A good way to start planning your job campaign is to determine the date by which you feel you must have made the job change. Then, plan backwards from this date. To illustrate:

Assume the new job you finally accept will be selected from at least three job offers.

Each offer will probably result from four or five interviews, and for each interview you obtain, you probably will have to send out five letters and resumes, and make at least five telephone calls.

It might take an average of one hour of job market research to find each prospective employer target to whom you will send a cover letter and resume.

Thus, the job you accept will be the result of

3 job offers
12 or 15 interviews
60 or 75 letters, resumes, and telephone calls
60 to 75 hours of job market research

On pages 76–78 are two Job Plan Forms. These are daily and weekly time schedules for you to use as you implement the specific job campaign actions called for in the coming chapters. It is a good idea for you to get a three-ring binder in which to keep these Job Plan time schedules, as well as copies of the other forms you will be using.

To use the Job Plan forms, sit down at the beginning of the week and make an analysis of what you want to accomplish in the coming week. List these planned activities on the Weekly Job Plan and Record as specifically as you can. Next, do the same with the Daily Job Plan and Record prior to each day's effort.

At the conclusion of each day and week, note what you have *actually accomplished* in the period, compared with *your objectives*, to make the next daily or weekly plan more realistic and effective. You will need many copies of the forms, so prepare them yourself beforehand.

WEEKLY JOB PLAN AND RECORD

Make copies of this form for each job target and for each week.

Week beginning: _____   Job Target _____

Major objective for the week _____

_____

_____

General job market research objectives for the week _____

_____

_____

_____

General objectives for outside contacts for the week _____

_____

_____

_____

Additional activities (book exercises, games, role plays, etc.) _____

_____

_____

_____

WEEKLY TIME CHART

Estimated number of hours to be spent

ACTIVITY	MON.	TUES.	WED.	THURS.	FRI.	SAT.	SUN.
Planning							
Self-research							
Job market research							
Telephone calls							
Letter writing							
Nonjob trips (libraries, interviews, etc.)							
Job interviews							
Meetings with third parties							
DAILY TOTAL							

Weekly total _____

DAILY JOB PLAN AND RECORD

Use a separate sheet of paper for each job target and for each day.

DATE _____   JOB TARGET _____

Job work hours scheduled from _____ *to* _____

Prime objective for the day _____
_____

Telephone Calls or Letters

PERSON/ ORGANIZATION	PHONE NUMBER OR ADDRESS	OBJECTIVE	RESULT
1.			
2.			
3.			
4.			
5.			

Specific Research Objectives

SOURCES TO CONTACT	OBJECTIVE	RESULT
1.		
2.		
3.		
4.		
5.		

Miscellaneous Objectives for the Day (people to see, places to go, interviews to schedule, etc.)

1. _____
2. _____
3. _____
4. _____
5. _____

Results of day's activities (list accomplishments and unsatisfied objectives)

ACCOMPLISHMENTS

_____

_____

_____

UNSATISFIED
OBJECTIVES

_____

_____

_____

11

ACTION SPEAKS LOUDER

This is the way Jim Thorpe described his recent job hunting campaign.

I knew that there was trouble back as early as February '74. That's when the parent company first started to rumble. They called my boss Tony Devlin up to a meeting on the 15th floor and when he came downstairs he looked like death warmed over. Right then I knew something was seriously wrong. But Tony didn't talk. Just walked around looking sick. Two days later he asked me to go to lunch with him. I broke my dentist appointment and went. Over spaghetti and meatballs he gave me the word. Seems that management of the parent had blasted him— but good. The performance of our college marketing network was lousy. A joke. Meaning we were a joke. From here on we were on the firing line. Unless of course we could do a turn around. Actually those guys upstairs weren't that unreasonable. They weren't asking to see profits. Just stop the flood of red ink.

After lunch I closed my office door and told my assistant to hold all calls. I sat behind my desk and practically cried. Six goddamn years trying to build this thing, and we hadn't met our projections for the last three. Obviously, as a college merchandising specialist, I was on my way to obsolescence. Then my tooth started to hurt and I called the dentist.

OK—time to dig out the old resume. Shape it up. Make a few discreet calls, get a few offers lined up, and then—zappo!—bail out before the shit hit the fan. I figured the department had a four-month life span. Maximum. I wasn't going to be around to hand out the termination notices. Including mine.

As things turned out it took seven months for the inevitable to happen. Probably because the parent was in such a turmoil themselves they didn't have time to notice our small divisional crisis. Until September. Then zonk!

Tony had resigned in May. Smart bird. All of those field trips must have covered a lot of interviews. Anyway, he's now with some food giant out in the midwest. But Tony always knew how to take care of Tony.

I was the sap. Not that I had any illusions that we would be around very long. But I never did make those discreet phone calls. The whole idea of the job hunt just gave me the creeps. I guess I had been hoping for a miracle.

So there I was on September 16th with the rest of the mice, getting my severance pay, and that wasn't too bad. I cleared out my desk, left the keys with the receptionist and walked all the way to Penn Station. A two-hour stroll with a couple of bar stops on the way. After faking the train ride into the city for two days, and bumming around from movie to movie, I finally decided to break the news to Mary. She always was a good girl. She took it better than I did. She got me moving.

I took a couple of hours and updated my resume. Wrote a cover letter to go along with it. And had about 50 of each Xeroxed down the street.

After that Mary and I screened the classified ads. In 10 days we picked out about 50 potential companies looking for sales, marketing, or merchandising types—especially with an emphasis on youth marketing—and mailed out 50 resumes.

I waited long after I was sure the last of the 50 resumes was filed away. Four weeks to be exact. Oh, I made a few phone calls to see if the resumes had been received. "Yes, Mr. Thorpe," said the voice on the end of the telephone. "I'm sure we've received your resume. You should be hearing from us if there is any interest. . ."

Nothing happened. With 50 letters you'd think I'd get at least four job offers. No. What I ended up with was nine form letter rejections and one application, which I filled out. When they called me and discussed the job they said it involved 50 percent travel so I told them to get lost.

By the sixth week I was a pretty scared college merchandising genius. Mary was worried too, and started talking about going out and getting a secretarial job. But who'd take care of Peter? Me? No way. I thought "OK, try again." Look at your resume? Maybe I hadn't really explained how great I was. Maybe it's too short. Maybe it has fleas. So I expanded a little. Then we combed the classified again and picked another 50 spots. Out went the resumes and the letters. Again the waiting time was librium time. I read every magazine in the house and got back issues of *Women's Day*. I put on 5 pounds from eating too much and doing too little. And the only time I saw other people was when I went to sign up for my unemployment insurance. With me and Mary stuck in the house together we started getting on each other's nerves. I decided to get out and do the employment agency routine.

I went to five agencies and filled out form after form. I tried to pick agencies that I knew specialized in marketing and merchandising. But it was all a waste of time. When I had my ten-minute interview with the guy in charge, he said nothing was happening in the college market. I didn't need him to tell me that. I'd have done better if I'd stayed home and painted the garage doors.

By now Mary had the real jitters. We discussed investing $500 in my seeing this career counselor I'd heard about last year. But when I called the phone was disconnected. He was out of business. Well, that saved me $500 but it sure made me feel queasy.

My second set of 50 resumes brought two positive responses. One said, "Call Mr. So & So in two months," the other had an application blank which I filled out and mailed back. I got a letter back that resulted in an interview with a Mr. McCoy. Actually, the job didn't really turn me on, but over the next day or two I thought more about it and saw that there might be some real potential. It wasn't directly related but it was in my general area. It was with a book publisher and it involved the coordination of their college travelers. As I thought about it I was sorry I'd been so lukewarm in the interview.

Over the next few weeks I had six more interviews including two in our local town. Two came out of agencies. Two came out of ads. I didn't send in any resume. I just showed up. Two were part-time local things I'm embarrassed about, they were so nothing. Out of it all I got one offer. But it meant relocating to Chicago within six months. And with the housing market the way it is, we'd never have sold the house. Anyway, I'm not too wild about Chicago weather.

Somewhere after four months of no paycheck Mary started fussing about getting a job again. What was left in our savings account dropped sharply, and Mary was hot to call her old boss and see if he had anything. Fit her in somewhere, she was a quality secretary. We hadn't been to a movie in weeks. We hadn't seen people either. I didn't like having to explain my unemployed status. Mary kept saying I was nuts—but pride is pride. Anyway, the gist of it was we had a rip snorting fight, and she ended up calling her old boss. I couldn't have stopped her without tying her up. She gave this character our tale of woe and asked if he might have a place for her. Well he didn't have anything for Mary. But he was an OK Joe. Anyway, he said he had a friend in the men's casual wear business who was looking for a salesman marketing type, who was also familiar with the college market.

Would I like to have an interview? Would I? By now, I'd work for a campus pharmacy. Anywhere. Anyway, I took the interview and got the job. Less money and less fun than the job that got away. But a job is a job is a job. It would take a crowbar to pry me out of here. I can't face a job hunt again! End of horror story.

Jim Thorpe's behavior was typical of most people's job-hunting campaigns. He took four months to get a job he disliked. With the right approach he could have saved two months and found work he would have enjoyed. At the root of Jim Thorpe's failure was lack of *positive action.* He sat around and waited for things to happen—but didn't make them happen.

This part of the book is about things you can make happen in your career life. You are about to become an Honorary Job Doctor. Reread what Jim Thorpe has told us about his job campaign. Think about what he did or did not do. In the space below, list the things that you feel could be improved.

Now compare your critique of Jim Thorpe's campaign with ours:

1. Timing

NONACTION. Jim waited too long. He threw away six months.

ACTION STEP. Once he knew the job would be terminated, there were many things he could have done in the remaining months to lay the foundation of a well-organized job search. He should have acted while still in possession of office facilities such as a telephone, a copying machine, a desk, and secretarial help, to say nothing of a paycheck and higher morale. In the office he was in daily contact with people in his field, yet he neglected to make those "discreet telephone calls." Had he faced reality sooner, he would have saved months of anxiety.

2. Job Plan

NONACTION. At no point did Jim Thorpe have an organized plan of action for finding a new job—not while employed or after dismissal.

ACTION STEP. As we've noted, every job campaign should have a well thought out job plan, which should include:

a. Job targets

b. A time budget (specific hours each day and week to be put in on specific job finding steps)

c. Weekly activity goals (number of resumes to be sent out, phone calls to be made)

d. Monthly goals (number of interviews to shoot for, offers to project)

e. A job plan notebook and calendar to keep you apprised at the end of each day and week whether you are falling behind your goals, staying abreast, or whether your goals are unrealistic and should be revised.

3. Resume

NONACTION. Resume writing is an important tool of all job-finding plans, and Jim Thorpe made no effort to research the art. He "updated" an old resume by adding his most recent experience—a frightened, passive way of handling this valuable tool.

ACTION STEP. A resume is not cast in concrete. It's the rare one that can remain unchanged after six years. A resume changes as its subject, the person it refers to, changes. Jim Thorpe should have sat down and thought about who he is *now*, six years older, wiser, and hopefully much more experienced. If he had, he might have discovered that he has a different view of where he has been and where he wants to go. This would have influenced the way he described his earlier jobs in order to bring them into line with new goals.

4. Cover Letter

NONACTION. He sent the same printed cover letter with his resume to every employer contacted. The letter had the same hit or miss luck of the resume. No wonder he got so many form letters in return—after all, he sent out a form letter himself.

ACTION STEP. He should have made an effort to find out as much as he could about the people to whom he was sending his resume, and the cover letter should have been appropriately personalized to relate to the specific needs of the companies he selected.

5. Research

NONACTION. Jim Thorpe did no job market research. He hoped his dream job would appear in the classified ads or show up in an employment agency file. This can happen. But the competition is enormous, and then again, what if it doesn't happen?

ACTION STEP. He should have used a variety of sources of information about possible job opportunities such as trade journals, business directories, newsletters, etc., to point him in the direction of organizations with opportunities.

6. Narrow Job Vision

NONACTION. He never stopped to consider in what adjacent or entirely different fields his college marketing experience might be applicable.

ACTION STEP. His college marketing skill required analyzing the needs of one segment of the population. If that segment "goes out of business," why not transfer the same analytic skill to an adjacent, livelier segment such as ethnic groups. Or housewives. Or if the youth market truly magnetized him, he might have explored manufacturers of youth-oriented products—soft drinks, bicycles, records, etc. Or, he might have begun with *himself*. Rather than seeing himself as the job title of "college marketer," he should have considered where else his talents lay with the college market now dormant. He should have evaluated himself as a total human being with other interests and problem-solving skills and proceeded from there.

7. Support System

NONACTION. Jim did not use the people in his life efficiently for aid and support.

ACTION STEP. He should have worked more with his wife, family, and trusted friends to critique his resume and provide more leads and help in the total approach to his job campaign.

8. Psychological Attitude

NONACTION. When Jim Thorpe was not going to employment agencies or waiting for answers to his letter and resume, he did nothing. He did not paint the garage doors, or clean up the basement. He did not start a study project. He moped around passively.

ACTION STEP. Three to five solid well-planned and scheduled hours every single day on job research, writing letters, making telephone calls, developing job leads, rehearsing interview techniques with wife or friends is enough time for most people to put in on job finding. The rest of Jim Thorpe's time should have been spent in other constructive activities—projects he enjoyed, that would have kept his morale, health, and efficiency in better shape.

In sum, Jim Thorpe's orientation toward his job finding campaign was nonactive. In this nonaction lay his failure to be more successful. Finding the right job takes positive action. It requires more thought, creativity, and more planning effort than just taking any job offered. To many people, the task of attaining a job target is rarely given the same uninhibited, well-motivated attention as is given to salaried work. Unfortunately, the tendency in the job finding situation is to be noncompetitive, passive, and constricted. But this need not be.

When job finding is approached in an organized, optimistic, action-directed way, with the right technique, it becomes a highly profitable and productive personal adventure. Not only do you meet potential colleagues and develop new work ideas, you also develop new interviewing and negotiating skills. With perserverance you will achieve your job target.

Once you learn these job-finding techniques, you have them for keeps, for all the remaining days of your work life. It's as reassuring as money in the bank. With this skill to attain work pleasure, you have more control of your future, a saner, healthier approach to the modern work world, and more safety from economic dislocation.

Keeping this new job-finding skill in mind, let's examine your own personal job-finding skills you utilized in your last campaign. How do they compare to Jim Thorpe's? Your answers to the questions below should give you a picture of what your skills were.

1. Prior to initiating your most recent job campaign—how many hours did you spend examining or considering more than one job family area that would give you work pleasure? _____
2. How much time did you spend considering more than one job target that would give you work pleasure? (Think of work directions as job targets.) _____
3. In how many different geographic locations did you seriously consider working? _____
4. Did you prepare a new resume? _____
5. If so, how many hours did you spend preparing it? _____
6. Did you review your resume with others to get their criticism or suggestions prior to having it typed or printed? _____
7. Did you conduct any "outside" research to line up potential job target leads other than screening obvious employment sources such as newspaper classified ads? _____
8. Approximately how many hours did you put into research? _____

9. Approximately how many specific names of potential employers did you come up with as a result of your job research? _____

10. How many friends, associates, ex-employers or other interested "third parties" did you contact looking for new job leads? _____

11. Approximately how many personalized, individual letters did you write on your own initiating some sort of job contact? _____

12. Approximately how many telephone calls did you initiate to obtain information about jobs—other than those in response to an advertisement? _____

13. How many specific offers did you seriously consider prior to accepting the one you took? _____

14. In sum, and only approximately, how many action hours did you invest in obtaining your current or most recent job? _____

If your answers were a little embarrassing, never mind. Think of it this way. You're in the landslide majority. Most people put a minimum amount of action time into their job campaign because they don't know what more to do. This book will show you what to do and how to do it.

One of the main reasons for lack of creative action in job finding is the mental states often brought on by job hunting. These inner obstacles often take the form of self-defeating excuses which on the surface look like sensible reasons for not doing something constructive; but when examined they turn out to be what they are—excuses. To train you to spot these dangerous, self-defeating excuses in yourself or others, let's play the Excuse Game.

THE EXCUSES GAME

1. Creative Job Finding Actions

Review these activities that have been used by successful job seekers, and check those that might relate to your own job campaign.

_____Spending money on important job aid tools, such as a course in a job-target field of work pleasure or books on the subject.

_____Making serious plans to turn a hobby into a profession.

_____Thinking seriously about working in another city, state, or country.

_____Contacting authors of books in your field of work pleasure to see what information they might have that could prove helpful to you.

_____Visiting the placement office of your old school, even if you haven't been there for 10 years.

_____Thoroughly evaluating your nonwork achievements and translating them into meaningful work-related opportunities.

_____Initiating a call for a possible interview, to a place for which you might like to work, although it is not hiring at the present.

_____Blowing $25 on long distance telephonic job exploration.

_____Obtaining the job sections of out-of-town newspapers.

_____Contacting the editors of trade magazines in your fields of work pleasure and interviewing them, either in person or on the telephone, for advice on your field.

_____Using good sales techniques to rewrite your resume and upgrade its sales appeal.

_____Contacting important people in the field of your work pleasure and asking them for advice on what's going on in the field, where the action is, and for possible leads.

_____Finding "unlisted" jobs by contacting accountants, lawyers, bank officers, friends, former co-workers, relatives, etc., who have business connections.

_____Personally visiting a technical or professional society relating to your field of work pleasure and seeing if you can get leads and advice from them.

_____Asking for honest criticism from anyone you trust.

_____Agreeing to pay an extra fee or "bonus" to any employment agency staffer who puts you onto a job you really want.

_____Having attractive personal letterhead stationery printed.

_____Spending three hours studying an organization in which you are interested, and with which you are going to have an interview.

_____Calling up a successful friend you haven't seen in five years and asking for a few minutes of work advice.

_____Asking for a job transfer if you are dissatisfied with your job.

_____Quitting your job.

_____If you are currently unemployed, setting up a buddy system with one or two other unemployed persons to help each other in your job-finding campaigns.

_____Obtaining the creative partnership of your spouse on a daily basis for helping you solve job-action problems.

_____Taking a couple of days off from your present job—either on sick leave or vacation time—in order to explore other kinds of work.

_____Getting an interview in a field in which it is highly unlikely that you will be employed, but which if you were, would give you considerable work pleasure.

2. The Excuses

Now, review items you've checked, and select three of the creative job actions that could conceivably apply to your own type of job campaign.

List one of these on each of the following forms. Then, under the column marked Reasons for Not Taking Action (Excuses) list all the reasons which you feel that a typical job seeker, or you yourself might find to avoid taking these actions. Even if you are not actually considering taking this job action now—dream up the excuses that might be used.

To show what we mean, here is a sample from the job action list of one of our workshop attendees—Harry Roman, a stockbroker from Phoenix who was interested in getting into horse ranching.

CREATIVE JOB ACTION: *Contact editors of trade publications in a job-target field and interview them, in person or by phone, for advice.*

REASONS FOR NOT TAKING ACTION (EXCUSES)	
1. *I don't know what the journals are.*	
2. *The editors are probably very busy. Why would they talk with me?*	
3. *What advice could they give me that I don't already know?*	
4. *I couldn't make these calls from work.*	—
5. *I'd never get past the secretary.*	

Here's another example of the Excuses Game. This example was from a woman named Diane Watson, a Civil Service cartographer working in Washington. Her job target was to become a recording engineer assistant, leading to the possibility of becoming a sound recording engineer.

CREATIVE JOB ACTION: *Spending money on a night course in Recording Technology*

REASONS FOR NOT TAKING ACTION (EXCUSES)	
1. Can't afford it	
2. Don't know of any good courses	
3. Too busy too take on additional time commitment	
4. My husband would object	
5. How do I know that once I take the course I'll be able to get a job?	

Now fill out *your own* Excuses Game forms on the following pages and see if you can invent some reasons or excuses that could possibly stand in the way of a person wishing to take this job action.

CREATIVE JOB ACTION: _____

_____

_____

REASONS FOR NOT TAKING
ACTION (EXCUSES)

1. _____

2. _____

_____

3. _____

_____

4. _____

5. _____

CREATIVE JOB ACTION: _____

_____

_____

REASONS FOR NOT TAKING
ACTION (EXCUSES)

1. _____

2. _____

_____

3. _____

_____

4. _____

5. _____

CREATIVE JOB ACTION: _____

_____

_____

_____

REASONS FOR NOT TAKING
ACTION (EXCUSES)

1. _____

2. _____

_____

3. _____

_____

4. _____

5. _____

_____

3. Overcoming Excuses

In this part we deal with overcoming excuses. We'd like you to change hats again, and get back into your honorary Job Doctor role. Go back to the three Creative Job Action forms you just filled out. Write the words Action to Overcome Excuses over the right of each form. Then, in the space below come up with a remedy or action which should answer or overcome the excuses listed on the left side.

Be a problem solver. If you find some of the excuses difficult to overcome—call in your support system and see what they might come up with. Before you do this, you might want to take a look at the remedies Harry Roman and Diane Watson listed.

Here is Harry Roman's list of excuses and his actions to overcome these excuses:

CREATIVE JOB ACTION: *Contact editors of trade publications in a job-target field and interview them, in person or by phone for advice.*

REASONS FOR NOT TAKING ACTION (EXCUSES)	ACTION TO OVERCOME EXCUSES
1. I don't know what the journals are.	1. Call someone in the field and ask - stop in at the library.
2. The editors are probably very busy. Why would they talk with me?	2. How do I know they are too busy? Just invent yourself a research project or survey. I only need 15 minutes or so
3. What advice could they give me that I don't already know?	3. They could give me leads to job titles, books, association people.
4. I couldn't make these calls from work.	4. Take a day off. Take two.
5. I'd never get past the secretary.	5. Tell the secretary that I'm doing an important top level project and was told that her boss was the best person to help.

Diane Watson, also, found ways to overcome her reasons for not taking creative action:

CREATIVE JOB ACTION: *Spending money on a night course in Recording Technology*

REASONS FOR NOT TAKING ACTION (EXCUSES)	ACTION TO OVERCOME EXCUSES
1. Can't afford it.	1. Work out terms, go without something else — work pleasure is a permanent pleasure worth the sacrifice.
2. Don't know of any good courses.	2. Call a dozen sound studios from yellow pages, check with Hi-Fi stores, write to Ampex.
3. Too busy to take on additional time commitment.	3. Give up an hour or two a day of less meaningful activities, get yourself organized. Use some vacation time to explore the field.
4. My husband would object.	4. Bring husband in on a positive basis. Make him part of the project — talk about future possibilities Increased income.
5. How do I know that once I take the course I'll be able to get a job.	5. I'll never know for sure but my chances could be increased immeasurably. It can't hurt — course contacts could be important job leads. Talk to the instructors before you register.

Postscript

Making excuses is a normal part of a job campaign—you aren't alone. It's how you overcome excuses that determines the success of your campaign.

From here on you will be presented with ideas, strategies and approaches which have proven successful, and, when properly used, are virtually guaranteed to get you into a satisfying job which will utilize your real skills and talents. If at a later date, you find that you are having trouble in your job campaign, review this book. If you find actions that you just haven't gotten around to trying, put them through the Excuse Game, and then, when you know how to overcome them—act.

12

THE HIDDEN JOB MARKET
What It Is. Where It Is.

You wake up one Sunday morning with the nagging feeling that you ought to start "looking around." There's something funny going on down at the place. Or one Tuesday afternoon at work you finally realize that you've been wasting the best years of your life doing a job a monkey could do. You want something better. Or you wake up at 10:30 A.M. on a Monday and discover that the nightmare is true—you were laid off on Friday, and you need a new job. Whatever the reason, you realize you're in the market for a new job and the thing to do is get the newspaper and scan the classified. See what's doing, Right?

Surveying the classified employment section and the employment agency listings in the newspaper is the classic, standard, and the most effortless way to look for a job. Which is what makes it right—and popular. That also is what makes it wrong. It puts you in direct competition with the rest of the job seekers—dozens to hundreds—who saw the same ad that attracted you. And all those people will be in there pitching when you get in there and start to pitch. This then makes the job easy to locate, but not that easy to get.

However, there's another much more imperative reason why the classified section should not be your only approach to job seeking. It has to do with *invisibility*. Only about 10 or 15 percent of the available openings in any given locality on a given day are in the public record. The other 90 percent or so are not listed in that day's paper, or placed with employment agencies. They remain in what is known as the *hidden job market*. In fact, some of your job targets might never be found in the newspapers or placed with an employment agency.

WHAT IS THE HIDDEN JOB MARKET?

The hidden job market is in people's minds. It is that vast reservoir of job information that people in companies, in associations, and other organizations have about what's happening on their own or on neighboring turf. It is made up of unreleased new plans, emerging new problems, the impending retirements, the expansions, and the contractions—the job that will be advertised in a few weeks. Last week's advertised jobs that haven't been filled. The jobs which were released to only one or two agencies.

The pressures of the marketplace force a company management to change direction constantly. Every time a change is made jobs open, jobs shift, jobs close. The people required to implement the change are seldom given the first priority in management's thinking. These new directions that can generate potential new job openings often are left dangling. Furthermore, where concretely defined openings occur, there is uncertainty about what to do. Months can pass between the time a potential new opening is recognized and the time the personnel department is contacted to put an advertisement in the newspaper, or place a request with an employment agency.

One Tuesday, Aron Hansen, who heads sales promotion for the Pacific market of a large beverage company, decides to leave. Or his supervisor who heads national sales asks him to leave. Or promotes him. Or Aron hits retirement age. Or he decides to take early retirement. Or . . . ? Only one thing is sure. The first to know of this change is either Aron or management—depending on whether he or they made the decision. The next to know are Aron's co-workers. And you the public are the last, if ever, to know. These decisions are arrived at slowly, and nobody considers putting a classified ad in the newspapers or calling an employment agency. Soon Aron Hansen leaves. Still nothing is done.

This is the hidden job market. A potential job exists for somebody if they knew how to find it. But how? Well, let's say there is a Sidney Ringley living in California who has been doing sales promotion in the cosmetic field. Sidney thinks he could bring a whole new flair to the food field, so one of his job targets is "food or soft drink sales promotion." The Hansen opening is just the job for Sidney. If Sidney does the proper job market research he possibly could uncover the position long before management makes up its mind what to do. He might very well be able to sell them on making up their mind to hire Sidney Ringley.

WHAT IS JOB MARKET RESEARCH?

Job market research is a system of well-proven investigative techniques that will provide you with the names, addresses, and phone numbers of organizations and of people within them who are related to your job target.

Job market research is an indispensable skill for exploring the hidden job market. Once you acquire the skill, you gain a new freedom from the bureaucracy you face when seeking a job through traditional methods. What it adds up to is that you act, you take the initiative, instead of sitting in waiting rooms and being on waiting lists, hoping for something wonderful to happen.

Select one of the five job targets you arrived at on page 67. You will concentrate on this job target throughout this part of the book. However, everything that applies to this job target will also apply to the other four, should you decide to go after them.

Job Target _____

Before we guide you through the phases of job market research, let's observe research-in-action as illustrated by George Hanna, age 36, a highly successful job market engineer. George has purposely changed jobs and companies three times in ten years, each time for a higher position. At each stage, George designed and implemented his own career plan, taking three to six months to make each move. So successful was his plan that it has carried him from a starting job as administrative assistant in retailing, making $9,000 a year, to what he is today, a vice-president of a medium-sized paper manufacturing company. He now earns $30,000 a year plus a large bonus.

George did the kind of research any good placement agency would have done if George were their only client. George is *his* own only client, therefore he gets all his own attention. He did the professional research necessary to identify for himself those companies that would want his skills and the people in those companies who could hire him.

Read George Hanna's report on himself.

I learned this idea of job research quite by accident, while I was working for my MBA. I was researching a school paper on the use of certain kinds of computerized financial systems in the retail business.

First, what I had to do was find out which retailers already had this type of system and what types of problems they were having. That question got me to the library where I found a copy of the *Directory of the National Retail Merchants' Association.* I picked out 50 large retailers to contact in my computer survey. It took me only two or three phone calls to a company to find out the name of the Manager of Data Processing and to talk with him. Frankly, I was surprised at the amount of information I was able to get from these telephone calls. Once in a while I'd have to send my questions in writing, but most of the time all I had to do was spend 15 to 20 minutes on the telephone. I guess it cost me 50 to 100 dollars in phone bills but it was worth it. I got very few turndowns. I went in person to visit four or five companies that were not too far from the suburb of Boston where I then lived.

I kept the project information in a large ring binder and before I was three-quarters done, the binder was fat with pages of information that included names of stores and companies, the titles and the names of the people who were in charge and working on the jobs, telephone numbers, detailed information about the kinds of systems and programs they were using. And a catalogue of the problems they were having. All kinds of good data. No one hesitated to give me information.

I also visited some equipment manufacturers. They were pretty glad to talk to me too, because I spoke their language. By now I was familiar enough with some of the problems they were having in the field to be able to discuss them.

I never finished the project because I ran out of money and had to leave school. I wanted to find any job with a decent size company in which I could use my financial and/or systems skills. After a couple of weeks off, I started the traditional job hunt. I went to seven or eight employment agencies, read the ads, sent out resumes, and generally waited for opportunity to knock. It didn't. For weeks nothing happened. I particularly hated being at the mercy of some personnel guy who was trying to coordinate interviews with 25 people—and it seems I was always number 26. I was leaving the personnel office of a large drug company one afternoon, bored and disgusted when the light snapped on. I said to myself, Stop! Why not use all that great information you collected on your retail financial project? Why not? My black ring-binder was going to pay back its investment.

From the information that I had collected a few months earlier I first picked out 10 specific companies within a 100-mile radius of Boston where I wanted to stay. I like the nearby skiing, the city, and my pad. I looked up the names of the people I knew in the ten companies, and gave each one of them a ring.

I told them I was going to be in their area some time during the week and asked if we could have lunch or a cup of coffee together. I never used the direct approach of saying that I wanted to work for their operation. That makes people nervous. What I said was I wanted some advice on where I could put my knowledge of retail financial systems to work. And the guy I was talking to was, I thought, the best man to give me the advice. This flattered him and it was true. He was the best man. He was working in the field. He knew what was going on. He could give me leads. If incidentally he happened to have a job opening in his firm—or know of one elsewhere—great. But let him suggest it. I wasn't pushing.

In all I made 75 or 80 phone calls. Visited 25 or 30 different people—all at my own expense. I kept my wife busy typing follow-up letters and thank-you notes and so forth. My original MBA project list almost doubled in size. Every time I talked with one guy, he'd have a couple of ideas about some other places and people. The list grew. The contacts grew. And it was all stored in my three-ring project binder.

Using this method and putting on a pretty intensive drive for interviews, I kept turning up more and more prospects. As a result, I got quite a few offers and I finally accepted a job in a medium-sized retail chain headquartered in Hartford.

My objective for the next job was to stay in the field of financial systems but to become a systems manager. To have more say in the decision-making process. I felt this meant working for a smaller company that hadn't gotten into computers yet, but was interested in it. Also, I wanted to get out of retailing and into manufacturing. I wanted to broaden my base.

In this second job, I didn't think about going to agencies or reading employment ads. I preferred to work at my own speed, determining the companies that were around, and then go in and make my presentation on how I could do a good job for them.

I started this campaign while I was employed, so I wasn't under the same pressure that I had been when looking for the first job. But I did set up a schedule. The first thing was to take a week off from work, and during this time spend about 20 to 25 hours building up new files, expanding into manufacturing. I talked to systems suppliers, broke out the directories and zeroed in on manufacturing concerns in the New England area with between 500 and 1000 employees. I used *Standard and Poor's*, *Dun & Bradstreet* and the *Standard Directory of Advertising*. I also had a lot of leads I'd picked up from people I met in the computer hardware field, and a collection of business cards from the times I'd been to the various computer association meetings and retail merchants meetings. These cards were quite useful. I did the basic research, lining up names and phone numbers in a solid five-day period. I knew it would take an uninterrupted momentum to get off the ground and keep moving. I had my three-ring binder going again and by the week's end, I had an organized list of 75 companies and maybe 100 individuals that I could contact. All with phone numbers and correct names and titles. Then began the process of elimination. I scanned the list and tried to get a feel of what these companies were doing. *Standard Directory of Advertising* lists major corporations and then some. They do it in a way that tells you who they are, what they do, names of products, names of executives, and so forth. This is very helpful. In those cases where I couldn't find any fill-in information on the company I called a brokerage house and asked for the company's annual report. They sent it to me immediately if there was one. Sorting over the long list of 75 companies, I narrowed it down to 40 top prospects for a manageable time budget.

I spread out my contacting over a four-month period. I started with the most potentially rewarding firms and proceeded down the line. My procedure would be to call the office of the top financial man in the organization to find out either from him or his secretary who was in charge of financial systems. I also asked whether or not they were computerized, and if so, what kind of equipment they used. Their answers gave me leads to the equipment manufacturers in case I wanted to find out more about the company, and how far along they were.

I have to admit to a little subterfuge. In telephoning I went back to my original pitch about a research project. It still worked. In fact, I designed a sheet of questions to be asked, Xeroxed it, and filled in the blanks as I talked on the telephone. My wife helped too. She made calls saying she was working with me on this research project. If things got too technical she would say I'd call back.

Incidentally, one thing was essential. Before we made our calls we always knew the names and titles of the people we wanted to talk to. It helped. This calling phase covered a three-month period. I worked at it for four or five hours a week from my office. My wife from home. We also asked the seemingly innocuous but very important questions when we made our calls. We asked: "Are you aware of any other organizations that are starting, or in the middle of planning to implement, a financial analysis system?" It was this last question that led me to the job I finally took. Every time I asked that question and got a response I wrote it down and checked it out immediately. Because that was the kind of job I wanted and the work for which I knew I was well qualified.

Along about the fourth month of my job campaign I went to see the vice-president in charge of finance of a shoe manufacturing company that had been mentioned by our IBM salesman.

Before meeting with him I had rehearsed my usual sales pitch on myself as though I were selling shoes. In the interview I described my experience in my present job, creating systems to handle the chain's financial analysis. I also made certain he realized that I had a pretty good knowledge of the shoe industry. Some of this knowledge I'd gained through my current job. But most of it I'd picked up just before my interview. I did this by talking to other shoe manufacturers, reading shoe trade publications and things like that.

My presentation worked. I got the job. The company knew they wanted to computerize their financial data but they hadn't even begun to think about equipment choices, let alone think about who to hire to supervise it. I turned up at the right moment. Salary increase of almost 30 percent—I was now up to $15,000 a year.

And then four years later I did the whole thing over again. Only this time I no longer felt I was a computer expert, but more of a financial pro. I went out for a vice-presidency. I got it in the location that I wanted—northern California. The company is medium size with a fine growth potential, the salary is $30,000 a year plus $1000 or so a month profit-sharing bonus. The company is in the paper business. What they liked about me was that I had not only a strong dose of programming systems but a solid knowledge of finance. Oh, by the way, I'd finished my MBA by going to night school during the intervening years. I realized it was important to have an MBA for the kind of top financial position I eventually wanted to get to.

What George Hanna's story tells you is that you can and should take your job campaign in your own hands. Take action. Don't be passive. George Hanna did quite a bit of research and really reached into the hidden job market. But in terms of dollar, work, and pleasure return for time invested, it was worth every minute spent. From reading his experience you should have deduced that job market research is actual detective work. It involves finding out the names of companies that could have openings in your job target field. It means learning the ins and outs of the hidden job market. Chasing down clues. Considering tips. Judging prospects. Following job leads.

JOB MARKET RESEARCH

This research goes on in libraries, on telephones, over lunches, during bank hours, and at the breakfast table as you make the moves of this game plan. Job market research comes in three parts:

1. Sourcing
2. Digging and sorting
3. Identifying possible and real openings

These probably are new ideas to you, but when properly understood and pursued, they will turn out to be invaluable. And they will remain a lifetime resource of job-finding techniques.

1. *Sourcing* refers to your looking for *sources of information* which might give you a clue about how you reach your job target. Sources of information include such publications as business directories, trade magazines, general newspaper and magazine information, even the Yellow Pages of the phone book. Sources also include economic news, product news, people news, trend news, and other news categories. It includes other people—second, third, and fifth parties who might "know something."

2. *Digging and sorting* is when you dig into your sources and then sort and list the names, addresses, and phone numbers of potential employers. You also list any other relevant information such as size of company, growth potential, head of department you're interested in, that can help you make contact with that employer.

3. *Identification* is the final stage of your research. You have obtained the names of employers who might relate to your job target. Now you probe these potential employers (by methods we will describe later), to determine whether they have or may need the kind of skill that is related to your job target. If they do, you next identify the name and title of the person in the organization who would be most likely to make the hiring decision for your job target.

We will now consider these three parts of job market research in more detail.

SOURCING

Before guiding you through the methods of sourcing let us clarify one point—we don't know what *your own* job targets are. Consequently, all the examples we give you will be *generalized*. However, when you come to fill in your Sourcing Inventory Forms on pages 110–113 your references should be *personalized*. For instance, in our Sourcing Check List, we note "Trade Journals" as a classification.

General Reading

Following are a variety of sources where you can find the names and addresses of potential employers that might lead you to your job target.

• *Your local newspaper.* Current and back issues. News articles, economic news, news relating to your field of interest, product news.

• *Out of town newspapers.* Current and back issues.

• *Wall Street Journal, The New York Times* (both carry job listings from all over the country). Current and back issues.

• *Classified telephone directories,* Yellow Pages, both local and those of other locations that might interest you.

• *General magazines.* For product ads and relevant articles.

• *Books* on your subject of job target interest.

• *College alumni journals* (see who is where now).

• *Club newspapers or magazines* for people news and ideas.

• *Newsletters* in your field of interest.

• *Special interest magazines and newspapers* in sports, music, home care, travel, crafts, etc.

Tips for Using General Reading Sources

• When reading newspapers, keep your eyes open for conventions and trade meetings of interest.

• We refer to back issues of newspapers and magazines because, surprisingly, the classified ads of three months ago sometimes can be more useful than those that appear today. You may find a company that three months ago was hiring for your kind of job target. It's a lead. What other openings do they have? And what about the Mr. X or Ms. Y who filled the job? Did he or she work out? If so, you might find out his or her name and call. Here's a knowledgeable colleague, recently hired in the field of your interest. If you approach this person properly you might get some useful suggestions as to where to go—potential openings he or she might know of, or particularly helpful employment agencies.

• Keep on the lookout for news about company relocations. Who do they lose? Who do they need?

• The Yellow Pages. If you are thinking of relocating, besides looking at the out-of-town newspapers, call the telephone company and ask for Yellow Pages for your target locations. One job seeker we knew ordered and received 20 different sets of Yellow Pages. He picked his job target field, which was furniture design, and then canvassed dozens of companies listed under *Furniture* in the Yellow Pages of the cities of his choice. He called the companies, got the names of people to talk to, and by astute questioning, found out who to call back or send resumes to. Eventually he wound up with a job he liked in a city he liked—and a sizable telephone bill that he was delighted to pay.

Directories

There are literally thousands of specific directories listing people, companies, products, publications, etc., in almost every possible field of interest, ranging from people directories such as *Who's Who* to major business directories—*Dun & Bradstreet, Standard and Poor's, Thomas' Register*, etc. In addition there are directories published by local Chambers of Commerce.

Once you have focused on your job target it is a relatively simple matter to locate one or more directories that can lead you to employers in your job target field. One way of deciding which specific directories relate to your job target is to contact people in the field and ask them which directories they know. It may take several calls, but it is well worth the effort as it uncovers good sources of information for your research. Most directories can be found in the economic or business section of your library, in business school libraries, brokerage firms, and in the offices of your local Chamber of Commerce.

There are also *super directories* that can point you to a directory appropriate to your job target area. One volume to turn to is *The Guide to American Directories* which lists thousands of directories in almost all employer categories. There is the *Encyclopedia of Associations*, which contains the names, telephone numbers, and addresses of thousands of different kinds of trade and professional associations. Then there is *Standard Rate and Data* which lists all business periodicals published, listing the name, address, and price of each publication, which enables you to purchase current or back issues.

These super-directories *do not* give you the names of employers in your job target field. What they give you are names of *other* sources in which you can find the specific information you want, such as employer directories for a given field, or—as in the *Encyclopedia of Associations*—the association that could put you in touch with employers in your job target area. For more detailed information on directories, see Part Four, pages 270–272.

A Real Life Example

Herman Collier's job target is to be a financial librarian. We asked him to name a directory that might be useful in suggesting companies, organizations, associations, etc., where he might find an opening, and he named *The American Banking Directory*. Banks need financial librarians.

Allison Cramer would like to do publicity work for an art museum or gallery. When we asked her to name a directory that might be useful, she couldn't think of one offhand. Then she made a telephone call to a friend who works in the office of a local art museum and came back with the name *Who's Who in American Art*.

Now what about you?

Offhand, name a directory that might be useful in giving you the names of organizations, associations, companies, corporations, etc., that might have a place for you in your job target area.

Name one _____

Did you have any difficulties? Who do you know in the field? Do what Allison did—pick up the telephone and call them. Ask for the name of an important directory in your field of interest. You don't know anyone in your field? Think of a friend you have who might know. Think. Call them. This is how you crack the hidden job market—by asking questions. And don't worry. If worst comes to worst you can always use the *Guide to American Directories*. That has everything.

Trade and Business Publications

Every business, profession, and endeavor from needlecraft to metallurgy has its own publication—usually several publications. There is a variety of magazines, newspapers, newsletters, and journals. Some are published weekly or monthly, others quarterly or annually. Those publications report ongoing events and trends in a particular business, profession, or artistic field with extensive information about organizations and individuals in the field. Some publications even include classified listings of jobs.

There probably are many publications in your field of interest. You may even subscribe to one or two. If you don't, you can always go to the library and look them up. You could ask the librarian for assistance, or you could find their names in *Standard Rate and Data*, a super-directory. If possible, go through issues one or two years old, and make notes on employers who might interest you. It's worth knowing who was hiring in the area of your job target in the recent past. Perhaps they have other similar openings, or reopenings. Read the articles too because they give you a lot of information about what's going on in the field. They also provide you with the right jargon for use on interviews. Check for references to books, reports, and individuals related to your job field of interest. Take down the names of the people who wrote articles you found particularly interesting and call the magazine.

While going through a publication, watch for product advertisements. See which companies are manufacturing what kinds of products. If any of the products correspond to your job-target field, it is important to add these companies to your Sourcing Inventory Form (p. 110) under Miscellaneous Sources.

A Real Life Example

Cora Wentworth's job target is social secretary to a celebrity. When we asked her what trade journals might be useful to her in developing job leads, she named *Variety, Backstage,* and *Broadcasting.*

Dave Currier's job target is the dry cleaning business. When we asked him which trade journal he would check he said he didn't know of any. Then he went to the Yellow Pages and looked up some names. He called Anchor Cleaning Service and asked to speak to the manager. When he got the manager, Dave asked him if he would suggest the names of two trade publications. The manager suggested *Dry Cleaning News* and *Clothesline.*

Name one trade publication in the field of your job target: _____

_____

If you didn't come up with one quickly, why not check the Yellow Pages, and do exactly what Dave Currier did. It's easy. People will be helpful if you go at it properly and politely.

Financial Reports and Analyses

Annual reports and investment analyses on companies are yours for the asking from brokerage houses, if the company is publicly held. In this way you can find out what the company is doing and what its prospects are. In addition, brokerage houses can give you clues as to trends in the field.

Government Reports

The Federal Government has information and prepares reports and studies on almost every activity—both commercial and noncommercial—that takes place. To get information, contact the Government Printing Office; if you know, for example, that the information on your particular job target would be in the Department of Health, Education and Welfare, or with the Environmental Protection Agency, you can contact those departments directly, and ask for a list of their publications.

Third Parties

A third party is anyone and everyone who could suggest information that would help uncover the names of organizations or people in your target field. It also refers to anything that might offer opportunities that would lead you closer to, or bring you directly into contact with, your job target. It's the old Who Do You Know Game and includes:

- Family members as well as distant cousins, and, if you're still talking, ex-mates, and current or past in-laws.
- Old school friends, professors, and teachers.
- Professionals—lawyers, accountants, your banker, your real estate broker, stockbroker, even your income tax man if properly approached may know something about an employer you're interested in contacting.
- Fellow employees or co-workers, or a boss from a previous job. Have a lunch or drink or a telephone chat with one of them. They may know something or somebody.
- Editors or writers of articles in trade journals or trade publications, newspapers, or newsletters in the field of your job target.
- Big name authorities in the area of your job target. Someone you know may know one of them.
- Employment agency people—consider college placement offices, trade association executives, officers in the local Chamber of Commerce, and other community contacts. With these groups of people you can be quite direct in your approach. It's their business to have ideas about job location.
- Priests, rabbis, ministers, insurance agents, merchants, congressmen, or suppliers. Your creditors may be valuable contacts because they want you to have a job too.

By now you should have a pretty good idea of how vital *sourcing* is to good research. You should have as long a list as possible of specific potential "sources" of information relating to your job target, as you can possibly think of, imagine, free associate, guess at. Go as far as your creativity and energy will let you.

It is important that this list of sources be well organized. The Sourcing Inventory Forms on pages 110–113 are made for just this purpose of organization. Under each heading on the form, list all the sources related to a specific job target.

If you can't think of enough sources, ask your spouse, your friends, a trusted relative, or a business friend.

Before you start, take a look at some segments of Fran Mitchner's Sourcing Inventory Form with the job target of photography.

Fran Mitchner

SOURCING INVENTORY FORM

JOB TARGET *Photographer's Assistant*

GENERAL READING

List here all of the names of basic publications with a general readership that you could screen for potential job target leads. Include any
special interest magazines that have a general distribution as well as
newspapers, books, etc.:

1. *Sunday Chicago Tribune – photo ads and articles, photo*
2. *credits – check back issues*
3. *Popular Photography*
4. *Camera 35*
5. *Modern Photography*
6. *Better Homes and Gardens (get names of photographers,*
7. *locate office, etc.)*
8. _____
9. _____
10. _____

DIRECTORIES AND BUSINESS PUBLICATIONS

List the names of specific directories and other business publications
which relate either to your specific job target area, or are general
enough to include information about organizations or companies
related to your job target area.

1. *Classified (Yellow Pages) under photographers*
2. *Midwest Camera Club – membership directory*
3. *Standard Rate & Data (look for publications under*
4. *photography)*
5. *Industrial Photography*
6. *Director of Professional Photography*
7. *Freelance Photographers' Handbook*
8. _____
9. _____
10. _____

THIRD PARTIES

List anyone who might be able to suggest information leading to the names of organizations, people, or agencies, that could lead you closer to your job target. If you have more names than the space allows, use extra sheets and attach them to the form.

1. Kodak Information Center (Visit)
2. Camera Stores
3. Advertising Agencies
4. Bobbie Rubinson
5. Photo Instructor from high school (call school for name)
6. Professional Photographers Association
7. Uncle Harry – works for company
8.
9.
10.
11.
12.
13.
14.
15.
16.
17.
18.
19.
20.

So much for Fran's sources. Now, fill out your own Sourcing Inventory Form for one particular job target. You will want to make copies of this form (pp. 110–113) for each of your job targets.

SOURCING INVENTORY FORM

JOB TARGET _____

GENERAL READING

List here all of the names of basic publications with a general readership that you could screen for potential job target leads. Include any special interest magazines that have a general distribution as well as newspapers, books, etc.:

1. _____
2. _____
3. _____
4. _____
5. _____
6. _____
7. _____
8. _____
9. _____
10. _____

DIRECTORIES AND BUSINESS PUBLICATIONS

List the names of specific directories and other business publications which relate either to your specific job-target area, or are general enough to include information about organizations or companies which could be involved or related to your job-target area.

1. _____
2. _____
3. _____
4. _____
5. _____
6. _____
7. _____
8. _____
9. _____
10. _____

FINANCIAL INSTITUTIONS AND GOVERNMENT SOURCES

1. _____
2. _____
3. _____
4. _____
5. _____

PROFESSIONAL SOCIETIES AND ASSOCIATIONS, COLLEGE PLACEMENT OFFICES

1. _____
2. _____
3. _____
4. _____
5. _____

MISCELLANEOUS SOURCES

1. _____
2. _____
3. _____
4. _____
5. _____

THIRD PARTIES

List anyone who might be able to suggest information that would uncover the names of organizations, people, or agencies, that could lead
you closer to your job target. If you have more names than the space
allows, use extra sheets and attach them to the form.

NAME   TELEPHONE NUMBER

1. _____
2. _____
3. _____
4. _____
5. _____
6. _____
7. _____
8. _____
9. _____
10. _____

Specialized Outside Parties

List editors or writers of trade magazines, newspapers, or newsletters in the field of your job target. If you don't know any personally, look for their names in the publications.

NAME   TELEPHONE NUMBER

1. _____
2. _____
3. _____
4. _____

List some Big Names in the area of your job target. If you don't know any personally, someone you know might; if not—you will have to research to find them.

NAME   TELEPHONE NUMBER

1. _____
2. _____
3. _____
4. _____

List all high school, college, or vocational school contacts—teachers, professors, school mates—who might be related to your target field.

NAME   TELEPHONE NUMBER

1. _____
2. _____
3. _____
4. _____
5. _____

Next are the professionals—lawyers, accountants, your banker, your real estate broker, even your income tax man. List anyone with professional contacts who might be a source of information if approached properly.

NAME   TELEPHONE NUMBER

1. _____
2. _____
3. _____
4. _____
5. _____

What about fellow employees or co-workers or ex-bosses from a previous job. Have lunch or a drink or a telephone chat with one of them whom you think might have information leading to your new job target. List some below.

NAME   TELEPHONE NUMBER

1. _____
2. _____
3. _____
4. _____
5. _____

GENERAL SOURCING TIP

By just sitting and thinking, you were able to come up with most of the information you needed up to this point. Now it is time to take positive action: make telephone calls, visit business libraries, either public or private, contact the Government Printing Office, stop in at brokerage offices, and do whatever is necessary to get the employer information you need. Do not stint on the time or energy put into sourcing. This early phase of the Research Game is crucial. When properly pursued it will be highly fruitful as a means of uncovering the job you want in the size, shape, and form you want.

13

THE HIDDEN JOB MARKET
Who and How

We now know that the hidden job market contains thousands of job openings and opportunities that have not yet reached the public. Because these opportunities haven't been advertised, it takes a particular effort to locate them before they become public knowledge. The different stages of job market research and our probing into the hidden job market accomplishes this. The first activity, Sourcing, has been discussed in Chapter 12.

DIGGING AND SORTING

Let us now turn to the second phase of job market research—digging and sorting. At this point you have located your sources of information—directories, trade journals, associations, newspapers in and out of town, the Yellow Pages, friends, accountants, etc.—and must begin to explore them for employers who might have positions relating to your job target.

First, review *all* the sources on your Sourcing Inventory Form (pp. 110–113). Put an asterisk (*) alongside the 15 or 20 publications, people, organizations, or whatever, that taken together could be primary sources of potential employer names.

Second, list each of these primary sources at the head of a Job Prospect Form. For example, if one of your starred sources is a directory, or a special interest publication, fill in the name at the top of its own Job Prospect Form. You should have 15 or 20 primary sources, and therefore, you will have to prepare 15 or 20 Job Prospect Forms, using the sample on page 117 as a guide, or duplicating it.

Next, read, phone, scan, burrow, and dig into each source for the names of potential employers. For example, if your job target was glassware design, one of your sources was undoubtedly *The Glass*

Digest. You will then get this directory, and under the column headed "Potential Employer," list all the companies that you find listed in the directory that seem worth considering in pursuit of your job target. You will undoubtedly be influenced in your selection by geographic location, size of company, style of product it manufactures, reputation, etc., depending on what your work pleasure–job target is. In addition to the name of the potential employer, write the address, the phone number, and whatever other useful information you have relating to the company.

See page 116 for an example of how Horace Anderson filled out one of his Job Prospect Forms. Sometimes a source may provide you with only one or two employer leads. In that case, you can put more than one source on the Job Prospect Form.

Last, when all your employer leads from these Primary Sources are listed and graded, transfer the information on the 20 or 25 most realistic and immediate possibilities for work pleasure to the Master Employment Target List on page 118. These Employer Targets represent the best possibilities extracted from all your Job Prospect Forms. As space is limited on the form we provided, you will have to prepare duplicates, adding extra sheets, as needed.

IDENTIFYING

Starting with the top name on your Master Employer Target List you will proceed down the list, and make initial contact with these organizations in order to answer two key questions.

1. Do they have a job opening or a potential job opening that coincides with your job target?

2. If so, *who* would you have to contact in order to be interviewed?

Let us make the following point very clear. You need not contact this potentially *very important person* just yet. You simply want to know *who he or she is.* What you want to do at this point, is qualify the 20 or 25 names on your Master Employer Target List, and eliminate those which turn out not to have any real job prospects for you.

On your Employer Target List, cross out those who turn out to be truly nonproductive. For others, make comments in the appropriate column. As you eliminate some names, go back to your Job Prospect Forms and find new ones. Continue this process of subtracting and adding until you identify at least ten organizations that are real job target possibilities.

JOB PROSPECT FORM

List all the employer leads you can find from this source, then rate the employers (A is best) according to which has the best potential.

JOB INFORMATION SOURCE _New York Yellow Pages_

JOB TARGET _Greeting Card Design and Illustration_

RATING			POTENTIAL EMPLOYERS	ADDRESS & TELEPHONE	PERSON TO CONTACT	COMMENTS
A	B	C				
			American Artist Group	200 Varick WA 4-3300		
			Becht, John B.	307 West 36th BR 9-4657		
			Gibson Greeting Cards	30 Rockefeller CI 6-2000		
			Drawing Board	7 West 39th 244-6488		
			Empathy Graphics	45 East 20th GR 5-8474		
			Modern Art Greeting Card	49-20 Van Dam LIC: EM 1-8842		
			Greeting Card Masters			

JOB PROSPECT FORM

(Use this form to record the names and ratings of potential employer leads from your various sources. Use a separate form for each source.)

JOB INFORMATION SOURCE _____

JOB TARGET _____
SOURCE _____

RATING			POTENTIAL EMPLOYERS	ADDRESS & TELEPHONE	PERSON TO CONTACT	COMMENTS
A	B	C				

MASTER EMPLOYER TARGET LIST

List the names of all employer prospects from your Job Prospect Forms whom you feel will be *most productive* as potential job targets. Continue to add and delete prospects on fresh copies of the form.

JOB TARGET _____

RANK	EMPLOYER TARGET NAME & ADDRESS	NAME, TITLE, & PHONE OF PERSON TO CONTACT	RESULTS OF CALLS AND COMMENTS

RANK	EMPLOYER TARGET NAME & ADDRESS	NAME, & TITLE, & PHONE OF PERSON TO CONTACT	RESULTS OF CALLS AND COMMENTS

Identification Tips

Ask the switchboard operator for the name of the person with the job title to whom you think you might report if you attained your job target.

If the operator doesn't know and switches you to personnel, ask for the name again. If they want to know why you want to know, make up a reasonable, nonthreatening business reason, e.g., you're taking an opinion survey on some subject in the field and you want to know the opinion of this man or woman.

If personnel can't figure out exactly who you should talk to (because there is no such job, or because it has a different title) try calling a senior vice-president in the area of your interest. If your conversation with him or her reveals that the company has no job title related to your job target, it might be a signal that they need someone like you. If you handle yourself properly, you may be able to create an opening for yourself.

You might also call the editors of trade journals in your field, and ask them what they know about the employer target you're interested in, and who would be the person to call.

For example, suppose one of your job targets is to be the Affirmative Action Director for a medium-sized company. (This is a new job area with responsibility for showing organizations how to apply the Equal Employment Opportunity Regulations to their business.) Mary Lou Fenster, who has long been concerned with the Women's Movement, selected it as a practical way of combining her strong interest in the movement with her other work pleasures of designing and implementing management programs. Mary Lou had been a public relations account executive for a PR firm, and decided that she was far more interested in the people her clients hired than in the products that her clients produced. She had attended and participated in several seminars on Equal Opportunity and had studied a number of publications from the Equal Employment Opportunity Commission. In her sourcing phase of job market research she obtained, among other sources, a directory of corporations showing number of employees from her local Chamber of Commerce. During her digging and sorting phase she combed this directory for medium-sized companies within a 50-mile radius of her home. She looked for companies which, she felt, might have need of an Affirmative Action Director, but which had not yet hired one. It was her feeling that larger companies would already have such a person so she skipped over these names. The directory yielded 25 employer targets within the 50-mile limit. To decide which of these firms represented really good prospects for her job target, she contacted each one with a prepared set of questions. On these fishing expeditions, where possible, she tried to avoid talking to that person who might ultimately be responsible for hiring her, if there was an opening. For that person she wanted to prepare a really finished self-selling presentation.

At this stage all she wanted to do was to discover whether the employer was or was not a *real* target with a possible job opening. If he was, she wanted to find out the name of the person who would be responsible for hiring her. Here is a sample of one of her telephone field trips (note that she is using an assumed name).

Mary Lou: Hello, Could you please tell me the name of your Affirmative Action Director?

Operator: Our what?

Mary Lou: Affirmative Action Director.

Operator: That's a new one.

Mary Lou: Well, you may not have one. Could you give me the name of your Personnel Director and his secretary?

Operator: Sure. James Ludlow. Addie Parks is his secretary. Do you want to speak with her?

Mary Lou: Yes. Thank you.

Ms. Parks: Hello. Mr. Ludlow's office.

Mary Lou: Ms. Parks?

Ms. Parks: Yes.

Mary Lou: Could you give me the name of your Affirmative Action Director?

Ms. Parks: What's your name, please?

Mary Lou: Grace Harrison. Who is your Affirmative Action Director?

Ms. Parks: We don't have one.

Mary Lou: I see. Well, thank you.

This company went to the top of her list as a company to be contacted for a possible job as Affirmative Action Director. They had none and were large enough so that they should. And she had the name of the contact too—James Ludlow, Director of Personnel. Then she called another company. She got Sylvia Easton, secretary to Hal Wallis, Employment Manager.

Mary Lou: Ms. Easton?

Ms. Easton: Yes?

Mary Lou: Can you tell me who your Affirmative Action Director is?

Ms. Easton: Well, my boss sort of is.

Mary Lou: Aaah. As part of his duties as Personnel Manager?

Ms. Easton: Yes, and a hundred other things.

Mary Lou: Uhm. I see. Well thank you. Our Women's Group is doing a survey on Affirmative Action, and we might want to talk with him if he's available some time. My name is Grace Harrison.

Ms. Easton: Well, he's very busy. But I'm sure he'd make the time. Except, I'm not sure he's into Affirmative Action that much. He's only been here four months.

Mary Lou: Well, thank you. I'll be in touch.

This company went on her list as a possible target. At least they knew they needed an Affirmative Action Plan. And maybe the personnel man had more than enough to do with all his other duties. Maybe she could present herself as a useful member of the team. And if he couldn't be sold, he might have contacts with other companies who might need her.

Then she called another company and they had a Ms. Betty Owens as Affirmative Action Director, and so she left that company on her Master Employer Target List but ranked it toward the bottom. She didn't scratch it entirely because if she ended up with only a few other employers to make her self-sale presentation, she might try them again. Things change. Betty Owens might move up, or out, and if neither, she still must have valuable information on what's going on in a field in which they were both concerned. She could check it out if she had to later.

The process of probing and identifying is a continuing one. You will find, as you go along, that you will be constantly revising your Master Employer Target List. For example, if you find on your first go around that some of the sources you selected turn out to be non-productive don't despair. Go back to your original sources and dig for more names. Or look for new sources. The variety of sources you use, and how you dig into them is the key to the mystery of the hidden job market.

Remember, just as you researched this one job target, you can research the other four or more. The techniques are the same; it is *sources of information* that differ.

Nothing succeeds like success. Sooner or later we believe you will have at least three job targets with three Master Employer Target Lists in your hand. There will be 15 or 20 names on each list. And you will know exactly who you want to reach in all 30 or 45 companies. How do you reach them? The next chapter, Getting Inside, will tell you.

14

GETTING INSIDE

It is impossible to achieve your job goals without an interview. No matter how good your list of employer targets, you will not get the job unless you are interviewed. You must be interviewed even if you have the best possible cover letter and resume. This chapter describes the strategies for getting you that all important interview.

If you've answered a classified ad and were offered a competitive interview—fine. Go ahead, take it and good luck! If an employment agency sends you on a competitive interview, again fine, and more luck. These easy interviews are standard, highly competitive, and no matter how good you are you can get lost in the crowd. Of course, with your job market research properly done, you should know more than most about the company. You will also have an outstanding resume, and the ability to control the interview. Given these extras you will stand out from the crowd. But you'll still have a lot of competition.

THE NUMBERS GAME

The interviews we want you to get are in the hidden job market. They're harder to find, as they haven't been publicly announced, but they're worth it. To get these interviews in the hidden job market, you should be able to answer Yes to all the statements below. Where the answers are No, go back and rework the required games and exercises.

	Yes	No
1. You have a solid understanding of activities which give you work pleasure and work survival.	___	___
2. You recognize your problem-solving skills and accomplishments.	___	___
3. You have chosen realistic job targets based upon your work pleasure and a recognition of your own abilities.	___	___

Yes   No

4. You have committed yourself to take action to get what you want from the job market.   ____   ____

5. You have done enough job market research to come up with the names of at least 20 employers who could satisfy your job target.   ____   ____

6. You are willing to analyze and overcome the obstacles and excuses which keep you from taking action to reach your job targets.

7. You have an effective resume.   ____   ____

8. You realize that there are enough companies that could hire you if you present yourself properly and that you will not be paralyzed by either a few, or a dozen rejections along the way.   ____   ____

9. You have a job plan.   ____   ____

DO IT YOURSELF

Let us assume that your answers to the previous exercise were Yes, and that you have the names of at least 20 organizations on your Master Employer Target List. Let us also assume that you have read the next chapter on resumes and followed the strategies it laid out so that you have at your fingertips a strong, persuasive resume already prepared. You are now ready to set up employment interviews with potential employers. What do you do?

In the space below fill in the names of three potential employers, with the appropriate data in each column. Let's discuss how you get these employers to give you an interview.

EMPLOYER TARGETS   JOB TARGET _____

Organization	*Person & Title*	*Company Address*	*Telephone*
1.			
2.			
3.			

We assume that the employers you listed appear on your Master Employer Target List. As such, they could possibly have openings which would fit your job target. As you take an active role in getting interviews with these organizations, you normally will have to handle many turndowns—people who can't, won't, or who flatly refuse to interview you. It's part of the game and everyone on all job levels has to deal with it. It is easy to see these turndowns as personal rejections. They are not.

In reality, you probably will have to make 5 to 10 phone calls for each interview you actually get. The pessimist in you complains, "What a waste of time—15 wasted calls." The optimist says, "You know, with an effort, I bet I can have two or three new interviews each week. What's 40 calls?" Take your pick. At every stage of your job plan you will be doing many things without immediate return. Follow our instructions, put in the time, the effort, the energy, and your number will come up Yes.

Door Openers

There are a variety of techniques to "get inside" for interviews. We will show you how to get the most from standard approaches such as mailing resumes and making calls, as well as some unconventional methods that have proved successful.

The ABC's

An effective presentation for getting an interview includes three elements:

A for Attention. You must be noticed. Your cover letter must be read or they won't read your resume. Your phone call must be listened to, or you won't be invited in.

B for Benefits. You must have something to offer the person you're contacting: a problem you can solve, a service you can render, an answer to give, a capability you have. And you must communicate this benefit in a sufficiently convincing manner so that the reader or the listener will want to hear more about you and how you can help him.

C for Closing. You must try to get the interview scheduled then and there. You have to ask for and get a specific time commitment. In sales parlance "closing" means "asking for the business."

ATTENTION—THROUGH THE MAILS

We'd like to introduce you to some written approaches which will help you get the attention you want from your employer targets. But first, let us show what you should *not do.*

An impersonal cover letter that says—

Dear Sir,
I am interested in talking to you about a position in your department . . .

OR

Dear Sir,
I understand you have an opening for an account executive . . .

will hardly get the same attention as a cover letter that opens with a personalized lead:

Dear Mr. Bieler,
I read your article in Professional Builder and I was struck by the fact that . . .

OR

Dear Mr. Bieler,
Your name came up at the premium show as a man particularly interested in imaginative ideas . . .

OR

Dear Mr. Bieler,
I have watched with admiration the way Dog Days has consistently moved ahead of its competitors and I believe . . .

To get attention you might even try some humor

Dear Mr. Bieler,
For years Dog Days has been Chadwick's favorite meal, but in the last year, I find it has gotten less and less shelf space in our neighborhood supermarkets. It occurs to me that . . .

ATTENTION—THROUGH THE TELEPHONE

The telephone is the most potent job-finding tool you have. In a matter of minutes, you can get in touch with virtually anyone in almost any sphere of activity that interests you.

Say you want to talk with the president or vice-president of a leading organization in your field. However, you don't know the person's name. You don't even know the name of the firm. How do you find out? Look up the subject in the Yellow Pages. Then call two or three people in the field. Ask for the name and location of the kind of company you are looking for. Once you have the information, call the company. Today, even at top levels, many executives answer their own phones. So, if you can find your person's phone number, chances are good that you will get through. If not, you'll get to speak to his or her secretary or someone else in the company who may give you a lead. Elapsed time: 10 to 15 minutes.

Good phone techniques can help you unearth a variety of valuable, nonpublic job data. It can carry your self-selling pitch to almost any ear in the world of employment. It can open doors, and can initiate interviews. But it can only perform these wonders if you know how to use the tool, and are willing to use it. Do you? Many people don't.

Most of us suffer what we can only call "phone fright," and experience a kind of paralysis when it comes to making a job-related phone call outside of the routine. We freeze. We come up with reasons to avoid it. We make excuses. Have a cigarette. Eat something. Three calls a week is about the best we can do.

A Practice Exercise

You can overcome this phone fright with a little practice. Start now and make ten telephone calls about anything at all; but make the calls to complete strangers. If it makes it easier, use a pseudonym. The calls need not relate to an actual work situation, and do not have to produce results. Just make them for practice. Here are some examples of the kinds of things you can call about:

• Call your local newspaper and ask to speak to the business (or other department) editor. Ask him or her some questions about how to find out what's going on in a particular area.
• Call a local utility company and ask to speak to the vice-president in charge of research. Ask him or her what they are doing in the area of solar research.
• Call a local department store and speak to the person who would be interested in introducing a new product line.
• Call the mayor's office and inquire about what is being done to provide job counseling to the unemployed.
• Call the sales manager of a manufacturing concern. Say you are doing a research project and want to know to which trade association the company belongs, and names of some other organization in the field.

In this practice, what you say is not that important. You must try to sound confident and relaxed, even though you are talking to important people. You will find that most of these authority figures will be willing to talk to you and to listen to you. So, go ahead. Make these ten calls now.

The most important aspect of job-related telephoning, whether you are digging for information, or trying to set up an interview, is that you organize yourself beforehand.

—Always prepare the names, phone numbers, and information for a group of calls before you make your first call.

• Be ready with a fast, interesting statement that immediately describes a specific benefit for the person with whom you are talking. Say something concrete that will hold their attention.

• If a secretary intercepts your call, and you don't wish to talk with her, hang up and try again—either early in the morning, or after she leaves, which usually is promptly at 5 P.M. But you don't have to avoid her. Be friendly, not huffy. If she asks, "What is this in reference to?" use the same opening lead as you would with her boss. If it's something the boss would pay attention to, so would his or her secretary.

• When you are on the telephone breathe slowly, sound relaxed and confident in your presentation. To achieve this you need practice. Make actual calls—both for fun, and for real. If possible, record your presentation and listen to it. Eventually, you should be able to spend at least six hours a week on the telephone, dividing your time between gathering job information, making contacts, and setting up interviews.

ATTENTION—THROUGH THIRD PARTIES

A forceful way of bringing yourself to the attention of people you want to see is through the use of other persons who might have more authority or standing in your job target field, or even have a connection with the organization you are trying to infiltrate.

The difficulty is to locate the correct third party, and then get him or her to take action. This can be achieved with a creative approach and the right attitude. Your third party could be

• someone in the organization
• someone in a professional society
• someone in a trade organization
• a trade journal editor
• someone in your local chamber of commerce
• someone in your alumni association who is in the same field
• a mutual friend
• a college professor
• an ex-boss or officer with a previous employer of yours
• a management consultant or placement counselor in the field
• a recognized expert in the field
• an important supplier of your target employer
• an important client of your target employer

A third party can help you in several ways. First, prior to your interview, the third party can find out from the prospective employer which particular aspects of the job offered are most important—and can then give you this information. Second, he or she can set up an immediate interview without the formality of sending a resume. And last, a third party can make an effort to see that your letter and resume are directed at the highest possible level of the decision tree.

Once you have located one or more good third-party contacts, here is how to use them to get an interview. First, in approaching the person you want to write the letter or make the phone call for you, make sure to present a clear outline of what you would like him or her to do, and why. If you wish him to send a letter for you, provide a good draft, and the specific name, address, title etc., of the person you want contacted.

Second, for a phone call, give a brief note of what you would like said. Using third parties to make our calls or send the letters is a special technique to be used in situations where you are unable to get through on your own, or the job target is in a new field and you need extra help.

BENEFITS—TELEPHONE

The presentation of the benefits you offer should use as many of the following elements as possible:

• It should be results or accomplishments oriented rather than task oriented. Instead of saying "I am a hard worker," say "I can get the work done in half the time."

• It should be concise and to the point. In your phone call don't try to explain a complicated mechanical process that you invented. You can do that in the interview. To get the interview talk about the payoff—the bottom line. The lead-in statement should be strong and short.

• It should be believable, within reason. Don't promise to double profits in 30 days!

• It should be measurable rather than a self-evaluation. Don't say "I'm very good at . . . ," instead say "Our sales went up for three quarters in a row," "There are three patents pending . . . ," "I'll bring in some sample designs . . . ," or "Our client list grew by 20 percent."

• It should use jargon relevant to the job target area. If you've been in the field you'll know these terms automatically. If you're changing fields, and have done your job market research in depth, you'll have picked up the lingo from your reading of magazines, journals, and talking to people. So listen, and take notes.

Put yourself in place of the employer listening to the following telephone lead-in statements. Do they work from the standpoint of benefits?

Hi. This is Roger Wey. I'm a graduate of Penn State and have a masters degree in finance, and would like to have an interview. Can you see me?

Hello. This is Sally Holly calling. I wonder if I could stop by to discuss a possible position with your company?

Hello. I'm sorry to bother you but I'm looking for a job in packaging design and thought you might have something. Do you?

They don't work at all. Nothing Roger, Sally, or Nameless said conveyed a real benefit to the potential employer. Instead all seemed slightly apologetic. They also made it necessary for the potential employer to try to figure out what, if any, use they might possibly be to the firm, even if there were an opening. An additional obstacle is that the callers had no clearly articulated position in mind.

Compare the previous statements with these revised versions:

Hi, Mr. Borden. This is Mr. Wey. I understand that you have recently expanded your cost control section and I'd like to talk with you about some research that I did for my masters degree in finance. I think it might be quite relevant to what you are doing. I wonder if I could stop by for a few minutes tomorrow morning to meet you.

Hello. This is Sally Holly calling, is this Miss Kavaliascus? Good. I wanted to talk with you about some work I've been doing in pattern design which I think would fit in well with your new look in coats. Could I stop by next Monday morning and show you the samples?

Hello. Roger Wade? This is Joel Turner. Jeb Tracey suggested that I call you about a series of new package designs I've put together. I think they could be adaptable to the new milkshake product you're planning to market."

The Positive Attitude

When the economy is tight, when jobs are scarce, when your first five interviews turn out to be negatives, it's natural to start to regard a job opening as charity—something an employer may give out of the kindness of his heart. This is absurd. Employers need employees more than employees need the employer. Without top quality problem-solving workers, very few organizations would survive. You must believe that an employer will hire you *any time, any place,* regardless of the unemployment rate, if you can show that employer that you have a positive value to offer—a benefit which is related to their needs and which will bring in a high yield on the investment of hiring you.

THE TELEPHONE GAME

You've read the revised telephone lead-in statements of Mr. Wey, Sally Holly, and Joel Turner. How well are *you* going to do when someone picks up the telephone, and you're at the other end? They say "Hello?" What do you say?

Prepare a one to three minute statement, that will be so persuasive in terms of conveying benefits to the person at the other end of the line, that they will be moved to invite you in for an interview.

Before You Dial

Pick a prospective employer target and describe him or her briefly.

_____
_____
_____
_____

Make up a description of the job target position for which you're calling to get an interview.

_____
_____
_____
_____

Prepare a one to three minute "commercial" about yourself, which you'll present to the prospective employer in order to induce him to interview you. Pretend you've been trying to get to talk to this potential employer for three days. He's just picked up the telephone and said "Hello?" Your turn: "Hello." Write out the balance of the statement you would use to help get an interview.

_____
_____
_____
_____
_____
_____
_____
_____
_____

Now write a second version.

"Hello._____

_____

_____

_____

_____

_____

_____

_____

_____

_____

Here's what Gordon Everitt wrote in his Telephone Game after the third try, and it got him an interview.

Hello? Lou Henderson? I'm Gordon Everitt. I've been studying your operation and I think I've come up with something you could use. For the past two years I've been doing research on a new compacting system which I think might be an ideal solution for your problem of disposing of old egg crates . . .

Want to play the game again? Pick another completely different lead-in statement.

Hello? _____

_____

_____

_____

_____

_____

_____

_____

_____

_____

More Telephone Practice

Pick a job target which is not necessarily on your own Job Target List. Make up an identity and name or role for yourself within this job target, and some particular piece of information you might want to discuss briefly with some prospective employer. In your local Yellow Pages search for the names of organizations that might employ this type of job target. List five organizations and their telephone numbers on the form below. Next, actually call each of them, and find out the name of the person who would employ you if you were really applying for that particular position. List this name in the proper column. Then call each of these employers over the period of an hour or two. The first thing you'll discover is how easy it is to reach people. Make up some piece of business to discuss with these "prospective" employers and attempt to get an interview by conveying a potential benefit, even if it is made up. Chat away, completely relaxed, since these calls don't matter. But they do give you good telephone practice. Go ahead try at least five of these trial calls. You can do more if you like. They can be fun.

Telephone Practice

Your invented job target role. _____

Description of the type of employer target you will call. _____
_____
_____
_____
_____

The idea you want to discuss or the benefit you want to convey.
_____
_____
_____
_____
_____

Organization	Person to Contact	Result of Call
1. _____	_____	_____
2. _____	_____	_____
3. _____	_____	_____
4. _____	_____	_____
5. _____	_____	_____

BENEFITS—THROUGH THE MAIL

An effective employment inquiry needs an attention-getting lead. It also needs one or two sentences or short paragraphs that compellingly state the benefits you may have for an employer. These benefits could lead him to invite you in for an interview. This is particularly true when you have had no response to a previous letter and resume, or when you want to avoid sending a resume and are making the initial contact via a letter.

Here are good benefit-oriented paragraphs:

After three years of concentrated effort on my part we had 150 new maintenance accounts. Twice that which Central Cleaning had. I believe I could do the same for your company and would like to talk with you.

OR

My design decreased oil consumption by 15 percent and turned the industry upside down. I have some comparable ideas that could fit your situation.

OR

The bank had never been on local television before. It was the best thing that could have happened to them.

OR

I helped build what was a three-man department—including myself—to one that now is staffed by 35 people, doing research and responsible for the company's major marketing decisions.

Now it's your turn. Write the opening paragraph for a cover letter you might send with your resume to an employer target.

(Name) _____

(Title) _____

(Company) _____

(Address) _____

_____

Dear _____

_____

_____

_____

_____

_____

_____

_____

_____
_____
_____
_____
_____
_____
_____
_____
_____

Now, write a letter that will get you an interview but makes initial contact without enclosing a resume.

(Name) _____
(Title) _____
(Company) _____
(Address) _____
_____

Dear _____
_____
_____
_____
_____
_____
_____
_____
_____
_____
_____
_____
_____
_____
_____
_____

CLOSING

In negotiations of any kind there is a stage called "the closing." There are some people who can make great presentations, but cannot close a deal. They don't seem to know how to wrap it up—whether the deal is a legal contract, a real estate sale, or, in your case, an interview. Many an applicant has done a superb self-selling job and wound up with the inane remark, "Anyway, if you ever happen to have the time sometime, maybe we could get together."

The interviewer didn't even have time to say "How about Tuesday?" before the telephone went click. Some people can't make closings.

You can. You want an interview—so push for it. Ask for it on the telephone, ask for it in the letter. Give the listener, or the reader, a choice of dates: "Would today or tomorrow be best for you?" That's some leeway, but don't give too much. *And don't take "no" for an answer.*

Put some urgency into your contact by implying that you are a person on the move, and that there are other job possibilities pending. If they don't see you now, you may not be around next week or next month.

OVERCOMING OBJECTIONS

Throughout your job search you'll meet people who aren't quite as eager to interview you as you are to meet them, so they give you "reasons" why they can't do what you want. These reasons are what we call *objections*. Listen to these objections, and then, instead of just giving up, see if you can, in a polite and firm way, counter the objection—not with an argument but with a logical reason why the employer should do what you want *anyway*.

Here's a sample of how it's done:

Prospective Employer: Well that sounds great. Why don't you send over a resume?

You: I could drop off a copy myself today.

PE: We're supposed to go through personnel.

You: Well, I understand that. Why don't I see you first, and then drop off another copy with them.

PE: I'm jammed up with meetings.

You: I could come by at five. Maybe we could have a quick drink?

PE: You know we're not hiring right now. In fact, we're cutting back.

You: That's why I called. I've some sound ideas on how to accomplish with 10 people what you've been doing with 20, and maintain the volume.

You do it, and overcome the following objections:

PE: Send us a resume.

You: _____

_____

_____

_____

PE: I'll be out of town for about three weeks.
You: _____
_____
_____

PE: The department budget for new employees has been cut. There's really not much point.
You: _____
_____

PE: We won't be hiring until next spring, why not contact me then?
You: _____
_____

PE: Okay, you win. Come in for an interview.
You: _____
_____
_____

INSIDE THE PERSONNEL DEPARTMENT

The purpose of the hidden job market research you did was to identify a hiring person *yourself,* and thereby circumvent personnel. If you make a favorable impression on the decision maker, you may then be sent to personnel to be processed—in which case, keep smiling and selling.

If you went around Personnel in your original contact, it's wise for you to have an explanation prepared as to why you did so. For example, "James Morrison of the National Jeweler's Association suggested I call Mr. Bixby, so I did." The purpose being to mend fences, soothe personnel's ego, and get everyone on your side.

Most of the time, Personnel deals with candidates who are sent to them by employment agencies they've contacted, or with job seekers responding to advertisements or other recruitment functions. Personnel usually can do nothing about an opportunity until a department head informs them of an opening. So Personnel is not your best lead to the hidden job market.

SPECIAL STRATEGIES FOR GETTING INSIDE

Over the years we've encountered many unique and creative ideas that job seekers have employed to get themselves inside ahead of the crowd. Some were so outlandish that they backfired. Others were not only creative, but served to get the job seeker his or her job target. Here is a sampling of inventive techniques that worked.

The Come-on Ad

John X pretended to be an employer. He inserted a blind box-number ad in his local newspaper, describing the position he would have liked to find for himself. The responses he got provided him with much useful information.

It identified people who had left or were planning to leave their jobs. Properly interpreted, this information actually provided a list of job openings.

It gave him an overview of salary levels and responsibilities which related to his own campaign.

It identified a variety of employers that applicants had worked for prior to their present jobs which were also potential targets for him.

It even identified a company in which he had been particularly interested. He had no idea that there might be an opening there but the letter informed him that one employee was planning to leave.

John X took the ploy a step further by actually contacting a few respondents, saying he had heard their name mentioned at a social gathering, or some such subterfuge, and generally queried them for information about their own jobs and the field. We won't tell you how he actually came to replace one of the applicants whose resume he received—but he did.

Breaking the Box Number Code

The difficulty in responding to box number advertisements is that you never know who the organization is, unless they are interested in you. This makes it almost impossible to do the kind of research essential to an aggressive approach.

Harry Y used the following rather simple approach to these ads. Using his brother-in-law's name, he wrote a fictitious letter-style resume, exactly in line with the advertised requirements for the position. His brother-in-law got an immediate response on company letterhead, and gave it to Harry. Harry then approached the company directly, never indicating that he knew there was an opening, and sold himself into a successful interview.

The Coattail Approach

As part of her job campaign, Amy Z followed the personal business columns in the *Wall Street Journal* and in trade publications. These columns name executives and managers whose moves to new companies are announced about three weeks after they settle into their new position. Amy called them up, congratulated them on their new positions and then gave them a pitch on how she had saved her previous employer thousands of dollars in expense-account costs. Not every call was followed by an interview, but she usually got permission to use the executive's name as a reference when she called his previous employer. After 31 calls and three weeks' time, she got the job she wanted at the salary she wanted.

USING EMPLOYMENT AGENCIES A NEW WAY

There are many thousands of private employment agencies around the country—and these agencies, with a few exceptions, can provide a most important input to your job campaign. But you've got to help them do their job. Don't say, as many applicants do, "Well, they're getting a fee, so I'll just sit back and wait." Use an agency the way you would an accountant or a paid consultant—by finding out how you can best work with them. With a little research you can find the right agency for your particular job targets and use it well.

Theresa A, a very capable job seeker, got the agencies working for her.

Well, first of all, I know that I'm damn good at my specialty— which is statistical analysis of sales information. I've got a masters in statistics, four years with one of the top polling organizations, and an ability to get a lot done in a short time. I also enjoy my work very much.

But then came a time when I decided I wanted to move to California. I wanted to live in L.A. or San Francisco, and I was sure I could find my kind of work there.

So the first thing I did was to pick three major corporations in each town—ones that I really didn't want to work for even though they were in my field. Each company was in a different industry; one was banking, one was oil, one was retailing.

Then I did something smart. I called each company and asked for the head of employment. When I got him on the telephone, I told him that I was trying to locate the best placement agency for people in my field. I left the reason for it a bit fuzzy. I then asked the personnel manager for the names of the two best employment agencies in town in the area of market research. All of the employment managers gave me the names of the agencies they used without hesitation. I also asked them to recommend me to someone in the agency. Naturally, they gave me the name of the man or woman at the agency that they did business with, and respected for their good performance.

With this information in hand, for both cities, I took a week of vacation days and went west. Once in town, I called each recommended agency and asked to speak to the recommended placement counselor by name. I told the agent that he had been specifically recommended to me by Mr. Collins or Mr. Aubrey or whoever—I said I would be in town for a couple of hours only and would like to meet with him briefly. The recommendations really did it! Not only were the agents flattered by having been recommended, they also felt, I'm sure, that it would be a personal favor to the Big Client to help me as much as possible. I didn't have to wait in any waiting rooms very long.

When I met with each of them, I had a list of suggestions worked out to help show them how to place me. As a result of my research, I had a list of 20 to 30 organizations in each area (with names and phone numbers) which could possibly use my statistical skills. I had a full packet of resumes for them, and an extra deciphering sheet to help them understand what I was talking about. Statistical research is so technical. I really briefed them on how to "pitch me."

I then told each agent that I was working with only 3 agents in a city, each with a different orientation. Which was true. And I said I'd be returning to town in a few days, say on Tuesday and Wednesday, and that I hoped they could set up some interviews for me with people on the list. They were also free to come up with any other situations that might be interesting. I said I'd call them the day before I arrived back in town, and review our progress. First of all—this super organization really blew their minds. But then they saw how I was really helping them earn their fees.

It worked like a charm. I waited a week and then checked back in with the agencies. Three of them had done a terrific job and set me up with, I guess, 18 to 20 interviews all told. I've gone through the interviews now, and have three job offers pending, with a couple of more probably on the way. What all these agencies did for me was the ground work in setting up the interviews.

15

THE RESUME GAME

Listen to excerpts from a discussion with Gil Preston, employment manager of one of the nation's largest brokerage houses:

If applicants only realized what happened to their resumes, most of the time, they'd probably think twice about mailing them in so fast. Depending on how many ads are running or how many employment agencies we've contacted about a particular opening we may have, I can get as many as 100 to 150 new resumes a day. Especially on a Tuesday or a Wednesday when the response runs highest. It's impossible to handle so much paper efficiently and find out everything each applicant is trying to get across. So naturally there's a weeding out process. The first ones to go are the four or five page essays. It took me a while to learn but I finally decided that if a person didn't say something to interest me about himself fast, he probably wasn't going to do it in the next 10 pages. As far as I know, my attitude is fairly universal.

At the other end of the spectrum are the "quick and dirty" resumes. Some man or woman needs a job. They type up a resume and don't think much about it. It's poorly put together, poorly organized, and doesn't say much about the applicant. Then they have one or two hundred printed up and mail them out to any advertisement that sounds vaguely right. Or to any company they can think of that just might have something for them. With a paycheck. Those kinds of resumes are easy, cheap. And they don't work.

My screening process is simple. I divide the resumes into three piles. The rejects—not for us. The possibles—worth a second reading anyway. The OKs—they're in our ball park.

How do I tell the OKs? I guess a lot of ways. Maybe the right buzz words. An articulate way of letting me know who the applicant is. How he's going to do things for us. Not the other way around. How equipped he is to get it done. I mean get the work that we need done. And how he or she communicates this to me like a real pro.

It's all there. Neat. Organized. Easy to understand. Good meaningful information. You feel like reading it. The opposite of OKs are the poorly typed and duplicated resumes. They're hard to read. Look sloppy. All over the lot. You can't help feeling that the applicants will think sloppily if this is the best they can show of themselves on paper. I read them, and sometimes I can find some good reasons to invite the person in, but the poor resumes really work against them, particularly when jobs are tough, like now.

After the first impression, a resume has to meet my red pencil test. I'm a speed reader. I go over a resume quickly. Every time something rings a bell in terms of our operation I hit it with a red check. After I've sorted out all the resumes, those that have a lot of red checks go into my "possible" or "OK" pile for second reading. At the second reading I'm more careful. I'm looking for cues and clues. Asking questions and making question marks where statements are made that I don't understand. Or where there are gaps in information. Or there's vagueness. Suppose someone says, "Improved sales significantly." I ask, how much? What's the dollar volume? Stuff like that. I write all over the margins.

After the second reading those resumes with more red checks and less questions go into my top priority file. Unfortunately, I'm sure that a good applicant who's written a vague resume will take a back seat to the person who has the same qualifications but prepares a well thought out resume. That's the way it is.

Those who come across best on paper get the interviews. The rest get printed rejection letters.

Over the years we've talked to hundreds of employers, managers, supervisors, job counselors, placement agents, personnel people, and here are some of the critiques we've heard about resumes.

• If a resume is too long and wordy nobody reads it. Not me nor the line manager I send it to.

• I make a real effort to read every resume I receive. But my eyes blur at some of the involved sentences, circuitous reasoning, and lack of any evidence of coherent thinking I often see on resumes. How can I hire somebody to write reports when he can't even explain to me clearly who he is and what he can do?

• I dislike wordy, flowery, life history resumes. I also have a pet peeve about bad spelling and typing and colored paper. When a person is looking for a $15,000 a year job the resume should look like the applicant is worth the money.

● A good cover letter is very important in influencing my thinking about whether or not I'm going to read the resume. When I see a printed cover letter that says "I am sincerely interested in working for your company," I think what kind of a fool does this person think I am? How many other companies did he send this valentine to?

A good way to practice resume writing is to practice ad writing. Here's an exercise to give you the feel of the technique with not that much effort. We want you to pretend to be an employer, and write an employment ad for your selected job target position. Write 50 words or less. Remember words cost money. The ad is to go into the classified section of your Sunday papers. Try to make clear every point that you think would be important in conveying the facts about the position.

JOB TARGET (POSITION)_____

_____
_____
_____
_____
_____
_____
_____

Now go back and look at what you wrote. Are there words you could eliminate? Facts that could be stated more clearly? Edit. Clean up. Cut it down. Remember, it's always harder to say something interesting in fewer words than to say the same thing in more words. And you're practicing how to write for someone who doesn't have much time to figure out what you want to say.

Resume writing is an art. It is probably the most important and neglected of all the arts of business communication. Top mail order writers who can sell anything from real estate to rock candy suddenly develop writer's cramp when it becomes necessary to sell themselves in a resume. In the job market, where a good resume can be the most vital of all instruments for making prime contact, people continue to approach resume writing half-heartedly, with the wrong thinking, and often with resentment.

What is a resume? It's not an autobiography. Nor is it your memoirs. A resume is an advertisement of yourself. It is an ad selling *you*. The purpose of this ad is to get you an interview. No more, no less. It's the interview that can get you the job. All the resume can do is get you invited in. During the interview you can fill in any details you think are appropriate to the particular position.

Usually, a resume is aimed at a general job area, rather than at a specific employer. In some cases a resume may be written specifically for a particular company and even a particular position within that company. This is an excellent self-selling approach and an extremely effective one. However, it may not be practical in all cases, because of the time and effort involved in so carefully personalizing a large distribution of, say, 100 resumes. This is what the cover letter will be used for.

TEN STEPS TO AN INTERVIEW-GETTING RESUME

On the following pages we will take you through an organized, proven procedure for preparing a compelling resume which will get you in for interviews. This is a step-by-step approach which has been distilled from hundreds of hours of work with individuals and their resumes. Please follow each step carefully, and participate to the best of your ability.

Step 1. Take the Employer's Point of View

Review your job target again. This time, from the point of view of your own future employer. Say to yourself, "I am Mr. or Ms. B. and I would like to hire someone to:

_____
(write in your job target)

OK. Remembering that you're the employer now, answer the following questions from that point of view. Once you get the feel of your potential employer's needs, you have a far better chance of communicating with him successfully.

1. "I want a person who knows how to perform the following specific tasks."

_____
_____
_____
_____

2. "I want a person who has had some of the following experience."

_____
_____
_____
_____

3. "If they didn't have the specific experience, I believe I would hire a person who could persuade me that he had the following equivalent abilities."

_____

_____

_____

_____

4. "I want a person with the following personality traits."

_____

_____

_____

5. "I must have a person who can solve the following kinds of problems for me".

_____

_____

_____

_____

How did you like being the employer? Were you able to answer each question easily and precisely? If you were, you should be able to write a forceful resume. But if you were like most employers, filling in the answers to these questions wasn't that easy. Were you a bit unsure? Most employers are. Employers, like employees, often have as much difficulty in deciding exactly what they are looking for as you have in describing exactly who you are and what you can do.

However, we cannot be too emphatic about the following point. *No matter how murky and obscure an employer may be about the specific abilities, experience, or personality traits that he might like to find in a new employee, he almost always knows exactly what problems he wants his employee to solve. That's what work is all about—* solving problems. And that's why Questions One and Five are the most crucial ones on the list. Reread them. If you've answered them only partially, or not at all, think about it. And try very hard to answer fully and completely. What are the tasks and problems that an employer in your job target area would want performed and solved?

After rereading and rethinking that crucial question, you must realize that your value as a potential employee depends on how well you can convince an employer of your ability to solve the problems he needs to have solved. The guiding principle in preparing your resume should be *defining and enhancing those problem-solving skills of yours that relate to your job target in such a way that conveys a benefit to a potential employer.*

This principle holds true in good times and bad, recession or upswing. If your resume can convince an employer that hiring you could be an asset to him, you will get an interview. The next step could be the job you want.

Step 2. Taking a Personal Inventory

In our experience, one of the most common mistakes of resume writers is to start right out in the upper left hand corner of a blank sheet of paper and keep writing until the final period in the lower right hand corner.

As an aid, fill out the Resume Preplanning Form which follows. This will provide an inventory of your skills, accomplishments, education, work history, and other facts about yourself. Using this form you will start to recall important information, which you can use when the time comes to write the actual resume. Filling out the form takes extra time, but it pays extra dividends.

RESUME PREPLANNING FORM

EDUCATION
High school
Year graduated _____
Specialization _____
Favorite subjects _____

_____

Best general areas (writing, speaking, acting, sports, politics, etc.)

_____

Hobbies from high school which continued to develop later

_____

Proudest accomplishments:

● _____
● _____
● _____
Work experience

_____
_____
_____

College
Years attended _____ Degrees _____
Grade point average _____
Honors (if any) _____
Major field _____
Favorite subjects _____

_____

Why? _____

_____

The most significant (to you) academic achievements _____

_____

_____

Your three most significant nonacademic achievements while in college

     1. _____

     2. _____

     3. _____

Work experience while in college

     1. _____

     2. _____

     3. _____

Extracurricular activities while at college

_____

_____

_____

Elected offices (if any)

_____

_____

Athletic achievements (if any)

_____

_____

Other significant accomplishments in college

_____

_____

_____

Other education or training (include vocational, military, corporate, schools, correspondence courses, etc.)

Course	School	Skills

HOBBIES AND INTERESTS

List your hobbies or interests and indicate degree of proficiency

_____

_____

_____

_____

_____

Do you see any work application of your hobbies and interests with or without further training? _____Yes _____No
If yes, explain _____

_____

_____

_____

MILITARY SERVICE

Have you ever been in the military? _____Yes _____No
Branch of service _____
Rank (highest attained) _____
Total years _____
List any special schools attended _____

_____

What were your major military functions? _____

_____

Describe any skills you acquired in the military which might have some commercial application _____

_____

What were your three most important accomplishments while in the military?
1. _____
2. _____
3. _____
Other relevant information pertaining to your military service

_____

_____

_____

SPECIAL SKILLS

Indicate your degree of proficiency. List additional skills as applicable.

A. Communications Skills

Skill	Excellent	Fair	Poor	Application to Work
Writing				
Talking				
Selling				
Teaching				
Organizing				
Supervising				
Motivating				
Analysis				

LANGUAGES

Speak	Read	Write

B. Creative Skills

Skill	Excellent	Fair	Poor	Application to Work
Painting				
Composing				
Writing				
Designing				
Acting				
Sewing				
Cooking				

C. Intellectual Skills

Skill	Excellent	Fair	Poor	Application to Work
Studying				
Researching				
Analyzing				
Organizing				
Problem solving				
Decision making				
Planning				

Job-Related Accomplishments

The purpose of this section of the Resume Preplanning Form is to inventory your *work* successes, your best job accomplishments. This need not be done in chronological order, but it would be helpful to you later to indicate after the date of the accomplishment the position to which it refers. Use a "live-action" word (such as invented, supervised, presented) to begin each sentence (see p. 152).

Describe a number of work/job accomplishments, if possible equal to the number of years of your working experience (describe 5 if you've worked 5 years, 15 if you've worked 15 years, etc.). Each accomplishment need not be in a separate year. State position, employer and year of each accomplishment. Accomplishments should relate to areas like profits or sales, increased efficiency, improved human relations, better designs, finer acoustics, or whatever it was in your job area that generally promoted and enriched your work product and/or contributed directly to the well-being of the company.

Year	Employer Position	Accomplishment

Have you had supervisory responsibilities? _____Yes _____No
If yes, describe scope, number of people supervised, type of people, type of operation for each recent instance of supervision.

_____

_____

_____

_____

_____

Nonwork-Related Skills

Include only problem-solving skills that are generally *outside* of previous or present jobs.

1. _____
2. _____
3. _____
4. _____
5. _____
6. _____
7. _____
8. _____
9. _____
10. _____

Summary

Now that you have listed skills and accomplishments from the past, the more recent past, and the present, look back over the Resume Preplanning Form and the earlier list from the Skills Interest Cross Index on page 42. In the spaces below write a short paragraph summarizing those skills and accomplishments you think would be most applicable to your current job target.

SKILLS

_____
_____
_____
_____
_____
_____

ACCOMPLISHMENTS

_____
_____
_____
_____
_____
_____

Step 3. Find the Right Words—Convey Benefits

A resume is a presentation in words. The words and phrases you use can make the difference between a resume that just lies there or one that gets up and grabs the reader by the shoulders and makes him pay attention. You write the wide-awake, full of life resumes by using live action words that carry the idea of live accomplishments and problem-solving skills, not of dead information.

Your aim in writing a resume is to convey immediate meaning and to suggest a benefit to your potential employer. Therefore, you must use words with strong impact. Avoid such phrases as: "I was responsible for . . . ," "My duties involved . . . ," "Project Manager," "Assistant Manager," "Staff Coordinator," etc. Instead, use *action words.* Action words convey a sense of participation, involvement and accomplishment. A partial list of action words would include:

designed	researched	trained
supervised	directed	reduced costs
implemented	analyzed	invented
developed	planned	managed
created	organized	negotiated

| conducted | sold | wrote |
| expanded | profits | presented |

An "accomplishment" is an action that produced a final beneficial result. "Information" is simply a statement of fact, such as a description of duties, job title, etc., which does not transmit the feeling of something achieved. Consider the following examples:

Accomplishment Versus Information

INFORMATION ORIENTED:

I was responsible for the organization and management of the entire Art Department. Hired and supervised designers, commercial artists and print specialists.

ACCOMPLISHMENT ORIENTED:

Directed eight persons in Art Department. Designed 22 product brochures which contributed to increasing sales by 50 percent in major market areas. Cut print production costs by 25 percent.

INFORMATION ORIENTED:

I was the Assistant to the Curator at the museum. My duties involved coordinating membership drives, meeting visiting dignitaries, planning and organizing events and schedules, assembling reports, and some secretarial duties.

ACCOMPLISHMENT ORIENTED:

As Assistant Curator, handled an average of 14 special museum functions each month. Coordinated four major membership drives which each added over 500 new members. Originated and laid out two outdoor projects which received national acclaim.

A resume is an advertisement for yourself. Follow these rules in preparing this important, self-selling ad:

• Use the minimum number of words necessary to convey your meaning.
• Avoid "wind up" words and phrases such as "my duties included . . ." or "I was in charge of the section which. . . ." Start right out with precise action words and benefits.
• Use short sentences. Don't try to convey too many ideas at once.
• Be sure your punctuation and spelling are correct.
• Don't be over-technical. Most resumes go through Personnel first.
• Leave out data that are not relevant to getting you an interview.

Read Before You Write

Before you start writing your resume, it is a good idea to familiarize yourself with a sizable collection of job advertisements in the field of your interest. If there are many such ads, clip them and read them carefully. The words and phrases used by prospective employers may give you a clearer idea of what they are looking for. If not too many ads relating to your job target are available, reread back issues of trade publications in your field of interest.

Step 4. Select the Best Format

You are now ready to start the task of organizing your resume. More accurately, you will organize the information in such a way that will help insure that it is read. There are three generally recognized formats or organizational styles for resumes, each with its own advantages and disadvantages. They are:

Chronological Resume

This is the most widely used resume format, and the one with which employers are more familiar (see p. 157). It is also the easiest to write.

In this type of resume, jobs are listed chronologically starting with the most recent and ending with the earliest. The most recent employment usually occupies the most space—although this is not required, particularly where this experience is not related to your current job target, or has been of short duration.

Dates of employment are given first, followed by name of employer, and your job title. For each position you held, start a new paragraph describing accomplishments on that job. You usually are expected to give both month and year of employment, but if you had a period of unemployment which you want to "bury," particularly in an earlier period, you can normally get by with just including the years—although you should be prepared to talk about these "gaps" in the interview.

Some advantages of the chronological resume are:

• Professional interviewers are most familiar with it.
• It is the easiest to prepare since its content is structured by familiar dates, companies, and titles.
• It can emphasize a steady employment record (when there has been little job hopping).

Some disadvantages of the chronological resume are:

- It starkly reveals serious employment gaps.
- It can put undesired emphasis on job areas that you might prefer to ignore.
- It makes it difficult to spotlight particular areas of skills and accomplishment unless they are in most recent jobs.

Functional Resume

The functional resume (see p. 158) categorizes your experience into a specific work experience or skills which you wish to highlight for a specific job target. It gives little or no regard to when and where the experience was attained.

Some advantages of the functional resume:

- It stresses your selected areas of accomplishment and experience which might be most marketable in your job target.
- It helps camouflage a spotty employment record or one with little actual experience in the job target area.
- It allows you to show real professional growth in desired areas.
- It is useful way to play down work areas which you may wish to deemphasize.

Some disadvantages of the functional resume are:

- Many employers are slightly suspicious of it and will want to see additional specific work history information.
- It is difficult to stress corporate or organization affiliations.
- It is harder for an interviewer to follow.

The Combination Format

This format presents a basic functional resume, with the addition of a list of company names and dates (see p. 159).

The combination format has a lot going for it, in that it allows the applicant the best of both worlds. You can stress the skill areas that are most relevant to you, and at the same time satisfy the employer's need to know names and dates. Titles should be included with the company listings, but can be eliminated without much negative effect if they are not in keeping with the job target.

Some advantages of the combination format are:

- It gives you the opportunity to emphasize valued skills and abilities.
- It helps cushion the impact of gaps in employment.

● It can be varied by increasing chronology portion and decreasing functional portion, or vice versa.

Some disadvantages of the combination format are:

● It tends to run longer than the other two forms.
● It takes the employer longer to read, he can lose interest unless the resume is well done, with strong holding power.

Which Resume Should You Use?

Consider your own employment history. How many jobs have you had? What do you wish to emphasize? Are there any gaps you want to soften? Are you changing fields?

Study the three examples we have provided (pp. 157–159). If you have difficulty in deciding upon which format to use, you might want to draft one functional and one chronological resume, and then decide after reading both. Once you've decided which format you will use, it's time to move on to drafting the resume.

CHRONOLOGICAL RESUME

This is a typical chronological resume. Shows major responsibilities and diversity of experience. No gaps.

Diane Tims
800 Main Street
Portland, Oregon 97208
503/710-5523

<u>*ADMINISTRATIVE ASSISTANT*</u>

Work Experience:

1971–1974   Administrative Assistant to Chairman, Department of Psychology—University of Oregon.

Responsible for smooth day-to-day running of department of 15 persons.
- Liaison with central university administration offices.
- Preparation of university and government surveys and reports.
- Preparation of agenda and recording of faculty meeting minutes.
- Prepared authorizations of expenditures of $175,000 budget.
- Prepared quantity audits, projections and financial statements.
- Interpreted and applied university and government policies.

1969–1971   Secretary to Chairman of Physics Department, Portland State University.

- Carried out administrative policies of section processing payroll, coordinating work schedules, ordering supplies and equipment.
- Scheduled meetings and appointments.

1968–1969   Secretary to Editor, Journal of Applied Physics

- Responsible for day to day journal operation, handling all general queries regarding journal, communication with authors, referees, and publisher, preparation of statistics, agenda, and minutes of Editors' meetings.

Education: B.A. Portland State University, 1968
Humanities major. Honor Student

FUNCTIONAL RESUME

Mr. Moran does not show names, and dates of employers. His work record is somewhat spotty (4 jobs in 6 years), so it is advantageous to present his background in functional format.

James Moran
3 Hemlock Drive
Silver Spring, Md. 20904
301-223-5944

DESIGN & DEVELOPMENT

Designed and developed four large scale communications systems. Performed studies for application of digital techniques to telephone networks. Analyzed digital multiple-access discrete-address system for use in satellite communications.

Also analyzed the effectiveness of modulation and error-encoding techniques against atmospheric-type noise. Other contributions were in the design of digital communications systems using different types of modulation techniques.

COMPUTER SYSTEMS ANALYSIS

Analyzed data from various test systems on secret military equipment and wrote programs for computerization. Planned and designed diagnostic systems for on-line real-time computer. Also programmed scientific data for IBM-360-40. Used FORTRAN.

DATA ANALYSIS

Analyzed data from planned tests to see if systems performed according to theoretical determinations. Analyzed data from six different test systems and prepared reports. Responsible for integration and reduction of special trajectory analysis data.

EDUCATION:

MSEE—George Washington University, 1969
BSEE—Columbia University, 1964
    Information Theory & Coding,
    Univ. of Maryland
    College Park, Md. 1972

MEMBERSHIPS:

Communication Technology Group—IEEE

COMBINED CHRONOLOGICAL AND FUNCTIONAL RESUME

As his experience is chiefly with one firm, it is best for this applicant to use a combined chronological-functional resume. It highlights his experience with Acme and only touches on the earlier experience which at this time in his career is not significant.

JACK E. NELSON
1000 21 Street, N.W.
Ft. Lauderdale, Fla. 33308
303/PO 7-8193

Offering a comprehensive background in sales, merchandising, marketing, and management in consumer package goods.

SALES MANAGEMENT: Responsible for planning and directing sales program for several companies. Made major policy decisions as to all phases of sales activities. Successfully built sales 85 percent above preceding year's business.

MARKETING PLANNING: Investigated the market for new products and new markets for established product lines. Introduced new chewing gum package to supermarkets after market study which indicated need.

MERCHANDISING: By close liaison with merchandising executives in major chains, developed point of purchase displays which gave added shelf space to company products and increased sales. Coordinated merchandising and advertising programs with stores. Developed new packaging concepts which made company products outstanding seller in frozen food cabinets.

SALES TRAINING: Hired and trained large crew of merchandisers and salesmen. Set up formal program to train them in company product and sales techniques. Wrote sales-training manuals.

SALES: Maintain close personal contact with buyers in major supermarket outlets. Have personally sold products to chains all over the U.S.

ACME CHEWING GUM COMPANY
SALES MANAGER—1964–1975
Started as Salesman and worked through sales ranks to current position in 1970.

GOODY GUM DROP COMPANY
SALESMAN—1960–1964
Sold candy to supermarkets, drug and variety chains, and vending machine companies.

EDUCATION: B.A., Florida State College, 1960

Step 5. Prepare a First Draft

Now that you have focused on employer needs, analyzed your history and achievements, developed some good words and phrases, and decided upon a format, we're ready to write . . . but only a first draft. Don't even attempt to make your resume look good on the first try—it won't work.

Begin with the idea that you are going to make at least two or three constantly improved drafts before you have a resume which is easy to read, has an attractive layout, conveys distinct benefits, and makes the person it goes to want to interview you.

How to prepare the first draft of your resume

1. Get several sheets of blank note paper, one for each position you have had, or skill or work function you wish to emphasize. Prepare an additional one for education and/or other information you want to include.

2. Reread the Resume Pre-planning Form and extract from it the dates, names, positions, accomplishments, and problem-solving capabilities you wish to emphasize. Write this information down on the appropriate sheets of note paper. Then add to this information any facts or accomplishments that can further improve your image. Remember to list facts in accomplishment terms, and to use action words which convey information as concisely as possible.

3. Look at the phrases and comments you have written down on the note sheets, and organize each into concise paragraphs. Concentrate on each area separately, paragraph by paragraph, rewriting and editing as often as necessary until the ideas are conveyed in the cleanest, briefest and most forceful form.

4. Now combine the paragraphs into a full chronological, functional, or combination style resume, and have this typed, single spaced, on one or two sheets of paper. If it is too long, edit it again. Make sure that the information is well written and concise, and that it communicates valid benefits to the potential employer. Check spelling and punctuation carefully.

Step 6. Edit and Critique

A good resume is virtually guaranteed by a thorough critical appraisal and careful editing and rewriting. This rewriting is aimed at reorganizing your resume in such a way that it will come alive for your prospective reader. You have three objectives relating to form and content:

1. *The elimination of extraneous information.* The longer the resume the less chance that all the information will be absorbed by the reader. This fact should be kept constantly in mind as you edit your second draft and plan the third rewrite. Most experts suggest you aim for a one-page presentation. Here are some items which generally do not belong in a resume, and simply take up space:

- Number and names of children
- Religion
- Sex
- Age
- Race
- Maiden name
- Spouse's occupation
- Social clubs
- College fraternities
- Hobbies (unless relevant to the job you want)
- Courses studied for which no credit was given
- Languages (unless relevant to the job)
- Nonwork related accomplishments (i.e., sport trophies, sewing prizes)
- References (unless they are recognized personages in the field or people you will want in your follow-up.

2. *An attractive layout.* You will want to be certain that the layout-margins, spacing, use of underlinings, headings, and white space results in a clear presentation which is both forceful and inviting. (More about layout in Step 7.)

3. *A strong writing style.* You want to be confident that the writing style is direct, interesting, and accomplishment-oriented.

The Process of Critiquing

Once you have completed your second draft—typewritten in the format and approximate layout which you have decided upon—it's time to look for more objective views. The outside critique of family, friends and trusted colleagues, or a placement counselor, is imperative. This essential step often is ignored because the applicant feels he or she had done a good enough job. Or because one doesn't want to bother anyone. Or one has reservations about involving others in such a private matter as a resume. We sympathize with these feelings.

However, intelligent feedback from reliable people is the best way of insuring that your resume does the job it is supposed to do—that it conveys an attractive, convincing picture of your capabilities.

There is an art to obtaining a good critique. You don't simply turn the resume over to a friend and say, "Hey, take a look at this. Do you think it's any good?" Most people don't like to criticize others, especially friends, and will probably reply with something like "It looks good to me." Therefore, your request for criticism must be made in a way that will give you valuable feedback.

Have the individual read the resume once or twice and then ask him to put it down and describe what he learned about you. The response will be the overall impression gained through the resume. This procedure is more valid when carried out with someone who doesn't know you too well.

Ask for criticism in terms of *improvement*—"Would you mind giving me some ideas about how I can make this resume more effective?" Review your critic's general observations, and then focus on specific questions such as:

Do you think the resume could be shortened?
How would you improve the layout?
Is the format clear?
Do I give enough information about my abilities?

Step 7. Design an Attractive Layout

Remember our analogy of the resume as an advertisement. One of the first criteria for a good advertisement is an attractive layout. A presentation which looks good—has the right amount of type for the space and has proper margins—will immediately draw your eye to the important points.

Your potential interviewer is inundated with paperwork. He or she must absorb and digest hundreds of pages of printed information each week—not only resumes, but reports, memoranda, technical papers, etc. What happens to your resume when it lands on top of this pile of paper?

Obviously, it could be ignored. When you lay out your resume, visualize it in the middle of a fairly high stack of other resumes and papers. It's around 4:00 P.M., your reader is tired, his eyes hurt, his blood sugar is a bit low, he needs a vacation, he's read 34 resumes that day, and found only four or five with even passing interest. Do you wish you could recall the resume? Get it back and have it retyped on a good IBM executive typewriter, allow wider margins, capitalize some key words, eliminate extraneous words, take out two whole paragraphs? Make it easier to read? Aah—the secretary just came in. There's an important meeting. He's getting up from his desk, leaving the room—great! Now you can get in there, pull your resume out of the pile and get back to this book before he even knows how poor it really looked. You're home safe—but it was a narrow escape. Don't repeat it. Let's do it right from the start.

After you've boiled your resume down to the most concise forceful expression of your skills and experience, emphasize the information you want to convey by creative but conservative use of capital letters, underlining, and spacing.

Keep in mind the final "look" of your resume. Pay attention to paragraph length and spacing. A top-heavy first paragraph is unattractive. No paragraphs should be bulky. It's better to have two short paragraphs than one heavy one.

Give less space to job experience that does not fit your current job target.

If a second page must be used, make sure the key information is on the first page.

Avoid unnecessary captions such as NAME, ADDRESS, etc.

Step 8. Typing and Printing

Use a top quality typewriter such as an IBM Executive with a clean or new ribbon. If you don't have one, pay a commercial service to do the final typing. Have someone proofread for typing errors. Take the typed and proofread version to a good local printer (check the Yellow Pages) who will print 100 copies on a good but not extravagant grade of paper. The cost will be nominal compared with the benefits which you will get from a well-prepared resume. Use off-white or buff stock. Keep the original in a sealed flat envelope for possible reprinting. Watch carefully for typing errors.

If you use a commercial resume service, make sure that they follow your layout, or that you specifically agree to any changes which they suggest.

Step 9. The Cover Letter

An individual cover letter accompanying a resume is as valuable to a resume as is a personal introduction to a potential employer. That personal introduction encourages the employer to read your resume— the cover letter must do the same.

The resume, as good as it is, is a printed form which focuses on your skills and experience in a given area. It is meant to be read by many potential employers in your field of interest.

The cover letter is meant to be read by one potential employer who received a copy of the resume. If you are sending a resume to 15 different potential employers, you will write 15 different cover letters. Each letter will have a somewhat different slant on how your skills relate to the employer's needs.

Therefore, each cover letter must be custom made, and be the result of some investigation into the specific problems which a specific employer needs solved. Sometimes you can deduce this information from an article seen in a trade journal, or from general information, or gossip about the company or the person. Or you can take an educated guess, and mix it with common sense. But whatever you do, the cover letter should be sufficiently personalized to compel the reader to read your resume. (See the sample cover letters on pp. 166–169.)

The cover letter relates the information in your resume to the specific needs of the employer, for example:

Dear Mr. Burns:

I would like to be considered for a position in your Art Department. As you will note from my resume, I have had three years experience designing display materials for an organization which had merchandising problems similar to yours.

The materials which I designed made a significant contribution to the overall promotion effort and resulted in a 30 percent growth in sales in the fall season.

I would like to meet with you next week if possible, to show you some of these materials.

Very truly yours,

Three elements are involved in writing good cover letters:

First, always address the letter, using name and title, to the particular person with whom you wish to have an interview.

Second, always refer to a problem-solving skill that you have, which will be further expanded in your resume and which can provide a direct benefit to this specific employer.

Third, the closing is as important as the opening. Try to suggest an interview time in your letter. Here are some examples of how to close a letter:

I would like to meet with you briefly on August 15, and will contact your secretary to see if this date is open or what an alternative date might be.

Due to travel plans, I will be available for interview only during the next two weeks. I hope we can meet. I'll give you a call.

I would like to stop by some day next week to show you an actual model of the new program.

Keep these points in mind.

The cover letter should be no more than three paragraphs long (half a page, centered).

Use printed personal letterhead. If you don't have any, get some printed at the same place that printed your resume.

If you are responding to an advertisement, try to use some of the words from the ad in your letter.

COVER LETTER

June 18, 1976

Dr. Robert Sayers
President
Seattle Community College
12 Rocky Mt. Road
Seattle, Washington 98101

Dear Dr. Sayers:

My excellent experience on the administrative staffs of two colleges should be of interest to you in your new drive to centralize administrative functions of SCC.

The enclosed resume will give you the highlights of my experience in handling the specific administrative problems of college departments.

We are moving to Seattle at the end of this school year. I will be in your city from April 10–24. If possible, I would like to arrange an appointment during that period to discuss your new organization, and explain how my experience could be beneficial.

Yours very truly,

Diane Tims

Enc: resume

COVER LETTER

James Moran
3 Hemlock Drive
Silver Spring, Md. 20904
301-223-5944

March 6, 1976

Mr. Wayne J. Anthony
Director of Engineering
Aztec Electronics Co.
70 Circle Drive
Rockville, Md. 20850

Dear Mr. Anthony:

I read in yesterday's "Electronics" about your new contract for manufacturing digital multiple access discrete communications systems.

I have worked on the development of similar systems for the Computronics Corporation and feel that this experience could make a direct and immediate contribution. Details are in the enclosed resume.

I would like the opportunity to discuss this with you sometime next week if possible.

Sincerely,

James Moran

Enc: resume

**COVER LETTER TO
EXECUTIVE RECRUITING FIRM**

May 2, 1976

Mr. Maxwell Harper
President
Harper Associates, Inc.
22 W. 48 Street
New York, New York 10036

Dear Mr. Harper:

You were recommended to me by Mr. Botson at CBS.

Perhaps one of your clients can use a successful sales manager with a strong proven track record and with heavy background in consumer packaged goods.

I know and am known by purchasing and merchandising executives in the major food, drug, and variety chains throughout the East. They can attest to my accomplishments.

As Acme, my present employer, is to be acquired by Rogers and Barley Ltd., I feel this is a good time to make a move. My current salary is $20,000 plus a bonus (last year $2,500) and car.

My resume is enclosed. Please keep me in mind for positions anywhere in the country where my experience will be of value.

Sincerely,

Jack E. Nelson

COVER LETTER
IN RESPONSE TO AN AD

May 12, 1975

Box 17A
New York Times
New York, N.Y. 10036

Gentlemen:

My four years of intensive personnel experience, plus my Industrial Relations degree from Cornell, qualify me for your job opening for an Assistant Personnel Manager.

I have just completed my military obligations where I had full responsibilities for employment, training, and employee relations for civilian as well as military personnel. My Cornell education covered union-management relations in depth.

A personal interview would give both of us the opportunity to explore this further. I am willing to relocate anywhere, and can visit your plant next Wednesday or Thursday as I will be in the vicinity.

Sincerely,

Donald J. MacArthur

Enc: resume

Step 10. Alternative to a Resume

Some people have job targets where resumes are inappropriate. Among these are people who have been out of the work world for several years—a housewife, a fine arts painter, someone who took a year off to travel, a person who has been ill or incapacitated, or one who is just beginning his or her career. This group also includes people who wish to make complete changes in their occupational area.

There are two ways to handle this kind of problem. The first is to have someone you know, who is in touch with your employer target, write a letter of recommendation for you. Better still, you write the letter, they redo it, on their own stationery, sign it and send it. The second way is to write a letter to your target employer, similar in form to the functional resume, and about two-pages long. It should be based on your history, your accomplishments, problem-solving skills, and how these relate to the job target you want. Your letter to your employer target should reflect the value your background can bring to him. Let your creativity be reflected in your letter through your use of accomplishment-oriented paragraphs. List benefits you can bring, despite the fact that your immediate experience is not in the area of your job target. A little research into the employer's needs will help you focus on these benefits.

RESUME
ALTERNATIVE

Letter to prospective employer from woman desiring to enter work force after many years at home. She has no real job experience. Mrs. Ashford is better off using a direct letter than a resume. As she has not held any full-time paid jobs, she emphasizes those aspects of her background most closely related to her goal: a job in marketing. Note she specifies her accomplishments in volunteer work and part-time work and school related to her job objective. She also uses the name of a mutual acquaintance to gain immediate attention.

Barbara H. Ashford
123 Douglas Street
Wichita, Kansas 67211
(316) 835-1122

February 19, 1975

Mr. Sheldon Sosna
Vice-President—Marketing
Household Cleanser Corp.
78 Washington Street
Wichita, Kansas 67208

Dear Mr. Sosna:

Our mutual friend, Burton Bell, suggested that I contact you concerning a position in your marketing department in which I could make a significant contribution. My marketing accomplishments include the following:

... As assistant to Fund Raising Director for Community Chest, I divided the territory into districts based on census figures and estimated contributions by district with 92% accuracy. This resulted in considerable cost savings in subsequent campaigns.

... As part-time market research supervisor locally for major soap company I determined viability of introducing 3 new products. Supervised seven part-time researchers in house-to-house survey. Survey reports were vital to later marketing.

... In last three state-wide elections, coordinated political party's vote analysis program in my district.

... Wrote sales promotion material for membership drive for United Cerebral Palsy chapter, resulting in largest number of new members since chapter was organized.

... Sold Avon products (part-time) for eight years. Always was in top ten of region.

My formal training in marketing includes:

    B.A.—University of Kansas—major in Economics.
    Special courses—Wichita State College:
        "Marketing Research Methods"
        "The Computer as a Marketing Tool"
        "Advertising and Sales Promotion"
        "Marketing Consumer Products"
        "Accounting for Non-Accountants"

I am confident I can be a valuable addition to your marketing staff and would appreciate the opportunity to meet with you within the next few days. I'll call for an appointment.

Sincerely yours,

Barbara H. Ashford

RATE YOUR RESUME

Use this form to rate your resume, or that of your friends, or to allow your friends to rate *your* resume. Grade the resume in each of the categories as either *Excellent, Average,* or *Poor.* Write in suggestions for improvement.

RATINGS

ITEM	Excellent	Average	Poor	SUGGESTIONS FOR IMPROVEMENT
Does it stress accomplishments over skills and duties?				
Is the resume clear? Is it easy to get a "picture" of the writer's qualifications?				
Is irrelevant personal information left out?				
Does it avoid self-evaluation?				
Is the language clear and understandable?				
Does it emphasize benefits for a potential employer?				
Does it make the reader want to read it?				
Is it well-printed on good professional looking stock?				
Does the layout invite attention? Do strong points stand out?				
Is industry/product line of past employers clear?				
Do the sentences begin with action words?				
Is it brief, to the point, and clear?				
Does it sell the writer's problem-solving skills?				

16

CONTROLLING THE INTERVIEW

It's 8:45 A.M. on a cold Wednesday morning. The traffic on the Bay-shore freeway is heavy but moving. Mike Stann is headed south from Maceyville and is looking for the right turnoff. He's driving to his 9:30 interview with Sten Shaw, the City Manager of Yerba Loma—a city of 30,000 inhabitants. Mike is applying for a job as city manager, and though it's the kind of job he knows is right down his alley, he's not at all sure he's going to get it. As he drives he thinks about the last five months of unemployment and his hands start to sweat. The voice of the radio announcer gets on his nerves, so he switches off the sound, and makes himself concentrate on the coming interview. . .

The two things that will get in the way are my quitting law school in the first year, and not having my MBA. But what the hell—I grew up in the business world. I helped my uncle run his hardware warehouse. Then with Illinois Bell as a junior super-visor. Then the meat packers. Why not city business? Business is business. General principles apply. . . . But I'm just not up to it. The last two interviews were total flops. Particularly that doctor and his hospital. Good lord, he never stopped talking once. Kept telling me what a great job he'd done. New beds. Walls painted. TV in every room. Zowie! What a deficit he's going to hang him-self with! He never saw a budget in his life. That hospital will go broke before any kid ever sees TV after having his tonsils out. . . . I wonder what this city management is like. This Farber fellow says it's all administrative. The kind of thing a small com-pany would need. Budgets. Reports. Employment. Records. Sys-tems. I know that stuff backwards. How is it possible I've been on the street for five months? What am I doing wrong? I'm really good. I bet he asks what I've been doing. Going to the movies I'll say. That should give him some jollies. . . . What'll I do if it doesn't take? I'm about out of savings. I could be a cab driver.

Except I'm a lousy driver. I never thought I was a loser but maybe I am. Poor Jan—Lord! I hope she's not pregnant. . . . I probably should have called old Koch. He was a pretty good boss. He'd have said "O.K. Decorate your resume. Change the dates. You left last month." Well, it's too late now. . . . If I had half the brain I thought I had I'd have done some research on what city management is about. Strike two. . . . I hate interviews. I feel like an insect under a microscope. There he sits whoever Mr. Big is, safe and snug behind his desk, and any minute, I say one thing wrong, or my button-down collar unbuttons and he pushes the switch which activates the trap door. Out I go. Down the chute.

Meanwhile, four miles away, Sten Shaw is making his morning commute to his office in the Municipal Building. He too is thinking about money . . .

. . . I'm City Manager. The town council appointed me ten months ago, and my greatest frustration in life is dealing with them. They make demands and have no sense of how the demands can be met. They haven't heard about inflation. Yes, we need new garbage trucks. And a new sewage disposal system. Hillside high school needs a new heating system. But how do they expect me to pay the bills? With funny money? "Be more efficient," they say. How can I be efficient with those jokers I have in my department? Bureaucrats. Red tape. Never rock the boat. At a quarter to five I look at my desk and it's stacked with papers, memos, reports—that say nothing. No solutions. All they tell me is how it can't be done. Everybody leaves at five o'clock. I'm at my desk till seven. Sometimes ten. No I haven't been as successful as I thought I'd be in getting things done. It's taken me six months to convince the council that I need a professional administrative assistant. Moffet won't do. He's a fool. I need a first-class, nonbureaucratic type. A professional. Someone trained in industry, who can get things done. Someone who understands budgets, cost effectiveness, purchasing. Such a person would be worth five of those I have in the department. And the department knows it. I'd fire them all. But where do I find someone? That last batch I interviewed were nothing. Each and every one of them sat there like lumps. Nobody said a word. Just answered questions. Maybe I talk to much. What was that woman's name? Walsh? Welsh? I don't remember any of their names. I got the feeling she was terrified of me. Maybe I don't know how to conduct an interview. How do you learn? . . . And how can you really judge? There's that information on the application blank and I'm supposed to ask probing questions. What questions? Wouldn't it be a pleasure if this guy I'm interviewing this morning was the guy? And I could get some real help? I notice he's been out of work for five months. Just let him have a decent explanation, and show some ability, and I'll hire him today and buy him lunch. I need some problem solving, or I'm not going to have a job . . .

Fortunately for Mike Stann, you were able to tune in to these two thought patterns. Right now Mike is pulling up along the side of a coffee shop, a few blocks from the Municipal Building. He has 30 minutes before he's due in for the interview. Why don't you stop in? Sit beside him, have a cup of coffee, and strike up a conversation. He needs help. Give him some advice on his coming interview. Sten Shaw is literally longing to hire him. But not the way he's coming in. Tactfully, suggest to Mike a few ideas that might help him get the job offer he wants.

In the space below, write down some of the good advice you might give him.

• What, for example, might you tell him about his attitude toward going into interviews? "Say, Mike, listen, your attitude is _____
_____
_____
_____
_____

• About that worry that you don't have a master's or a law degree. Here's how to play it— _____
_____
_____
_____
_____

• Another thing, you should be certain to emphasize the following problems you can solve: _____
_____
_____
_____
_____

• When the City Manager says to you, "I see you've been unemployed for five months," you should say _____
_____
_____
_____
_____

• A final word. If at all possible, call up and get the interview post-poned for two hours—or until the afternoon. You could say your car broke down, or give another excuse, then you have all that extra time to visit the Yerba Loma library, do a little research, and make a few telephone calls. Here are some of the facts worth finding out about the city and the job that would make a useful impression on Sten Shaw. You can find them out in a couple of hours. _____

_____

_____

_____

_____

Good show. We thank you and Mike thanks you. The rest of this chapter will be devoted to returning the favor. We will give you some insights into methods of getting the most from the interview, which is the most vital phase of the negotiation between you and the employer.

INTERVIEW CONTROL

The interview is an inescapable part of the employment process. Good performance in the interview is essential to landing the job that you have targeted for your work pleasure.

Many applicants take the interview as an employer-run show—"They ask the questions, you answer them." But this isn't the way it is.

You can be in charge of your own performance by learning how to control the interview. Controlling the interview means keeping it moving in the direction you want it to go. Making certain to get across the selling information that you have prepared in advance, and which is designed to get you the offer. It means asking the questions you want to ask and not being thrown by a surprise objection or question. It means that you are in charge of your own presentation, at the same time making sure that the employer doing the interviewing feels that he or she is in charge.

INSIDE THE EMPLOYMENT INTERVIEW

To many people the job interview is a subtle, unavoidable form of verbal torture. In fact, all an interview is, is a meeting between two human beings for, hopefully, their mutual benefit. The employer representative wants to hire you, as much as you want the job offer—once he finds the person to solve a particular problem his tension ends. He has his new employee and he can go on to other problems.

An interview exists from the company's point of view because neither a resume nor an application form can tell everything about a candidate. From your standpoint the interview exists because the advertised job description, a telephone research call, or other in-depth job market research can not tell you enough about the nature of the organization and the job target within it for which you are aiming.

At its best, an interview is a structured conversation in which the employer tries to make an inward prediction—based on his experience and on what he knows of your past history—as to your future performance in his company. He then compares you with other candidates. You try to convince the employer of the benefits to him of hiring you. But you must also look out for yourself—evaluate and rank work pleasure, personal growth, and paycheck represented by the job being discussed in comparison with other job offers.

What the Employer Wants to Know About You

During interviews, the employer attempts to do the following things.

• To verify the accuracy and/or completeness of the resume, application form, or letter, and to fill in any gaps or apparent contradictions.

• To quantify the kinds of information which you gave. (For example, you were a building manager. How many tenants lived in the building? What was the rent total? Were you responsible for handling customer accounts? If so, how many? how often? Did you handle $50,000 in billings every month or $150,000? It makes a difference.)

• To measure your verbal skills.

• To ask questions about your experience and accomplishments, and evaluate their pertinence to the specific job.

• To judge personality factors which may be relevant, such as attention to detail, sense of responsibility, etc.

• To describe the position and note your response.

• To determine your salary requirements.

PREPARING FOR AN INTERVIEW

The best interview results in an offer, and this interview starts long before you appear in the interviewer's office. Most applicants do nothing to prepare for their interviews. How to prepare for your interview is what a large portion of this chapter is devoted to. The advance preparation will give you considerable advantage over other candidates competing for the job.

Interview Planning Form

Take a look at the Interview Planning Form on pages 182–183. You will need a copy of this form for every interview you take. The purpose of the form is to give you a means of organizing in advance all the information you can possibly get which you think might be relevant during your job target interview. The various items on the form are explained below.

Part I: About Your Employer Target

Employer name, address, time, and date of interview. Get the correct address. If there are multiple offices, the interview might be at an address other than the one with which you've been in touch. If the location of the building is unfamiliar get explicit directions so you are not late.

Individual giving the interview. Get the exact name and title of the person with whom you are meeting. Also, get the name and title of the person who would make the hiring decision.

Job description. Although you feel you are familiar with the nature of the job you are being considered for, write down as detailed a description of it as possible. Don't be shy about calling the secretary or the person who is interviewing you to ask for additional information.

Salary range and benefits. Prior to your interview, it is important to accumulate as much information as you can about the salary range in your job target area. If you know the range, you will be in a better position to quote a salary that will get you the offer you want. If appropriate, add questions on hours, training programs available, and so on.

You can get this information by contacting officers of trade associations or people you know who are in the field. Another tack is to contact a placement counselor who deals in the field and see if he can give you an idea what the going rate at this or comparable companies might be. If a placement counselor got you the interview, he will know what the salary range will be—and how much you can get. You also can read the classified ads that deal in your field and see what salary range is stated.

Products and services. You should know the major products and/or services that the employer produces or delivers to the public. You should also know what the department or section of the company for which you are being interviewed is responsible for within the company.

Competition. It is important to know the relative position of the company within the industry. Are they among the larger or smaller firms? Are they growing or declining? The more you know about your potential employer's competition, the more you may show yourself to be of value to them. Furthermore, while discovering information about the competition you may discover new employer targets.

Image. How does the company's public image compare with its industry image? Find out what people in the same business think of them.

History. The higher the job level, the more you must know about the company's past, present, and future. At any level it's wise to know what major changes occurred in the recent past, and what trends are apparent in the near future.

Day-to-day problems. Prior to your interview, try to find out the kind of day-to-day, month-to-month problems faced by the person who could hire you. Those problems could be budgets, turnover, sagging contributions, supply shortages, complaining customers, low productivity, overload or overwork, poor organization—whatever. You want to get this information in *as specific terms as possible.*

Other information. There are special areas of information about every employer target. You should try to find some of these facts prior to the interview. Use the allotted space on the preplanning form to list any incidental, but relevant, information.

Part II: About Yourself

Use Part II of the Interview Planning Form to organize the data about yourself in such a way that it will satisfy your interviewer that you are well-qualified for the job target.

Review resume. Is all the information complete? Can you account for all the time since you started work? If there are gaps, have an explanation planned. If you are not sure of the dates of specific events, check.

Accomplishments. In your interview you will be asked to provide information about previous positions you held, and about education, and special training or skills. List at least one accomplishment from each experience that is slanted toward your present job target.

Private life accomplishments. Often, accomplishments in one's private life can contribute to one's aptness for a job in the work world. Write down these accomplishments on this part of the form.

Your problem areas. Try to anticipate any areas in your record that could possibly stand in the way of your getting the job offer. Review these areas, and prepare as strong a case as possible to meet the anticipated negatives during the interview.

Questions to ask the interviewer. In this part of the form, list the specific questions which *you* want answered during the interview, for example:

- What are the day-to-day duties involved in the job? (Do they meet with your concept of work pleasure?)
- What are the working conditions?
- How much authority will you have over decisions?
- Given what you can deduce about the personality of the company, what is your growth potential one, two, and five years hence?
- Who does your future boss report to?
- What happened to the person who last held the job you want?
- Find out about turnover.

Use the Interview Planning Form for every interview you will have. Fill in as much information as you have, and try to obtain any additional information from the available sources. Review the form prior to the interview and during the interview if necessary, in order to be sure that you present yourself in the best possible way and therefore be more certain of obtaining a job offer.

INTERVIEW PLANNING FORM

(Prepare this form in advance of each interview you take)

PART I: YOUR EMPLOYER TARGET   JOB TARGET: _____

Employer Name: _____

Address of interview: _____

Phone: _____ Date & time of interview: _____

Persons to see: _____
_____

Travel instructions: _____
_____
_____
_____

Description of position applied for: _____
_____
_____
_____
_____

Salary range: _____

Products & services of employer: _____
_____
_____

Competition: _____
_____

Day-to-day problems of employer target: _____
_____
_____
_____
_____
_____

Public image: _____
_____

Company history: _____
_____

Other information: _____
_____
_____

INTERVIEW PLANNING FORM

Part II: About Yourself

Review of resume data: _____
_____

Work accomplishments: _____
_____
_____
_____
_____
_____

Private life accomplishments: _____
_____
_____
_____
_____

Anticipated problem areas: _____
_____
_____
_____
_____
_____

Questions to ask the interviewer: _____
_____
_____
_____
_____
_____

Other information: _____
_____
_____
_____
_____

THE INTERVIEW FORMAT

At its best, an interview is a structured conversation between the interviewer and you. It will be contained within a specific format that makes use of specific types of questions in order to satisfy both your goals and those of the interviewer. As stated earlier, it is meant to enable the interviewer to predict your future performance in the job under discussion, and to enable you to predict the desirability of the job. Throughout the interview you will be exchanging three primary types of questions—open end questions, closed end questions, and probe questions. Take a look at how you and the interviewer use each type of question.

Open End Questions

The Interviewer wants to listen to your general discussion of a subject which he can later explore with you in more depth: "Tell me about your work experience at your last two positions."

You will use open questions to obtain as much information as possible from the interviewer. You need this information to help you evaluate the job and the company, and also to use as clues to kinds of answers you should give to impress the interviewer most favorably: "What attributes would you say are most necessary to fill this position successfully?"

Closed End Questions

These are questions that can be answered in one or two words. They tend to sound like a ping pong match, with fast response on both sides. They generally keep the control of the interview firmly in the hands of the person asking the questions—which is usually the interviewer. The major disadvantage to the questioner is that one really doesn't have the time to evaluate the answers given before it's time to ask the next question.

Interviewer: You say you grew up in the hotel business?
    You: Yes.
Interviewer: You have a degree in hotel management from Cornell?
    You: Yes.
Interviewer: In your position with Saddle River Resorts were you responsible for the purchasing of the furniture?
    You: Yes.

When this line of questioning prevents you from expressing ideas you want to communicate, parry with the straight answer and then continue immediately,

> You: . . . Not only was I involved with the purchasing of equipment for the resort, but I also ran the kitchen. You know I studied at the Cordon Bleu school, for one year after graduation. Originally we had much the same kind of restaurant problem you have here, but it was through my reworking of menus that we eventually turned a profit. Would you like me to tell you a little about it . . . ?

How can the interviewer say "no" to you, if, as you've discovered, the resort restaurant is his major problem. So he nods, and you get the green light. In this way you are able to make your point, *control the interview*, without the interviewer ever feeling that he's not in charge.

Probe Questions

These questions are a form of cross check or request for more specific information about an area already discussed, but about which one or the other of you wants further information.

> Interviewer: You mentioned that your previous supervisor was quite difficult to work with. Could you tell me more about that . . . ?
>
> OR
>
> Why do you want to change fields after 10 years in education?
>
> OR
>
> What exactly were your responsibilities as production manager?

Sometimes, probe questions are simply an effort on the interviewer's part to get further clarification. Sometimes they have other purposes: to uncover contradictions, inconsistencies, unfavorable attitudes, and so on. Be prepared for them by knowing before the interview what your weak points are, and having well thought through answers.

On your part, probe questions serve two purposes. Though it is important to be a good listener, the surest way to impress people with your seriousness is to ask intelligent, penetrating questions about the position and the company.

You: Tell me more about the company's policy on promoting from within.

OR

Why did you decide to give up the computer after only one year?

OR

"Will the company back this new product with national advertising?"

TWENTY QUESTIONS

Listed below are 20 questions which come up in a variety of interviews. Not all are related necessarily to your own interview since questions vary from one job target to another.

Answer each question in the space provided below it. You can write your answers in an abbreviated form, since some of the actual spoken answers may be too lengthy to write in a short space. The object here is to put down enough key points to give you an idea of what answer you would actually be able to give if one of these questions were asked.

Write in the appropriate space the name of the employer and a brief description of the job target for which you would be likely to be interviewed. Address your answers to this prospective interviewer—speak them aloud if you wish.

YOUR JOB TARGET _____

THE NAME OF THE EMPLOYER TARGET _____

ABBREVIATED JOB DESCRIPTION _____
_____

1. What was your most important accomplishment during your school years? _____
_____
_____

2. Which subjects did you like best? _____
_____
Why? _____
_____
_____

3. What was your poorest subject in school? _____
Why? _____
_____
_____

4. Why did you leave your last job? _____

_____

5. Can you work under pressure? _____

_____

6. What is your biggest weakness? _____

_____

7. How long would you stay with us if this job were offered to you?

_____

8. What other positions are you considering? _____

_____

9. What can you offer us that someone else cannot? _____

_____

10. What did you like least about your last job? _____

_____

11. What position and salary do you expect to hold in five years? __

_____

12. Why are you interested in working for us? _____

_____

13. How long do you think it would take you to make a positive contribution to our organization? _____

_____

14. What is your opinion of the company you currently or previously worked for? _____

_____

15. What about the position under discussion interests you the least? What interests you the most? _____

_____

16. Do you like to work individually, or as part of a team. Why? __

_____

17. Can you supervise people well? Give an example. _____

_____

18. What do you think your co-workers think of you? _____

_____

19. To date, what have been your two most important career accomplishments? _____

_____

20. What is the minimum salary you would accept? _____

_____

Look back over your answers to the Twenty Questions. Ask yourself each question out loud, and then answer it without looking at your notes.

If you have a tape recorder, use it, and when you play your answers back, critique them. You may have another person critique them with you, or fire the questions at you.

THREE TOUGH QUESTIONS

Next, think of the three questions you would find most difficult to answer—the questions you hope the interviewer won't ask. List them below.

1. _____

2. _____

3. _____

Now take a deep breath and verbally compose answers to the three questions you hoped wouldn't be asked. Do it again and again, until you have what sound like satisfactory answers. In order to remember the answers, list the key words for each in the space below.

1. _____
2. _____
3. _____

INTERVIEW CONTROL TECHNIQUES

When answering questions that occur in an interview it is important to keep the following in mind:

• Watch for verbal and nonverbal feedback from the interviewer. Do his eyes wander, fingers tap, are there signs that his interest is wandering? If so, shorten your answer, and switch to another topic.

• Leave out superfluous detail, and stress all the benefits you can convey.

• If you don't know the answer to a technical or factual question, say so. Nobody knows everything.

• If the interviewer is someone who knows little about your particular skill or technical field, don't rub it in. Discuss the subject in a general and interesting manner.

• Don't agree when you don't agree. An honest difference of opinion is acceptable, if it's put in a thoughtful, nonhostile manner.

• Save some of your strongest self-selling points for the end of the interview.

• Take your time, think about your answers before giving them, and try to remain relaxed. And listen, listen, listen. The earlier you can get the interviewer to talk about the position, the company, or the department, the more you can sense what he is looking for and the more directed your answers can be.

• Refer to your own questions about the job and the company as you go along. Make sure to convey the impression that *you too* have to be sold.

ANATOMY OF AN INTERVIEW

Interviewing styles will vary greatly from employer to employer, and from person to person. Some managers and supervisors, as well as some personnel people, are very poor interviewers, though they may be otherwise excellent at their jobs. Regardless of the personalities involved, there are several standard stages in an interview.

Stage 1: The Opening

At the interview start, establish a cordial rapport with your interviewer. Shake hands, introduce yourself, and make small talk to put both of you at ease. Note the surroundings, the office decor. Pay attention to any personal touches which will give you some idea of the interviewer as a human being, not an authority figure. Remark on any trophies, paintings, or other signs of the interviewer's interests. Don't overdo it, but if the interviewer is responsive, you can explore these interests for a few minutes. (Make sure to remember all relevant personal conversation, and after the interview note it on your Interview Critique Form, pages 207–208. It may have use for you in the follow-up stage.)

The average interview will last anywhere from 20 to 60 minutes, depending on the job level. In the opening minutes, the interviewer should tell you how much time is scheduled. If he neglects to do so, ask, "How much time do we have?" Then note your watch so that you won't run out of time before making the points you want to make.

If the interviewer talks at the opening, *listen attentively.* If he waits for you to begin, do so, and have a well-prepared lead that relates to your job target, for example, "I must say that I'm quite impressed with your marketing approach—building a family of products around an established toothpaste name. Where did the idea originate?" This kind of open question forces the interviewer to answer. The object is to get a reading on the interviewer's style, how open he is, how much he knows about the job target itself, how much he knows about you, whether he has read your resume and application.

Interviews that you have "created" within the hidden job market particularly require that the opening statement be your responsibility. The following kind of opening question can give you a wealth of information about the job target you're aiming at:

"Mr. Popenoe, I'm glad to have this time with you today. I wanted to explore some ideas relating to my experience with management controls, and how they might relate to your department. I wonder if you could give me some idea how your organization is structured, and what kind of controls now exist?" Then listen.

In those cases where you know there is a specific opening and more about the nature of the opening, you could ask, "In your view what are the most important requirements of the job?"

Stage 2: Information Exchange

After about one-third of the interview has elapsed, you should know what the employer is seeking in the position, and the day-to-day requirements of your job target. In the second part of the interview, the interviewer will want to get more information about you in the following areas:

Education, training, and skills. Degrees, grades, major subjects, specific skills, and other training related to the job target area. Schooling will be less important when you have been out of school over five years.

If you are recently out of school, and your grades are not high, concentrate on extracurricular activities, after-school jobs, etc. Stress initiative, responsibility, and hard work.

Work experience. If you've been in the work force for three or more years, this experience is more important than schooling, especially if you are applying for a position in the same field. Traditionally, the interviewer begins with open end questions, asking you to explain your past jobs starting with the earliest to most recent. When answering, spend as little time as possible describing responsibilities and accomplishments in jobs that are over five years old. Of course, you should stress these jobs if they were significantly different from your most recent experience, or if they are important to your new job target.

During the interview you may refer to your resume, to written notes, and your Interview Preplanning Form. Use this material as a reminder of accomplishments, but don't appear to be reading a script.

When describing previous positions, do so in a way which emphasizes problem-solving areas most related to the current needs of the prospective employer. And as noted earlier, keep watch for nonverbal and verbal signs of the employer's response to your remarks. If he shows signs of losing interest during your presentation break up your remarks with questions to him such as, "Is this the way you handle it here?" or "I think that what we did might be similar to the kind of problem you face in scheduling—is that right?"

Your questions will be based, of course, on your pre-interview research in preparation for achieving your job target.

Personality factors desired. These are never clearly spelled out, nor easy to determine through direct questioning. But if the interviewer has done his preplanning, he will have five or six specific personality characteristics in mind, which he will try to uncover. Below is a list of the most common personality factors that show up in job descriptions. Prior to your next interview, try to imagine which four or five might be most important for your specific job target.

Appearance	Motivation	Initiative
Self-confidence	Attitude	Creativity
Self-expression	Resourcefulness	Punctuality
Alertness	Stability	Aggressiveness
Maturity	Leadership	Neatness
Sense of humor	Growth potential	Attention to detail
Intelligence	Team work	Versatility
Warmth	Innovation	Easy, relaxed manners
Sensitivity to feedback	Perseverance	Vitality
Naturalness	Honesty/sincerity	Hard working

Stage 3: End Game

This is the final quarter or so of the interview. At this time you must make an appraisal of how well you have done so far. If no clues have been forthcoming earlier, ask, "Does my experience seem to fit with what you are looking for?" or "Is there any area of my experience that you'd like to know more about in relation to your needs?" Then, *listen closely* to the answer. If the answer is noncommittal, push—"I think that my experience would be valuable to your organization. Don't you agree?" or a similar question would be appropriate.

Most applicants never ask this question, but they should. If you haven't "made it" with your interviewer, the time to find out is now, not two weeks from now in a form letter rejection. If you've made a positive impression, such questions won't change the interviewer's mind. If the interviewer expresses uncertainty that you are the best candidate, try tactfully to find out why. "Is there some particular area of my qualifications that you feel doesn't meet your requirement?" In a nonhostile way inquire about specific points that might keep you from getting the job. Suppose the interviewer says, "The problem I see is your lack of familiarity with the new IBM 370 storage retrieval technology." If you have an answer handy, give it in a positive way—"I can see why you're concerned about that, but the 370 is not that different than the 360 with which I've had extensive experience." If you don't have a quick answer, say you'd like to think about the point he raised. Think about it. Then get back to your interviewer with an answer in a follow-up letter or a telephone call.

Your Difficult Questions

Bring up the questions you had prepared about the job and company, or those questions which occurred to you during the interview. These questions show serious concern and a concrete understanding of the company's problems. Such questions "Do you have five-year projections for this division?" or "Are you satisfied with the profit margins that you've developed in this product line?" are not aggressive questions. The answers represent the kind of information that a serious candidate would want to know about a company he is considering becoming affiliated with.

THE PERSONNEL INTERVIEW

If your interview was with the personnel department as many will undoubtedly be, your concluding objective is to try to get a commitment for an interview with the proper hiring authority. "Do you think it would be possible to meet with Ms. Walters now, or this afternoon?" Or, "When would the earliest time I could meet with Mr. Barlow be? I have several other job opportunities pending and before I make any decision, I'd like to explore this one more fully. Would it be possible to set up a meeting this week?"

UNSUCCESSFUL INTERVIEWS

If you, and/or the interviewer, have decided that you are not suited for the position, that's not the end of the line. Having established this relationship there is still much that can be done. Ask your interviewer about other positions in other organizations, or about people you might contact in extension of your job search. Get names and addresses and write them down.

Most important, try to get as much feedback as possible as to why your interview failed. This information should pertain to how you came across personally, areas in your resume that might be improved, etc.

Don't be embarrassed to ask. If the questions are put in the proper way, and you communicate a genuine, nonhostile desire to learn, you will be surprised at the cooperation you receive.

RICK SNYDE'S INTERVIEW

We would like you to look carefully at an abbreviated version of an actual interview. Except for the names, nothing about it is fictitious.

We'd like to evaluate this interview from the point of view of the candidate's effectiveness. As you read the following text, use the margins to make notes and comments about how well the candidate did, or how he could have improved his performance, and have had more control of the interview.

Art Bell: Hello Rick. My name is Art Bell. Sit down please.

Rick: Thank you Mr. Bell. Nice to meet you.

Art Bell: You've come in response to the opening we have in our Marketing Department?

Rick: Yes, sir.

Art Bell: What's your education in marketing?

Rick: I've a BS degree in general Business Administration. I'm currently studying for an MBA in marketing at New York University. My BS is from the University of Pennsylvania.

Art Bell: What's the subject of your MBA thesis?

Rick: The title is "Marketing the Concept of Population Control in the United States."

Art Bell: Challenging idea. Is it finished?

Rick: Not quite. As you know I'm currently employed full time. So I have to do my research nights and on weekends. But that phase is almost over. I should be able to sit down and start writing in about two weeks. I should have it on my advisor's desk by April. I expect to graduate in June.

Art Bell: Very good. I see from your resume that you've had one job since completing your undergraduate work.

Rick: Actually I've had several. Part-time jobs while I was going to graduate school.

Art Bell: I'm really interested in your full-time position.

Rick: The company is small. We're in the recruitment publication business. What we do is carry advertisements and general guidance articles to graduating college seniors and separating military men.

Art Bell: What do you do for the company?

Rick: Originally I was hired as Sales Manager. I called on Personnel Directors, College Relations Officers and such, to sell them advertising space in our publications.

Art Bell: Stop there. The word "manager" has the connotation of supervision and planning. What you were doing sounds more like selling. Was "manager" just a title or did you have managerial responsibilities?

Rick: More a title, with some managerial responsibilities. I did have one full-time salesman working for me, and I structured his calls. I was also responsible for the hiring, firing and so on, and the daily activities of three office support people.

Art Bell: Was most of your time spent in the field or your managerial responsibility?

Rick: Sixty percent selling, 40 percent managerial. Most of my work was strengthening relationships with people we already had as clients, getting advertising renewals, and so forth.

Art Bell: Were you successful?

Rick: Given the state of the employment market, and the fact that right now there is not much college recruitment going on, I think I was fairly successful.

Art Bell: What would you say was your most important contribution to your company to date?

Rick: Well, times being what they are, the company's had to retrench, and let go many staff members. I seem to be capable of doing many jobs at once, so I've taken over the responsibilities of many of these people. For example, the actual magazine production. Because of cutbacks we had to let go our Production Manager. I worked with him prior to his leaving, learned as much as possible about the job, and now I supervise it, and we've a part-time person to keep all the ends together.

Art Bell: You are energetic. Why are you interested in changing now?

Rick: The industry situation. There's no demand for our product right now, so I don't think my position will lead to any growth. I think the company is going to suffer some serious financial problems and it may ultimately hurt me.

Art Bell: We have more than one marketing position open. If you had your choice, where do you think you might make the most contribution?

Rick: In a staff position. I have book knowledge, right now, not practical experience. I'd do best under the guidance of someone with practical know how. As long as I was allowed to progress as quickly as I'm capable of doing.

Art Bell: What is your long range goal?

Rick: Marketing vice-president of a relatively major corporation in say, 20 years.

Art Bell: How do you plan to achieve this goal?

Rick: Hard work and constantly learning as much as I can. Being aware of what others are doing, what they're doing right and what they're doing wrong and learning from them.

Art Bell: Well then, would you prefer starting out in a marketing research activity or in, say, a sales administrative area?

Rick: Given my long range goal, I think I'd prefer sales. Yours is the kind of product that requires that your marketing people know exactly what your salesmen go through when they walk into retail outlets—what are the problems they run into, what are the buyers like, and so forth. I don't think a marketing man should get this knowledge second hand. He should experience it. So, I guess, I'd like to start in sales.

Art Bell: Are there any questions you have?

Rick: Yes, I'd be interested in learning a little about your advertising agency. How closely you work with them. How much of your advertising do they do and how much is done in the house?

Art Bell: I can't answer that myself. When the time comes you can talk to our Advertising Director about that.

Rick: OK. Fine.

Art Bell: Anything else? Or would you rather wait until you speak to Mr. Brady. He makes the decisions, you know.

Rick: I think that's all for now.

Art Bell: Fine. I'll see if I can set up an appointment between you and Brady. Why don't you wait in the reception room.

Rick: Of course. Thank you very much.

Well now, what did you think of Rick Snyde's presentation? What good points did he make? What did he miss? Or was he all good or all bad? From the interviewer's standpoint answer the following questions:

1. How well was Rick prepared for the interview?

_____

_____

_____

2. What do you think of Rick's answer to the question of why he is changing jobs?

_____

_____

_____

3. Were Rick's questions relevant to the job under discussion?

_____

_____

_____

4. How well did Rick relate his prior experiences to his potential abilities in the new job?

_____

_____

_____

5. When asked about significant contributions to his current job, did his answers show him off well? Explain.

_____

_____

_____

6. What is your opinion of Rick's response to the question concerning his long range objectives?

_____

_____

_____

7. Are there any other ways in which Rick could have improved his interview?

_____

_____

_____

We now turn to our critique. First, the positive points:
• Rick was familiar with his work and articulate in discussing it. Many people have difficulty describing the kind of work they do, even though they may have done it for years.
• He knew what he wanted, and he had prepared information

relating to the kind of product and sales problems the company interviewing him might encounter. He knew the company was consumer oriented selling to retail chains.

• He answered questions fully, without wandering to unrelated matters, and spoke with self-confidence.

These are the negative, or weak points of Rick's self-selling:

• He could have done a better job in translating his prior experience into a benefit for the company interviewing him. He implied that his current experience gave him problem-solving capabilities for a job in marketing, but he then failed to show a clear connection to the current job target.

• When asked about his most significant contribution to his current company he discussed the diversity of jobs he could handle. This had little to do with his expressed goals of sales leading ultimately into the marketing department. It would have been smarter to talk about what he had achieved in sales, and relate that to this new company.

• When asked why he was changing jobs he painted a gloomy future for his present place of employment. Instead he should have taken a positive view, and said he needed a more challenging job.

• In order to demonstrate his knowledge of the new company he raised an irrelevant question about work relations with the advertising agency. The answer to this question had little profit for him in terms of the job he was interviewing for. The interviewer recognized it as a meaningless question, and dismissed it. The time could have been better spent on questions regarding the sales and marketing department.

• When asked his long-range objective, he said to be vice-president of a major corporation. This is a foolish answer to a foolish question. One cannot be specific about 20 years from now. He could have said "It's difficult to project that far in the future, but most immediately I would like to work in the area of sales leading into marketing, and I would like to get a full understanding of your product line and see how together we could improve your market penetration."

• When asked whether he had further questions, or did he want to talk to the decision maker, Rick missed the opportunity to find out more about the person he would next interview.

• When salary was not brought up by the interviewer, it was Rick's place to ask what the salary range was. By not asking, he was ducking an important piece of information.

SALARY MINIMUM

The salary question can be one of the touchiest points in an interview, and the interviewer as well as the applicant often will avoid it as long as possible.

As mentioned earlier, before going to an interview one should know as much as possible about the salary range. When the interviewer asks, "What is the minimum salary you will accept?" try to find a point between what you know is their top and the money you feel you can command—even if it is higher than the "maximum." If what you want is far above their maximum, try to convince them of your worth, and see if they could go up a thousand or so. You can also handle the question of salary by saying, for example, "That depends on many factors. I'm considering a number of possibilities, and the growth potential here, my interest in the work, peripheral benefits and factors such as that will necessarily influence my attitude toward salary. I'd like to reserve that decision for now." If you are asked your present level of earnings, a certain amount of reasonable exaggeration, which includes expectation of a bonus or a salary increase, is not unacceptable. Actually, most firms do not search out a verification of present earnings, so if you are somewhat expansive, it undoubtedly will go undiscovered. Finally, before agreeing to discuss salary concretely, try to make sure that an offer is going to be extended. Then state what you believe is your maximum worth, or remark that you have an opportunity available right now at the $20,000 level. Seldom will a firm withdraw an offer simply because you feel you're worth more than they want to pay. Instead they bargain. If a company won't budge from their first salary offer, you might compromise for an earlier than normal salary review, stock options, a bonus, etc.

PRACTICE MAKES PERFECT

In a way, an interview is reminiscent of a tennis match—what you say influences what the interviewer says, and what the interviewer says influences what you say. A good interview can be a satisfying experience for both parties—the negotiation could effect each of their lives. Still, it is an experience that most individuals have only a dozen or so times in their lives—if that often. It is also an experience which, from the applicant's point of view, is clouded by nervousness, worry, and anxiety.

The interview presents a situation in which there are two role. The applicant frequently accepts without challenge the fact that the employer representative has all of the power: It is he who schedules the interview, and it is he who asks the questions. It is taken, therefore, that the applicant's role is to be polite and give the other party what he wants.

But it is not so. As we have said before, the employer needs you as much as you need him. You aren't just an applicant for a job—you are a unique being, with a combination of skills, capabilities, and interests. You must not confuse the job description with yourself. The interview, even more than the finest resume, is that point where the human element takes over and where you can transmit your special qualifications and attributes directly and most convincingly to the prospective employer. It is your best chance to play down your shortcomings and to maximize your positive values in terms of your job target.

Given your normal job lifetime, you will never take enough interviews to become really proficient at the art. So the best way to attain a high level of professionalism and relaxation during the interview is through structured practice. Through this structured practice you will learn how to transmit your unique and special value.

One form of structured practice is to take interviews for positions you are really not interested in, and to ask for, and get as much feedback as possible from the people who interview you. Another, even more productive way of obtaining useful feedback on how you can improve your interviewing techniques is through the use of the *role play interviews*.

Role play interviews are structured practice interviews involving you and a friend, family member, or another job-seeking friend. The basic requirement of role playing interviews is that you project yourself into the role, and allow the situation to become as realistic as possible. In the following interview role plays you will practice taking the roles of both the applicant and the potential employer, in order to obtain greater insight into the interview situation. If possible, you should have an audience of one or two other people during these interviews. They are there to critique your performance and tell you how to improve it.

How to Set Up the Role Play Interview

On the following pages are several role playing exercises describing applicants and employers. Before you practice "being yourself" in a role play interview, warm up with one or more of these exercises, in which you are really taking another person's part. You and your partner should each copy the pertinent information on the role plays. Study your roles to give yourself an understanding of the interview that you will be conducting.

• Start by playing the part of the employer in one of these exercises. Your partner plays the role of applicant.

● If possible and practical, have someone else present who will take notes on the Interview Critique Form on pages 213–214. On this form your critic should note the areas in which your interview could be improved—both as employer and as applicant. If you have a tape recorder use it and then listen to the interview later.

● Next, check the time, conduct a 10 to 15 minute interview as realistically as you can. As employer, do everything possible to determine whether you wish to hire this applicant. Ask probing questions, open end questions, etc. If either of you can't answer a question on the position, make up the information as you go along. It doesn't matter how "correct" your information is, since these are imaginary positions; what does matter is that you learn to perfect and polish your interviewing techniques.

● When you have completed the interview, give your impression of how the "applicant" could have improved his or her performance. Obtain the same feedback on your performance from the other party.

● Repeat the same role play interview. This time *you* take the applicant's role. Go through the same process including the critique. Encourage negative criticism. In addition, ask for constructive criticism—ideas on how to do better.

● Having gone through two imaginary interviews, one as employer and one as applicant, you are ready for the main event. You now play yourself. Provide your partner—who is playing the employer—with as complete a description as you can of the position and the organization. Give your partner a copy of your resume. Finally, have your partner interview you within the 15 minute time frame. Try to get the job. Put as much of your real emotions into this exercise as you can. When the interview is over invite the same critique as you did in the previous exercises. Repeat the interview a few times, with different partners. Repetition will make it easier, more comfortable, will prepare you for the unexpected question, and will help you develop the instinct for controlling the interview.

● Practice these role-play interviews as often as necessary. Interview role playing is fun, but more important, it is a proven strategy to insure the best outcome of real interviews leading to job offers.

Copies of an Interview Critique Form appear on pages 207–208. Use these to criticize the role plays, the actual interviews, productively.

INTERVIEW ROLE PLAY 1

The Employer

The Allwell Hospital Center Incorporated is a 350-bed hospital which will be completed within 6 months.

It is part of a larger medical organization affiliated with a major university. Although for the first few months the new hospital will be under the supervisory administrative control of the university, the idea is to have it completely independent of day-to-day control after the initial operating procedures are worked out.

The hospital will be one of the most modern facilities of its kind, with the strongest possible financial foundation. In terms of administrative management, the objective is to use the most sophisticated management techniques, computerized personnel and accounting records, and an advanced pharmaceutical purchase, inventory, and control system.

In short, they plan to do everything right from the start to the finish.

The Position

(Sent to you, the interviewer, from the Acting Director for whom you now work at the university. You are working temporarily as Personnel Manager for the hospital. He is now away on vacation.)

BUSINESS OFFICE MANAGER

Responsible for patient admissions, patient and third party billings, credit and collections, cash forecasting, and related systems and procedures including the hiring of administrative staff. Must have recent college degree with study in related field. 2–4 years experience in hospital administration is essential. Knowledge of computer systems is desired.

Position offers an excellent opportunity to apply new ideas in a progressive environment.

Salary between $15–18,000 plus good fringe benefits—free medical care.

The Applicant

Resume

Major George Hopkins, Ret.

CAREER OBJECTIVE: To translate over 20 years of military experience into productive work with an organization in the health care field.

EDUCATION: Medical Service Administrative Training Program 1966–67 (Special program for staff level Army Medical Officers—conducted in cooperation with the Walter Reed Medical Center).

U.S. Staff School, 1962

U.S. Military Academy, 1954. Major–Military Science

Various administrative and career military education and training programs over entire military career.

EXPERIENCE: *1970–76 Officer in Charge,* Amarillo Base Hospital.
* Administrative Officer (separate from the medical staff) of this 250-bed medical facility connected to the Amarillo Army Helicopter training base.
* Set up and administered all aspects of hospital management including all record keeping procedures in accordance with hospital operating manual and specifications.
* Designed new system to handle processing of large number of Vietnam veterans who were processed out of this base in 1973–74.
* Served as consultant to base commander on health and recreation policy.

1965–70 Assistant Officer In Charge, Personnel Records Division, U.S. Army Command Center, Washington, D.C.
* Responsible for implementing the transition from a manual personnel records system to a computer and microfilm system designed by the Control Data Corporation.

1954–1965 A variety of specific army assignments which were not related to my most current work in medical and health services area.

SALARY: Negotiable.

INTERVIEW ROLE PLAY 2

The Employer

Hartford Printing Corporation is a $20 million company which has over its 15 years earned an enviable reputation for very good four-color work, and has won many awards for quality printing. In the past few years the company has expanded its plant capacity—and switched largely from sheet-fed to web-(rolls of paper) fed presses.

The transition in this production area has resulted in a number of service problems with the work force, which have resulted in plant inefficiencies, small labor disputes, and unfortunately, has contributed to two years of moderate losses.

Management has decided that it needs to implement a program of upgrading its work force through better hiring, better training, and better line supervision. This goal has been assigned to the Personnel Department, and the present position opening stems from this.

The Position

PERSONNEL ASSISTANT

The person hired will have complete responsibility for what is now known within management as "Project Upgrade." He or she will report to the Personnel Manager and will implement and help plan the two year task.

Applicants should have experience in interviewing, an education specialty in training or industrial relations. Degree is desired (but not essential if a sufficient theoretical basis has been established in practice) to enable the candidate to help create innovative new approaches to on-job training, management by objective, and employee motivation.

A knowledge of patterned interview techniques and EEO regulations is desired.

Salary range $10–12,000.

The Applicant

(This applicant graduated from college last June. He was scheduled to come in for a plant interview, but at the last minute decided to take the summer off. It is now October and, having heard about this position from the placement office, he dropped by, and was granted our interview.) Here is his resume:

WENDLE MORTAIN

CAREER OBJECTIVE: Personnel Management

EDUCATION: BS Psychology, Harvard, 1974
Major Field—Industrial Psychology

EXPERIENCE: 1972–1974—Placement Office Assistant—Student Placement Office. This was a part time job—working 10 hours per week—interviewing students and referring them to jobs in school files. Called companies to solicit openings and followed up on referrals. Interviewed and referred student applicants to part-time jobs both on and off campus. Also helped design school Affirmative Action Program.

Also conducted independent (of Placement Office) job counseling service run by the Student Honor Society.

1973–1974—Vice President of Student Honor Society

1971–1973—Part-time work, tended bar (served as manager in owner's absence), did odd jobs, etc., to provide supplementary income.

INTERVIEW ROLE PLAY 3

The Employer

Your company, *The Provent Corporation,* is a manufacturer of heating and ventilating equipment for industrial establishments. Customers range in size generally from light industries of 100 manufacturing employees to major corporations with multiplant installations.

Sixty-five percent of your sales are through architects, engineers, and builders connected with original plant construction, and the balance is in updating existing equipment in older plants. A new area of growth is in response to the requirements of a recent occupational safety regulation which has had the effect of requiring many plastics and chemical manufacturers to upgrade their ventilating equipment over the next 18 months. Your product is well designed to meet these new requirements, and your president has decided to launch a major marketing effort for this purpose.

At present your sales are concentrated mainly in the Midwest, but, in line with another corporate objective, have been expanding into the rest of the nation. Corporate sales have risen to $75 million from $60 million two years ago.

The Position

ASSISTANT SALES MANAGER

This position calls for a person with a technical background who has had direct sales experience with the type of customers which you now have, and which you hope to obtain as part of your growth. The field sales force now includes 10 salespersons plus a dozen or more manufacturers' representatives that work on their own but must be kept motivated and informed. The Assistant Sales Manager is responsible for direct liaison with the sales force and manufacturers' reps, for recruiting new field sales staff, and for implementing sales programs which have been approved by the Sales Manager.

The person employed will travel 8 to 10 days per month, and will also be responsible for training and motivating both new and old salespersons. The person in this position will also be responsible for calling on certain "target accounts" that lie outside of the area now covered by the sales staff.

Other duties would include the day-to-day administration of field staff, handling customer complaints, and participating in sales planning with the Sales Manager.

Salary is $15,000 annum base, plus an incentive bonus based upon increased sales. The bonus could add as much as $5,000 per year to the salary.

The Applicant

(This man has answered your newspaper advertisement, and has been invited in on the basis of the following brief resume.)

JOHN P. STOKES

EDUCATION: BS, Lehigh University, 1965, Mechanical Engineering.

EXPERIENCE: *Not presently employed.*

October 1971–1974: Sales Manager, Applied Products.

Supervised a sales force of 18 persons involved in selling prefabricated manufacturing components to chemical manufacturers and processors. The components were used in the transporting of liquids and gases in the manufacturing process. Personally recruited and hired new salesmen, and trained them. Sales volume increased during tenure from $10 million to $17 million, including two new government contracts which represented business that the corporation had never previously been involved in. Reported directly to the Vice President/Marketing, and was responsible for all projections and reports.

1969–1971: Application Engineer, Air Pollution Control Division, Polutech Corporation.

Responsible for all application engineering, estimating, systems design, proposal preparation and overseeing of installation of air pollution control devices. Supervised 8 people. Was responsible for 20% sales growth in new applications.

1967–1968: Start-Up Engineer, Biegler Corporation.

Supervised the installation of new piping systems in paper plants.

CURRENT SALARY: $18,000

INTERVIEW CRITIQUE FORM

Use this form to critique the applicant's performance in the Role Plays as they are performed, then discuss your critique. (This form can also be used to evaluate real interviews.)

IDENTIFY INTERVIEW: _____

What is your general overall impression of this interview?

     Excellent____   Good____   Fair____   Poor____

     Explain:_____

     _____

     _____

Critique the interview in each of the following areas, and be prepared to explain your choices.

CONTROL - *How well did the applicant keep the interviews under control?*

_____ Maintained strong positive control without becoming overagressive.

_____ Was generally in control, but could have improved by _____

     _____

_____ Other_____

     _____

UNDERSTANDING OBJECTIVES - *Did the applicant have a good understanding of his own strengths <u>and</u> weaknesses? Did he know how to present and sell himself?*

_____ Applicant discovered what the company needed.

_____ Applicant found out enough about the job. Is it what he's looking for?

     _____

_____ Applicant forgot to <u>ask</u> several key things about the job.

     (Example)_____

_____ Applicant failed to <u>mention</u> several key things about himself in relation to the job.

     (Example)_____

INTERVIEW CRITIQUE FORM

LISTENING - *What percentage of the time did the interviewer listen?* _____

PRESENTATION - *Did the applicant provide enough information about himself to interest the interviewer, and do this at the right time in the interview?*

_____ Applicant was well presented.
_____ The presentation was accurate and good, but the timing was bad.
_____ The presentation was only perfunctory.
_____ The presentation was poor.

_____ Other _____

_____

EDUCATION, TRAINING AND SKILLS - *Were these well explained beyond the information presented in the resume? Were weak spots dealt with?*

_____ Very well covered.
_____ Not very well explored - could have yielded more information.
_____ Didn't require any explanation.

_____ Other _____

_____

PERSONALITY FACTORS AND JOB INTEREST

_____ Is this a special problem in this job? _____

_____

_____ Did the applicant take these factors into account? What was left out?

_____

_____ Other _____

_____

EVALUATION - Would you hire this applicant?

_____ YES

(Why) _____

_____ NO

(Why) _____

17

FOLLOW-UP

Let's pay a short visit to the Sargasso Sea of the job campaign:

Roger B: I sent 75 resumes to well-selected employer targets. I got answers from seven. Four of them turndowns. I must be doing something wrong. The three interviews I did take didn't work out too well either. Two negatives. I'm waiting to hear from the last one. I want that job.

Marty K: I don't understand it. All that work. Individual cover letters—and I had 14 really good leads. Names of the right people—some referrals, and so forth. But now it's been four weeks. I should have heard something from somebody.

Carol L: I had four interviews, which was really more than I expected. I flubbed one—but I think I'll probably hear from one or two of the others. At least I hope so.

Peter J: What I really mind is not the research, not the time spent writing and rewriting my damn resume—what I mind is the slowness of the companies to make a decision. It's like the old Chinese water torture. One place said I'd hear something in 10 days. It's now almost three weeks—I resent this waiting around, twiddling my thumbs.

Steve M: Employment agencies are worthless. I've been to or sent my resume to at least a dozen of them. Not one, not one of them called me back. It burns me.

Lillian L: Do you think they lost my resume? They said I would hear from them within a few days. That was three weeks ago. They haven't checked out my references. I called one and found out. The waiting around is more exhausting than the work I did to get the interview.

Art P: I talked to him on the phone. He sounded very interested. They sent me an application to fill out. I got it back to them in three days. I guess I'm buried in some file drawer somewhere. Should I call him again? Will I be making a nuisance of myself?

Tenance F: They turned me down flat. And I still can't figure out why. I know that I would be perfect in that spot. I really resent their attitude. Now I have to start all over again.

These people are marooned, becalmed, and going nowhere in their job search. They did many of the right things: developed employer targets, sent out what they thought were well-constructed resumes, personalized cover letters, and in many cases, got interviews.

But three weeks later—after having made contact by telephone, the mail, or through an agency-initiated interview, they've still heard nothing. Things are at a standstill. The ball is in the other fellow's court and he's not around. What do you do if you find yourself in this kind of spot?

You do *not* sit still and do nothing. You follow up.

But before you follow up on those "other people," let's do a little following up on yourself. Where have you been indecisive or blocked or lazy in *your own* job campaign? What areas could use more attention and more positive actions? Check off any statement on the list below which applies to you. List additional ones that apply, which we have not mentioned.

_____ I haven't thoroughly worked out my list of accomplishments and skills.

_____ I haven't mapped out a job plan yet.

_____ I've asked some people for information on my job target, and they haven't gotten back to me. I haven't gotten back to them either.

_____ I could have put in a little more time on thinking through my resume.

_____ I skipped a number of games in this book and haven't gotten to them yet.

_____ I have several phone calls to make to employer targets and have been putting them off.

_____ I planned to send letters to a number of employer targets but I haven't done it yet.

_____ I sent out cover letters and resumes weeks ago. No response.

_____ I was going to get in touch with _____ and haven't.

_____ I have an interview scheduled with _____ and haven't found out much about him, his department, or the company.

_____ I want to go to _____ (employment agency) and see what's happening. I haven't.

_____ I haven't heard from _____ and they said they'd be in touch with me.

_____ What ever happened to that interview with _____ _____ ?

Additional statements:

_____

_____

_____

_____

_____

_____

If the previous list revealed a number of *inactions,* you need some follow-up on yourself. Take action! Do it now! You can't just now? Why not? Go back to page 86 and review the format of the Excuses Game. In the chart below, fill in the areas of inaction. Next, list your reasons for this inaction and how you can overcome them and get active.

EXCUSE	OVERCOME
1.	
2.	
3.	
4.	
5.	
6.	

What is it in the corporate employment process that makes the follow-up necessary? The process is carried out by people, and often gets jammed. Before we get into specific strategies for following up, consider this early morning conversation between a supervisor and the personnel manager.

Supervisor: What else can we do, John? I'm dizzy with all the people I've seen. We've run ads in newspapers, and trade journals. We've talked to all the agencies. I've even called the association on my own—but nothing. Nobody fills the bill. And I needed someone last month.

Personnel: Harry, are you sure you're not being too particular?

Supervisor: I don't know anymore. No one really rang any bells. One or two did stick in my mind, but this isn't my game—interviewing. Didn't someone strike you?

Personnel: Harry, it's your department. I only sent through people I thought might qualify. But you're the one who has to work with them. How can I tell you who to hire for purchasing. It's like you telling me who to get as a Personnel Assistant. It doesn't work that way.

Supervisor: You're right. I know it. And I don't remember anyone clearly.

PHONE RINGS

Supervisor: Hello?

Vaughan: Is this Mr. Donnelly?

Supervisor: Yes, who is this?

Vaughan: This is Carol Vaughan. We talked two days ago about a spot in your Purchasing Department, as your assistant?

Supervisor: I remember, I think . . .

Vaughan: I'm the woman who told you that in addition to my working experience I had a great deal of experience with various consumer groups as a volunteer.

Supervisor: The consumer's union lady?

Vaughan: Right. That's why I'm calling. When we had our interview you told me one of the things you expected the department to do was to branch out into consumer products in the next two or three years. Well, since our interview, I've been doing some thinking, and I realized that given what's happening in this industry, my total experience with consumer groups would become more and more valuable as time went along. For example. . .

Supervisor: Ms. Vaughan, say no more. Could you stop in today so that we could talk a little further?

Vaughan: I'd be delighted to.

Supervisor: Fine. Let's make it three. Bye!

HANGS UP PHONE

Supervisor: Well John, I remember her. She's perfect I think.

Personnel: Even if you don't remember her, she had the sense to call you back. In the state you're in she is perfect. Good for her.

FOLLOW-UP TACTICS

The object of a good follow-up is to get a *fast* and *positive* response and to push for getting the job offer. Those are two quite separate objectives. If the response is absolutely negative, you want to find it out quickly and keep moving. On the other hand, the essence of follow-up strategy is to intervene at those delicate moments when the decision-making process is in flux and weight it toward a positive outcome for you. If the timing is right, you could even reverse turndowns.

Avoid the wait-and-hope syndrome. Hope and act instead. Have on hand some proven, practical follow-up strategies.

Tactic 1: Urgency

As you have your interviews, whether they are at the Chicago headquarters of Playboy, the main office of Club Mediterranee, or Chase Manhattan Plaza, you will notice that almost everyone you meet is busy. There are phone calls, paper work, schedules, and reschedules. There are meetings upon meetings, and then more phone calls. The work machine seems to be full of people who are fighting to stay busy.

It's different with most applicants. If you are working, and looking for a new job, then you sit in a waiting room and wait tensely for interview time, so you're not late getting back to work. If you're out of work, it's worse. With no job to return to, you can take all day to get through what you could do in an hour or two. You can wait hours in a waiting room, because the waiting itself gives you something to do.

Waiting tensely, or waiting peacefully, either way, too much waiting around is not productive in a job campaign. You must impart a sense of urgency to every step in this campaign. And you must do it in a way that communicates itself to the prospective employer.

After an interview . . .

Mr. Speese? This is Tim Hogan. We met last week. I showed you those three-color illustrations from the book I'm preparing on birds. Remember? Right? Well, there's a freelance project in the offing in a few days. It's in Salt Lake City. Before I schedule it I'd like to know if you've decided when to hold the second round of interviews?

After mailing a cover letter and resume to Mr. Testa, call his secretary:

Do you think Mr. Testa has seen my resume yet? I'm going out of town on business next week, and I'd like to see him before I leave. Would you please check it out for me? I'd appreciate it. And I'll call you later today to find out if that's convenient?

Tactic 2: Additional Information

This is an adaptable follow-up device. It can be used at any point in your job campaign *after* you have made your initial contact with your employer target. It concerns additional information you didn't give when you first met the employer or talked with him, when you had your interview—whenever. This information should add new benefits to your approach and give you a new positive push. It is both a means of staying in touch and of giving the employer another reason to make you an offer.

The following excerpts from conversations are examples of additional information being conveyed by telephone or letter.

Ms. Rolfson, how are you? Say, I left my application and resume with Mr. Gordon last Friday, and I wanted to attach this report to it. I think he'll find it's important. Would you see that he gets to see it? I'll stop by in a couple of days to pick it up. It's rather confidential, so I don't want to leave a copy.

Mr. Barton, this is Dr. Rodgers. We met last week for an interview. I remember that we briefly discussed that new process for coating tin oxide on Pilkington float glass. Well, I've just gotten hold of the way they do it during the actual float process. If it works it will bring down the cost of coated glass by 200 percent. Would you like to meet for a drink after work, and I'll describe it to you? It can be an important part of your project.

Mr. Alexander, about our interview yesterday. I must have really been quite pressured. I forgot to mention one whole area of developmental work which I did. And the more I think about it, the more I feel you should know about it, because my experience would be quite helpful to you. Can I stop by for a few minutes tomorrow and discuss it?

Dear Mr. Wilson:
Here's a postscript to our pleasant and brief meeting in Atlanta. Enclosed is my new resume, a far more detailed listing of the experience I have that is most directly related to your new Energy Conservation Department. As you can see, application of some of these ideas could be most useful to you.

Very truly yours,
Sam Southworth

Dear Ralph:

I enjoyed our last meeting very much, and am delighted that you decided that you can use my services.

I think that my recent experience with the FTC & SLA gives us a considerable edge when you begin to lay out the program for bar displays.

Before you reach a final decision about your salary recommendation, I wonder if we could get together briefly. In the interviews we've had we never discussed salary in depth. This is important both in terms of the initial salary, and my long-term career planning.

Very truly yours,
Angus Drake

Tactic 3: Repeat and Recap the Benefit

If at first you don't succeed, repeat, repeat again. That's why TV commercials repeat the same sales message over and over. Your self-selling commercial will not suffer from repetition. It will be remembered. Therefore, if you don't hear a word from a prospective employer, follow up with a repeat and a recap of the benefit you have to offer them. Write or telephone and remind them *who you are*, and *what your problem-solving capabilities are in relation to them.*

Dear Mr. Green:

In my letter of June 15th which accompanied my resume, I pointed out several new product development areas which could be added to your present output with a minimum of expense, and considerable success. My past two years' direct experience with this type of project would, I believe, add significantly to your marketing capability.

I've enclosed a copy of my resume, and hope that we might be able to meet briefly to discuss the possibilities. I'll call you in a few days to see if we can arrange an interview.

Very truly yours
Amie Greenleaf

Hello Miss Pastile, this is Benjamin Glick. I'm following up on my letter of last week. Just to recap briefly: I've been working for three years with a small publishing venture in Berkeley. We produced a new line of inexpensive how-to-do-it books which were marketed in supermarkets and discount stores—quite profitably I might add.

My role was to take the specific subject areas which we had

decided upon, and locate writers and illustrators that we felt would do a good job with the subjects and help them get the job done. I completed 12 different titles, which have each sold in excess of 50,000 copies.

Do you think we could get together for a half hour tomorrow? Any time in the afternoon would be good for me.

Dear Mr. Wilson:

I certainly appreciate your decision not to meet for an interview at the present time. I know how difficult it is when budgets are cut back.

But I do think that there is one very good reason to get together now rather than in the future.

As you will note from my resume (I've enclosed another copy for your convenience), in the position I held as assistant administrator at the Will Rogers Center, I was also in charge of all purchasing and office procedures. What is not fully shown is that an extremely important element of my job was involved with cost controls.

During my four-year tenure there, through internal procedures, I accomplished a 20 percent reduction in the budget for office supplies and materials. Also, by redesigning all the forms which were used in the control of our primary operation, I was able to help bring about even greater savings.

I think that this experience could be quite valuable to your department now. If you could spare a short amount of time I will show you how these savings were effectuated.

> Yours very truly,
> John Sullivan

Tactic 4: Response to a Question or Problem

Something has come up in an interview or a phone conversation, and you use this question or problem as a lead to your follow-up. The question or problem could be one concerning the position, the company, or one which relates to your own qualifications. Sometimes, coming up with a practical solution to the question or problem will require your going back and doing a little research. But having learned how to do this, it's not that hard.

For example, in an interview for a position as Food Service Manager for a large hotel, the hotel manager mentioned that one of the major problems they have is with high staff turnover. You make a mental note. A week after your interview you send a follow-up letter in which you say something like:

I've been thinking about your problem with high staff turnover. One technique which you might want to consider is the idea of incentive bonuses for people who have stayed for a certain duration. I know that this has been tried successfully with a West Coast hotel chain, and worked out quite well.

Now, just how did you know that? A few hours in the library, reading back issues of the biweekly *Nation's Restaurants News* and a call to an ex-professor at the Cornell School of Hotel Management yielded the information. It's simple when you know how.

Here are a few other examples of how to use problems as opportunities for positive follow-up:

Mr. Love? Hello, this is Ciba Thomas calling. You may recall our meeting last week at the Skagway Club. I'm calling to ask you a couple of questions about the job we discussed. You said that one of the problems you were having was the work load distribution among the various garages. I've been thinking about the problem and if I had a clearer picture of garage locations I believe I have some ideas that could be useful to you . . .

OR

Dear Mr. Gordon:

I was remembering our meeting two weeks ago with Mr. Benjamin and his associates. I was very impressed with your description of the Galaxy expansion program. Very creative.

You might recall that in our discussion we touched on several areas of mutual interest regarding audio training materials and the federal government. You mentioned that you might want to incorporate some of my ideas into your own planning.

Since our discussions I have taken the liberty of developing some of these ideas, and would like to present them to you.

Yours very truly,
Jack Thomson

Or when you have been turned down for not meeting the specific job description:

Dear Mr. Montifiore:

During our telephone conversation last week regarding the position of Fashion Coordinator you mentioned that you would prefer someone with at least five years experience with a department store. I understand why this is important to you, but I believe my experience with Easee Patterns would be as appropriate and even more useful.

As part of my job as Fashion Coordinator for Easee I visited over 50 major retail outlets yearly, setting up fashion shows and other promotional events that featured our patterns. This was done over and beyond my work on the Easee Pattern Book.

During these country-wide visits I had occasion to meet with many top department store executives, and deal with the variety of problems each store faced in doing their fashion merchandising. I believe that the solutions I brought to the multiplicity of problems confronting each retailer give me a diversity of experience that should be of enormous value to your operation.

I'd like to stop by next week, and take a few moments to show you my portfolio. I'll call your secretary to see if we can arrange an appointment.

Yours very truly,
Karen Bantan

Dear Ms. Lovitt:

I have received your letter concerning the position as Shipping Supervisor. I am sorry you feel that my lack of a degree would disqualify me for this situation.

One thing I neglected to bring out in our interview, and, as I now notice, was not detailed in my resume, were the extensive courses I took while serving in the U.S. Army. These courses would have led to a degree except that my transfer to New Jersey, and then to active duty, prevented their completion.

Another, possibly more relevant, aspect of my service experience included responsibility for the shipping and receiving of an entire training unit. In this assignment I received a formal letter of commendation from General Steven Roberts (copy enclosed).

I wonder if in light of this new information you would reconsider your decision, and agree to meet again, so that I can provide you with more details. I will call you next Monday.

Your very truly,
Marcy Waller

Tactic 5: Going Over Personnel

If your initial contact with the company was through personnel, there is no doubt that this tactic is risky. So if possible use it before you have been officially rejected by personnel. The best time to use it is when you've been unable to get a response out of personnel. In other words, as soon as possible.

The tactic does not work in reverse. If your initial approach was at the hiring level you won't gain a thing by then contacting personnel, unless it is to find out about alternative positions.

When going beyond personnel to the supervisor, you must do so in such a way that the decision maker is not put in the untenable position of implying that personnel was not on its toes. People up the line generally have a sense of protection for the decision of subordinates. There is also a built-in suspicion of people, like you, who are bucking the system. But it can be done.

First, if you are rejected by personnel—acknowledge their decision and imply that it was probably your fault that they did not have all the information they needed. Don't say they were wrong. However, be prepared for the fact that the "higher up" you want to see may have made the decision himself, and had personnel send out the letter. So don't pretend that you haven't been turned down if you already have.

Second, if possible, try to get in your appeal to high authorities before you have been "officially" notified of a rejection. This way you are not necessarily defying the system—just trying to be helpful.

Here is an example of an approach that worked:

> Mr. Stiles, this is Steve Rind, I'm sorry to interrupt you—I realize you're busy, but I'm in your neighborhood now and felt it would be valuable for both of us if you would see me for a few minutes . . .

> Several weeks ago I sent in a resume in response to an advertisement about an opening in your section as a Contract Negotiator. I've had three years solid experience in negotiations in both commercial and military projects, for an organization like yours.

> I've heard from personnel that I am "being considered" for the position, but I'm in a bit of a spot. There are two other situations which I'm now considering, and I'd like to know as quickly as possible about your opening which I'd much prefer.

> Since you are the one who will make the final decision, I'd like to bring a copy of my resume over and meet with you for a few moments.

Tactic 6: The New You

If the job is worth it, you can redo your resume to zero in on the job. When you do send a new resume, don't send the original. Send a printed copy even though you are possibly only going to use one. This seems wasteful, but it gives the impression that you have a variety of situations under consideration.

Here is a sample of the type of cover letter that you might want to send with a revised resume.

Dear Ms. Horwich:

I enjoyed meeting with you and your associate last week. It was a highly instructive interview. I never realized that Bard Ltd. was moving in so many directions.

Enclosed is a copy of my revised resume. You will note that I have provided more details about my experiences with Wise and Kalins—which I previously only touched on. I have also highlighted the photographic tie-ins.

Under the circumstances, you can see why I feel confident that I would be able to contribute to the expansion of your midwestern conventions, once given the chance.

Thank you for the introduction to Ms. Josephs.

Hoping to hear from you soon.

Yours very truly,
Bernard Mann

Tactic 7: Third Party Follow-Ups

One of the proven methods of getting you out of the file drawer and closer to a job offer is to have people other than yourself take positive action. These other people generally fit into one of the following three categories:

1. Placement or referral agents, school placement services, etc.

2. Other third parties, including inside contacts, trade journal editors, association officers, or any other people who have helped you "get inside."

3. References or prior employers.

Let's examine how they can help you.

The placement counselor or agent, or another third party who has referred you to an employer for an interview, most often has a relationship with the person at the organization to which you were referred. He can use this relationship to expedite action. If nothing is happening he can find out why. If there is a problem he might find out what it is.

For example, if the employer has narrowed his decision down to two or three candidates, and you are one of them, an agent could ask a question like "What are Harry's strong and weak points for the position?" He would be more likely to get a direct answer than you would. Armed with this information from the agent, you might just happen to drop by or call up, or provide some additional information to build up your case.

Both prior to your interview and after it, there are some things that a third party can do to help you. For example, he or she can,

- Find out from the potential employer, prior to the interview, what particular aspects of the job are the most important, and what the salary range is, and give you this information.
- Make sure that the resume or interview is directed at the highest possible level on the decision-making tree, and follow up to see that it gets there.
- Find out the immediate reaction to the resume or interview, and help you decide how to reinforce positives and overcome negatives.
- Imply a sense of urgency in making a decision, suggesting to the prospective employer that you may be considering other situations.

REFERENCES

One of the most effective follow-up techniques is through the use of one of your references. It is particularly valuable when your reference is a person of some standing in the field—an official of a prior employer in the same field, a college professor, a politician, etc. Use this person as a reference on your application or resume. This is an exception to the usual rule of not including references on resumes. Put one or two on—if you know that they will make an effort for you, particularly if they are "visible" personages in their field.

Whether it is after your interview, or before, you may feel in need of some positive encouragement in your campaign. At this point, ask your reference to call the individual who is responsible for the hiring decision, and to give a strong presentation of how you are the right person for the job.

The pitch goes something like this:

Hello, is this Mr. George Meade—Chief Industrial Engineer? Yes?, Good—this is Dr. Bustamonte, Head of the IE department at State College—how are you?—Good, Terrific, I hear you fellows are really doing great things over there. Say, by the way, a young fellow—former student of mine, Bill Brotherton, put me down as a reference on one of your employment applications a few weeks ago. Now I've been doing some traveling since then, and I was afraid you'd tried to reach me when I was away.

So I thought I'd take the initiative and give you a call to talk about Mr. Brotherton, whom I recommend fully. In our view he is an outstanding candidate, and one that would make a terrific contribution. He's one of the best . . .

The caller would then end with either a question or comment such as "What was your opinion of Mr. Brotherton? Are you considering him for the position?"

In this way the caller could gain some insight into how you stand with your prospective employer, could unearth any potential problems, and at the same time reinforce the positive aspects of your abilities. Finally, he brought you to the attention of the potential hirer.

Tactic 8: I'm Harold—Try Me!

When you have been turned down flatly in your approach to a job target, the rule is *Don't take no for an answer!*

If there is a job you truly want, and somewhere along the line you've reached a road block, don't just pick up your marbles and leave. It is possible to make an extra effort, and often turn the situation around, or at least obtain valuable additional feedback which will help you in future job seeking. The first step in this approach is to *find out what the objections were—why you weren't hired.* Only a very small percentage of job seekers even consider this tactic. The prevailing tendency, upon receiving a negative response is to withdraw—hurt, rejected, depressed, discouraged.

The adage among top salesmen is, "The sale doesn't begin until the prospect says *No!*" This means that he must meet and overcome the real objections or restrictions which the potential buyer has.

The same goes for you. As a job seeker or a salesperson selling yourself, you must face the objections that an employer might have. This is a natural part of the process of getting what you want. There are many kinds of turndowns, or objections, that you will encounter in your job campaign. Some of these we have discussed before, and will recap briefly here:

A form letter in response to a letter or resume you sent. Saying sorry—no openings, or, nothing for you just now.

• A turndown on a request for an interview—either by phone, mail, or in person.

• A letter or telephone call after an interview at the personnel level informing you that "despite your fine qualifications we are unable to make an offer at this time."

• Or, no response at all.

The essential and first step in dealing with these turndowns is first to find out as clearly as possible the *real* reason for the turndown. The reason you have been given may not be the real reason at all. The rather innocuous bureaucratic expression, "Unfortunately, at the present time we have no openings which fit your qualifications," may cover a number of possible reasons. They may range from

Hey, we've got too many applicants for this job already—we really don't want to consider any more people.

OR

We've narrowed our search down to three candidates, and will probably decide on one of them.

OR

You don't have the specific experience we seek.

OR

We didn't see what we were looking for on your resume.

OR

We've decided to hold off for a few months on this position.

OR

You don't have the degree of education we seek.

to any one of several dozen possible reasons—including the fact that the employer might actually have someone in mind who they think is better for the position. So what is it—why were you turned down?

The rejection may come in response to a mailed-in resume from someone you've never met, or talked with. In this case it will be more difficult to find the real reason than if you had contact with a real person. This, of course, is one of the reasons we are against the indiscriminate mailing out of resumes—it gives you no personal connection.

It is different when your rejection comes from someone you have met or talked with. Here, good telephone technique can get you the kind of feedback you need to possibly overcome the turndown, or at least to tell you something that will improve your next interview. For example,

Mr. Mack, this is Harold Steinmetz. We met two weeks ago regarding the position in your Collections Department. I got your letter today saying that you had decided that I wasn't the best one for the job. I want to thank you for the fast response, and the courtesy of the personal letter.

I'm calling to ask you a favor. Could you possibly give me a bit more information about where my qualifications fell short. I have no quarrel with your decision, but it would be valuable for me in my future interviews to know where my strong points and weak points are.

Then you sit back and listen, and take notes, encouraging Mr. Mack to go on, particularly with the areas in which he feels you could have done better, or been better qualified. *Encourage negative responses*— this is the best and also the most difficult feedback you can get. Don't try to defend and answer these negatives—not *now*.

If Mr. Mack is reluctant to give you the information you need, you can ask specific questions such as, "Could you tell me if you felt that my daily interest accumulation method had any applicability to your business?" or personal things such as, "Are there any specific ways in which I could improve my interviewing presentation?"

It's not easy to get this information, as most people don't want to have to criticize. So, your skill in handling this difficult situation can make an impression—it says: Here's a person who is really interested in this job, and can take criticism and learn.

After you have gotten all the feedback you think you can get (or stand) you switch to Phase Two:

> Thank you very much, Mr. Mack, you don't know how much I appreciate this. It's a rare person who will be so frank and candid, and you've been a help to me. I'll think about what you told me.
>
> There's just one other thing I'd like to ask you. Could you suggest the names of any other concerns like yourselves, where I might make a contact for a similar type of position—or is there a particular agency you know that is good in this field. Or would there be someone in another part of your company that might possibly have something appropriate for me?

As we mentioned in Getting Inside, parlaying contacts is very important. It can be done at every stage of job seeking—once you've made contact, during an interview, or during follow-up.

This probing for additional leads, whether within the same organization or out of it, is a proven way to get personal referrals to other job situations. This is a fine time to do it. Your Mr. Mack is probably feeling guilty at having crossed off such a nice person. Usually he will try to be as helpful as he can. With his name you may be guaranteed two or three new interviews in a related field.

Take good notes, stay open to information. Then—Phase Three— can you overcome the objections?

If you have a good grasp of the real reason for the turndown, and a solid response to it, you can respond to it once Mr. Mack stops talking. Otherwise sign off nicely, wait a day or two to put together your thinking and then call. Or write and then call. But whatever you do, it should be positive and confident, not argumentative or defensive.

It could sound like this:

> Mr. Mack, you know I've been thinking about what you said. About the fact that I didn't have enough experience in the area of consumer credit type accounts of the number and scope that you have in your organization. Well, you are completely right. But there is an area of my experience that you might want to look at again.

When I came to my present position we were only collecting 48 percent of the total assigned accounts. Within *one year* we were up to close to 60 percent—an increase of over $100,000 dollars each year. That was my doing.

And I think this ability is something that could be useful in your organization. Why not consider hiring me on a trial basis. If within 120 days I haven't proven myself to be able to deal with the larger number of accounts, as well as raise the percentage of collections, then we'll both know it. But I believe after three months you'll find you made the right decision.

Try me.

Part Three

SUPPORT SYSTEMS

18

PERSONAL SUPPORT
SYSTEM

Job seekers often see themselves as solitary and out of touch. They view job seeking as something that has to be done alone. With this attitude you carry an emotional burden that is unproductive, as well as being unnecessary.

While you are job seeking, and conducting your search program, you need all the help—both practical help and morale building—that the people in your life can give you. A prime source of this help, of course, comes from those nearest you—your spouse if you have one, your friends, your relatives, and other people who are close to you. These people make up your *Personal support system*. These people can help in critiquing your resumes, they can carry out job market research, make telephone calls for you, join you in the interview role playing game, etc.

If you are unemployed, an important part of your support system can be other job seekers, at the same level as yourself. Try to find three or four others who are in the market, and meet them once or twice a week at one or another's house. Use these meetings for planning, discussions, and working out new ideas and joint projects of research and/or follow-up. Working with others can increase the speed and effectiveness of your job finding.

SUPPORT SYSTEM PLAN OF ACTION

The first thing to do with the people you want to use for your personal support system is to motivate them to help you. You must convince them that their help is essential to your job campaign, and may even be the key to its successful outcome—as well it may be.

When you have identified this personal support system, start out by letting each participant read this chapter. It really is written for them. After they have read it, discuss frankly the specific actions that they can take to help make your job search more productive. Following are some examples of specific areas in which your personal support system can and should help.

Emotional Support

Whether the feeling is justified or not, it is not unusual to feel emotionally insecure when beginning a job search. If you are unemployed, the question of financial security will increase the distress. It is hard to avoid the feeling that somehow you are outside the system, looking in. Furthermore, the prospect of rejections, an inevitable part of every job campaign, can lower the spirits of the bravest. Unless you see these rejections for what they are—doorways to success in obtaining job targets.

Memo to Personal Support System

Here's how you can help the job seeker get over some of the emotional unease which can interfere with a job campaign:
  • Look upon the time of job change as one of opportunity. It is not a "red alert."
  • Take a practical interest in the process of job finding. Pay attention to his or her successes, small and large, and reward them with approval. Accept rejections and disappointments as a natural part of the job-finding process.
  • Get the job seeker involved in things other than the job campaign. The world doesn't stop because someone looks for a new job. It is not a good idea to immerse oneself totally in job finding. Keep their sense of humor alive during the job campaign.

FINANCIAL SUPPORT

If you are unemployed, the time of job change is a time to conserve resources—to budget, plan, and to call upon all the support you can to help keep you going as long as necessary to obtain your desired job targets. Your personal economic situation may require obtaining financial help from family and friends. If it does, don't be embarrassed to ask. Wouldn't you respond if they were the ones asking for assistance?

Before you call Uncle Charlie, or Mom, or your in-laws, do a little arithmetic. Work out a budget, calculate how long you can comfortably (not luxuriously) get along on the assets you have, including unemployment insurance. Then, make a *realistic* appraisal of how long it will take you to conduct your job campaign. Then add a month or two to give yourself the advantage of turning down any job offers that are wrong for you. If then you find you have to borrow money from friends and/or family, put the figures before them. Let them see that you are well organized and have a realistically thought out plan.

Memo to Support System

• If you are a wife, husband, or someone sharing financial responsibilities, do what you can to help work out a practical, realistic budget. Write it down, and help keep to it every week. Help in the overall financial planning.

• If money has to be borrowed from friends or family, do what you can to help put these requests forward in as persuasive and business-like a way as possible.

• Limit discussion of money and economy to times when essential. It doesn't help to dwell on the subject endlessly. Try to absorb as much of the pressure as possible.

• If you are working, are there any conveniences of your job (such as an available telephone, office supplies, etc.) that you can put at the disposal of your friend?

BRAINSTORMING

Throughout virtually all chapters of this book we ask you to look at the idea of work and jobs in a new way. We invited you to explore new avenues of personal pleasure and accomplishment that might lead to work. The free associating you did in relation to job families and job targets could represent major changes of career direction. In the chapter on the hidden job market you discovered imaginative ways to do job research, and created new ways to get interviews and do follow-up. Originality was required in much of the job-finding process which we described and now, when it comes to inventiveness, your support systems of family and friends can be most productive. Ideas grow faster and better when worked out with others. Use one or two members of your support system for once a week rap sessions in which you discuss some of the ideas you are exploring about your career campaign and job plan. These do not have to be formal meetings. They can be as simple as meeting for a cup of coffee or a drink after hours. Or a walk after church or a movie.

Memo to Support System

• Don't wait to be asked to participate in the creative parts of your friend's job campaign. Look at some of the earlier chapters of this book. See where you can contribute with new ideas.

• Think of other people out of work, and help organize weekly meetings for discussion and planning.

• Don't be shy about suggesting your own ideas about areas of work or research from which your friend might profit. See if you can extend your thinking and your friend's beyond the rigid confines of the conventional.

• Keep a book of your own in which you list ideas and suggestions for your friend's job campaign. Keep eyes and ears open.

THIRD PARTIES

You should know by now that we set great store on all the contacts, friends, associates, etc., you can possibly think of, who might be useful to your job campaign. Point your personal support system onto third parties. Have them think of and list as many names as possible of potential contacts for you to approach for leads.

Memo to Personal Support System

• Write down as many names of people as you can think of who might know, or have ideas about, work areas or people that your friend should know about. (You might want to read the chapter of this book called The Hidden Job Market.)

• Call a few of your friends, relatives, and acquaintances to see what leads they might have which could be valuable.

FEEDBACK AND ROLE PLAYING

An important aspect of every good job campaign is to develop and use ways of finding out how you are impressing others, particularly potential employers in such areas as your resume and interviews. Get the most accurate feedback possible, *before* you approach prospective employers. That way you will know how to make the best impression when *it counts*, in the actual job campaign.

Use your personal support system as much as you can to critique your resume, your phone presentation, and your interviews, prior to actually putting the information to work for you in your campaign. Go through interview role plays with different members of your personal support system until you are satisfied that you have perfected your skills.

If there are specific items of your job campaign that are giving you problems, discuss these openly with one or two friends or family members. Invite constructive criticism.

Memo to Personal Support System

• Feedback and critique are there to provide as much helpful information as possible, to help your job-seeking friend or relative improve performance in presenting himself to a potential employer.

• Be as direct as you can in suggesting alternative solutions. The art of good criticism is to learn how to say "I think this would be better" rather than "You are wrong."

FAMILY COUNSELING

Let's consider the impact on a marriage of your losing a job, or making the kind of career change that entails starting at the bottom or being trained for a new field. In either case your income could be curtailed for a period and force a change of life style. How will your spouse take it? The success of any job campaign depends on your own positive attitude, which in turn is influenced by the attitude of your spouse. In those marriages where you are in agreement, and are optimistically committed to your job-finding campaign—wherever it takes you—there will be no conflict. But homes have split up because of one partner's job loss or career change that brought with it a move to a new community or less affluent way of life.

Changes in family income can raise questions that should be dealt with immediately and openly explored for answers. For example, if you are a husband, and your income was the mainstay of the family, will your wife consider working in order to help out, so that you can pursue your job campaign properly? If she can't and won't, are her reasons sound? How would you feel about her taking a job? Another question: If yours is a marriage in which both partners have careers, what happens if you find your ideal job target in another part of the country? How will your spouse feel about making the move; will he or she be willing to change jobs too?

In working out the answers to these questions, and dealing with the other pressures that job changes bring about, you might find that the relationship can become strained. If you reach the point where you can't resolve the emotional load we suggest you consider family counseling. Don't be embarrassed by the idea, hundreds of thousands of couples do it. Write to *Family Service Association of America,* 44 East 23rd Street, New York, N.Y. 10010. They are a well-recognized, nonprofit organization which has been operating for over 60 years. They will put you in touch with an accredited family-counseling agency near you to help you work out the serious family strains.

19

PUTTING THE GOVERNMENT TO WORK FOR YOU

Federal, state, and local government agencies spend many millions of dollars each year providing programs and services designed to help people prepare for, locate, and obtain new jobs.

The largest provider of employment services is the Federal Government, through the auspices of the Department of Labor. The states, which share with the feds the responsibility for unemployment insurance, and most localities of any size, which operate programs under CETA (Comprehensive Employment Training Act) use federal money to finance local programs to help people—primarily at lower income levels—to get training and work.

You can find out more about the availability of job services by contacting your local employment service or CETA office, your State Department of Employment, or by contacting the US Department of Labor, Washington, D.C. 20213 and asking for a directory of publications—which can lead to many resources.

Many job seekers, especially in the professional, management, and administrative fields, have spoken with disdain about the level of service received from the "Unemployment Office." This is an understandable reaction because state employment counselors must of necessity handle a large volume of people from many walks of life who are unemployed, and in many cases desperate for a new job. With jobs on the tight side, their work isn't easy. But as a highly motivated job seeker, you should know that if you invest your own time and energy to make the most of the services that are available, you will find the relationship quite productive.

WORKING WITH THE EMPLOYMENT SERVICES

As in working with other third parties or with placement counselors, you must consciously motivate USES counselors to help you. Do as much as possible to make their job—helping you—as easy as possible. Don't go in with the "I don't think you can help me, but I'm going to try you out anyway" attitude. Instead, be as specific as possible in describing the kind of help you need, and as familiar as possible with the services which are available. If you are working with a counselor who isn't helpful, go back another time and get another. If the person you work with is good, express your appreciation by sending a brief thank you note, and by using some of the techniques you learned in the follow-up chapter.

A partial listing of the services that are or should be available to you at your local employment service or CETA office follows. However, you must keep in mind that the level of competence of counselors, and the services provided at USES offices, vary from state to state, and location to location.

Labor Market Information

The United States Department of Labor and the Employment Service have more statistics on employment, unemployment, and job availability than any organization in the world. They can tell you what skills are in demand in what locations, and what types of occupations are in trouble.

Even in tight employment markets when some fields are laying off, others will be expanding and some locations will be doing better than others. If Detroit is in trouble, and there are massive layoffs in automobile production you might find that there is a severe shortage of mechanics in the auto repair field in Akron or Seattle.

USES offices are geared to develop and make available localized job search information materials such as employer directories, directories of community services, training opportunities, pamphlets describing specific jobs, and other relevant labor market information. This material is available to employers, the general public, and to applicants.

Job Banks

The *Job Bank* is a computerized job order distribution system for display of current openings in a given locality. In many states you can have access at your USES office to listings in other parts of the state, or in the surrounding region. In using job-bank listings, be sure to find out what geographic area they cover. If a location you are considering is not included, find out how you might have access to that information.

By law, all employers doing more than a minimum amount of business with the federal government are required to list job openings, at all levels, with the USES. Although there is strong evidence that this regulation is not being fully complied with, still it increases the job listings in the professional, technical, and administrative areas.

Job Information Service

Here you can view listings (either in book form or on microfilm) of all current job openings, and select the jobs (which do not contain employer names) for which you feel qualified. If the USES screening counselor feels that you are qualified, you are referred, without an extensive interview, to the employer. As in the job bank, check to find out what localities are represented on the microfilm.

Job Development

Depending upon the office work load, and degree of motivation of the counselors, it might be possible to have USES put in some time to develop some positions for you—that is, to call employers that you or they have selected, even though these employers have not registered an opening.

This active job solicitation might be difficult to obtain in a tight job market, when counselors are under more pressure. Try to convince the placement counselor that you have worked hard to develop your list and that his cooperation would be very valuable. Tell him that you are aware that, according to official sources, this is a service he is allowed to offer—and you might find him surprisingly helpful. A letter to his supervisor, praising him for his very real effort would, of course, be much appreciated. He likes to succeed too.

Relocation

Up until recently, there were funds in the Department of Labor to pay the travel expenses of individuals who were unemployed as a result of the aerospace layoffs a few years back. These people had to relocate to other towns and cities in order to find the specialized technological jobs that no longer existed on the West Coast or in whatever cities they were living.

The Trade Act of 1962 authorizes relocation, subsistence, and transportation for people whose jobs are affected adversely by foreign trade. Under such circumstances the USES can get involved in travel or relocation. There are also other special circumstances in which the USES could possibly help with relocation. So, even if you are one of the many for whom relocation allowances are not mandated by law, you might still try for an allowance if you have a bona fide job offer pending and cannot afford the travel expense.

Professional Offices

Several years ago the USES set up special Professional Offices where college-educated and professional people could get the same caliber of service they would get from a good professional employment agency. There is an increasing number of offices which provide service to applicants in the fields of photography, advertising, sociology, education, communications, etc. The potential of these offices to help the professional is greater, and in a few offices the counseling experience is equal to the job targets and the candidates.

You can find out where the nearest Professional Office is by contacting your local employment office or the regional Manpower Administration office for your state (see the list at the end of this chapter). If there is a professional office near you, you should use it if you can. Go first class, it doesn't cost any more.

Counseling

All USES offices offer career counseling to applicants as one of their services. According to the official literature: "The goal is to enhance a person's employability and enable him to develop his job potential." In practice, this counseling is generally most effective for people with very basic job problems: need for career direction, medical rehabilitation support, or to overcome other barriers to employability.

Apprenticeship Training

If you are between the ages of 17 and 26 (or older if you have had military service) and want to go after a career in one of the traditional apprenticeship areas—aircraft fabricator, brick layer, carpenter, printer, silversmith, tailor, etc.—you may be able to qualify for federally supported apprenticeship training. This is a four-year program in which you get paid for working and learning a trade. For information ask your State Employment Office for their brochure describing the program.

Other Services

There are dozens of other services provided by the CETA, your Employment Service Office, or out of Washington. These services range from specialized computer "registers" of particular job areas, to films and pamphlets describing particular careers, to aptitude testing. The only way to discover all of the available services is to visit the offices—obtain brochures and publications and get to know a good counselor who is willing to devote some time to you.

Inter-area Placement

Here are some things which USES offices can (and should) do to help you find work in other areas.

• If there are four or five organizations in other cities that you would like to be referred to, or which you have contacted, a manager or counselor at your office could probably send your resumes airmail to the managers of offices in the cities you indicated, with the request that they call the employers and make a presentation of your qualifications.

• If you wanted to have your qualifications checked against the jobbank listings in another location, this should be reasonably easy to arrange if you are convincingly serious about your willingness to relocate.

• If you need specific job market information concerning which fields have openings in what areas, you may get permission for a phone call by your counselor to a counselor in another locale.

• If you were planning your own trip to another locality, you should arrange in advance an appointment with a specific counselor (by name) in that city.

• If your USES office won't make these intercity connections for you, make the contacts yourself by phone or letter. Use research techniques to get the name of a counselor in the office you wish to have helping you. Should you get resistance from the bureaucracy to your request for specific steps to help you find work in another area—put your request to a higher supervisory level or call the regional office or Washington, D.C. These days the USES puts out a good deal of information emphasizing their dedication to linking all internal job markets by high-speed computer so this kind of feedback could prove quite embarrassing to officialdom.

Following is a list of the regional Manpower Administration offices and the states they serve.

LOCATION	STATES SERVED
John F. Kennedy Federal Bldg. Boston, Mass. 02203	Connecticut, Maine, Massachusetts, New Hampshire, Rhode Island, Vermont
1515 Broadway New York, N.Y. 10019	New Jersey, New York, Puerto Rico, Virgin Islands
P. O. Box 8796 Philadelphia, Pa. 19101	Delaware, Maryland, Pennsylvania, Virginia, West Virginia
D.C. Manpower Administrator Patrick Henry Building 601 D Street, NW Washington, D.C. 20210	District of Columbia
1371 Peachtree Street, NE Atlanta, Ga. 30309	Alabama, Florida, Georgia, Kentucky, Mississippi, North Carolina, South Carolina, Tennessee
300 South Wacker Drive Chicago, Ill. 60606	Illinois, Indiana, Michigan, Minnesota, Ohio, Wisconsin
555 Griffin Square Building Dallas, Tex. 75202	Arkansas, Louisiana, New Mexico, Oklahoma, Texas
911 Walnut Street Kansas City, Mo. 64106	Iowa, Kansas, Missouri, Nebraska
Federal Office Building 1961 Stout Street Denver, Colo. 80202	Colorado, Montana, North Dakota, South Dakota, Utah, Wyoming
450 Golden Gate Avenue San Francisco, Calif. 94102	Arizona, California, Hawaii, Nevada, American Samoa, Guam, Trust Territories
909 First Avenue Seattle, Washington 98174	Alaska, Idaho, Oregon, Washington

20

INSIDE THE EMPLOYMENT AGENCIES

There are between 8 and 10 thousand private employment agencies, "search firms," and other placement offices operated as independent businesses. There are probably 100 thousand men and women with the sole objective of placing applicants similar to yourself in new jobs. And if they don't perform for you, they don't get paid.

There are as many variations in quality as there are agencies or as there are placement counselors. The quality of service may vary even within an agency, among specific counselors.

Some managers, placement counselors, and executive search consultants are at the top of the ladder professionally. They have a strong background in one or two areas of specialization, strong contacts in the industry, a good reputation, and incomes in excess of $50,000 per year. Others are inexperienced salesmen, with little or no sensitivity to the field in which they refer people for jobs, with a defensive attitude, a lack of organization, and a superficial understanding of what it takes to match employer and employee.

Not all employment agencies are right for you. The way to find out which agencies provide the best placement services for your job target is to question several employers in the field, in the localities in which you wish to work. Find out from them which agencies and counselors they use, and why. It is generally quite easy to get this information, simply ask the personnel manager or the department head, if there is no personnel office. You then visit these agencies and counselors, and tell them that they were recommended.

FEES

When selecting an agency you should know at the start if the fee is paid by the employer (Employer Paid Fee), by you (Applicant Paid Fee), or by a combination of both. In some cases (Negotiated Fee) the matter is to be decided between you and the employer when the hiring decision is made.

Over the past few years the question of who pays the fee has been resolved more and more in favor of the applicant, that is, the employer pays the fee. Today there is only a relatively small percentage of jobs above the clerical level that require the applicant to pay a fee. But during certain labor market conditions, or when it comes to choice locations (Miami, San Francisco), you may still have situations where applicants are expected to pay the job fee.

However, applicant paid fees are not entirely a disadvantage. If an agency saves you weeks of searching by coming up with an attractive position that you yourself couldn't or didn't come up with—it's worth the fee. Most agencies allow an applicant to pay placement fees over a short period, or to charge it against a credit card.

Be sure to read your contract with an agency before signing it. Be cautious about any clauses that call upon you to guarantee fee payment if you accept a position, and then, for whatever reason, leave the job after a week or so. These clauses have been sources of problems in some agency/applicant arrangements.

If such a clause exists on a contract you are to sign, try to have it deleted or changed. If you worked at a job for less than 30 days, you shouldn't have to pay a fee for it, even if you are the one who decides that the job is not right for you.

The first thing a good employment agency can offer is incentive. Since most agencies don't get paid if they don't produce results, you have an organization whose motives are the same as yours—to find you a job you will take. A qualified counselor with experience in your field can be an important source of field information: who's hiring, what the salary levels are, etc. An agency generally is a small independent business, and therefore can be flexible in its approach to helping you locate the right position. Agencies are not restrained by bureaucratic rules. They can make unlimited phone calls, send letters, and take other steps if you have motivated them sufficiently.

Most good employment agencies have the capability of developing jobs for you even with companies that have not registered an opening with them. They are not afraid to get on the phone and make exploratory calls for possible openings. This is a service generally not equaled by nonprofit placement services such as the United States Employment Service, college placement offices, or other institutions.

There are plenty of agencies to choose from. If you don't find the service you want with one, there are many others that could prove more helpful. You can work with three or four agencies in different parts of the country at the same time. But be careful about working with more than one or two agencies in the same geographic area. A counselor will be offended if he finds out you are also working with a competing agency.

Many agencies for technical, administrative, and professional people have arrangements with agencies in other cities around the country. They will work with these agencies in attempting to locate a position for you. If you are considering looking for a position in another town, check to see if the agency which was recommended to you in your home town has affiliates elsewhere.

There are several "networks" of agencies which have facilities for duplicating and distributing your resume to scores of different locations (see Chapter 25).

Good agencies are most frequently run by top professionals with a broad understanding of their own placement practice, and a good knowledge of the world of business and industry. If you can find an agency which specializes in your particular field, and can make contact with the agency manager or with a top counselor, you have a powerful ally in your job campaign. A good agency counselor is a valuable "third party" when it comes to final negotiations for salary. Moreover, he or she can be a valuable source of feedback on your performance during the interview with the employer.

HOW TO GET THE MOST FROM PLACEMENT COUNSELORS

The art of getting what you want in your job campaign, as you have learned from previous chapters, is having an organized, action-oriented approach at every stage, never just drifting aimlessly.

The normal placement agencies' procedure is to check current files; if there is nothing on file, they will make a few calls. If this produces nothing, the counselor's instinct will be to look for the next applicant. It is up to you to see that the counselor sticks with you as long as possible and takes those extra steps: research, more phone calls, creative thinking, or checking other sources.

Briefly, here are some pointers on getting what you want from placement counselors:

• Find out in advance, from persons in the field and employer contacts, who the good placement offices are, and who are the best people, or the managers, in those offices. Use these "referrals" to get you the service you want.
• Once you meet with an agency, try to make a fast determination if you think that they can and will really do a good job for you. If not, don't waste your time and theirs. Go find a better agency relationship.
• Once you have located a good agency in a given geographic area,

stick with it for at least a week before looking for a second agency to work for you as well. Don't irritate the first agency with immediate competition.

• In your first meeting with an agency counselor, present yourself in a positive way, as you would in an employer interview. Convince the agent that with the two of you working together he will be able to line up a good job for you, and a good fee for himself.

• Whether it be an employment agent, college placement counselor, or association secretary, treat people as equals. Be neither condescending nor obsequious.

• Bring in good copies of your resume, and a list of employers (compiled through your own research) who might want to hire you.

• Offer to help the agent in any way that you can: research, revising your resume, etc. Don't take the attitude: "You're getting paid for this—you do the work!"

• Find out precisely what the counselor plans to do—and what his time schedule is. Take notes on this.

• Follow up with the agent every few days, or according to a preset schedule. Don't bug him, just check to see if he's doing his job.

• If things aren't working, drop by and try to find out *why*. You are looking for specific reasons, i.e., he's had no time to make the calls, or the people he called were out; or negative responses; or uncertain responses. Offer ideas on how to improve the situation.

• Keep at it. If you aren't getting the service you want, find another agency to supplement your own job research.

A NOTE OF CAUTION

Because the profit motive is a strong one in agencies, keep in mind that the way a counselor sees his task will differ from the way you see it. You want to find the job target which will give you the greatest long term potential for personal fulfillment and growth. The counselor wants to make a fee.

The agency objective is to get you hired. You will rarely hear them advising you *not* to take a particular job because it's not good for your future.

Because of the relative ease of entry into the business, you will find many employment agencies whose service leaves much to be desired. Many counselors have little or no experience in the fields in which they are doing placement work. Some counselors work on straight commission, and being eager to place applicants, they exaggerate or misrepresent a particular position. Many agencies with less than inspired management will only tap the surface of possibilities in your field. They have no time for counseling an applicant on his overall career goals, fields of interest, or job search techniques. In fact there really are only a few organizations either capable or willing to provide in-depth, overall career counseling.

EXECUTIVE SEARCH CONSULTANTS

Search consultants are in the business of seeking out specific people to fill key spots in corporate managements. Search consultants normally work only in salary ranges of $25,000 and above. Their activities are triggered by specific requests from employers. They rarely work through the personnel departments of organizations, and pride themselves that the person they are seeking for a particular position is not "on the market." They generally work on an hourly retainer basis with their employer clients, getting paid whether or not they find the right candidate.

It does no good to send unsolicited resumes to these firms, but there are ways that they can be helpful to you.

Use your research techniques to find out the names of a few top executives in the field of your job targets. Call these executives, and ask them to recommend a good executive search firm, and an individual name that they know, or have had experience with. Call these consultants and say that they were recommended by Mr. A, and that you would like to buy them lunch, or meet for a cup of coffee or a drink after work.

When you meet, describe your specific objectives, discuss your job targets, and, if you establish a good relationship, you could be rewarded with a wealth of information about your field, people in it, and even some specific job leads.

You can obtain a list of these executive search firms by writing to the American Management Association, 135 West 50th Street, New York, N.Y. 10019.

COLLEGE PLACEMENT OFFICES

Most college placement offices maintain a good library of materials related to counseling and specific opportunities available for students and alumni. In many cases they have directories, books, and other information which could be valuable in your job campaign.

Placement directors at colleges are generally most concerned with setting up campus interviews, and coordinating the large influx of placement activity that arises each winter through spring. If you can see them during times when they are not swamped in scheduled activities, and if you have specific areas about your job campaign to discuss, you could find them to be of some assistance in coming up with names or contacts of employers who are hiring.

One problem is that these offices have never really worked out much of a program of reciprocity. So if you went to the University of Pittsburgh, and are now working in Boston, there is no "formal" way for you to get job counseling or assistance from Boston University. But try anyway. Get the name of the Placement Director, find out when he or she will be in, and then drop in. Explain your situation, and see if you can get help. Or else call the Placement Director at your own school, and ask him if he would call the office in your area, and see if he can set up an appointment for you with the person you want to see. It has worked for others.

Also, while on campus, find out the names of a few professors or assistants within your job target area. Visit them. See if you can get them to cooperate in your job campaign.

ASSOCIATION PLACEMENT OFFICES

Many professional societies and associations have placement services for their members. These can be as elementary as a set of 3 x 5 cards kept by the receptionist, to a complete register of openings published monthly.

It is worth looking into the services provided by an association in your field, whether you're a member or not. (You can join when you've gotten the help you want.) In addition, you can meet with the association officials, and probably get some valuable help from their contacts and information.

FORTY PLUS CLUBS

This is a self-help organization designed to help those who have at one time been executives, earned at least $16,000 per year, and are over 40 years of age.

This 35-year-old club is a volunteer cooperative job search organization. Members help each other by donating their time, a given number of hours per week. There are several committees set up to do the various tasks of the club: the Public Relations Committee informs the public of the club's existence and purpose; the Job Counseling Committee is responsible for counseling members, reviewing and sometimes revising resumes—and for applicants' morale; the Marketing Committee contacts companies throughout the country in search of possible job openings; and of course, the Placement Committee coordinates the members and the jobs available.

The club requires a membership fee. It boasts a new membership turnover every three to four months. The largest and oldest club is located in New York City with a membership ranging from 125–150 members at any given time. The Forty Plus Clubs are independently operated and have several locations throughout the United States and Canada: Chicago, Cleveland, Denver, Honolulu, Houston, Los Angeles, New York, Oakland, Philadelphia, Washington, D.C., and Toronto.

21

EDUCATION AND TRAINING
FOR NEW JOBS

Until recently our society had been convinced that a four-year college degree was the only path to a successful career. We now know that this isn't always true. Much of our formal schooling, though providing us with a valuable education, doesn't prepare us to make a living at work that will give us pleasure.

In many cases our formal training can actually work *against* our work pleasures. The 19-year-old boy who elects to study engineering, architecture, or business administration, may have very little idea as to the day-to-day work in these fields. Consequently, ten years later he is still working in the field, because that's his "profession," while his real pleasures could lie in an entirely different direction.

New technologies, new political alignments, and new economic or environmental considerations affect the work world many years before they influence the educational establishments. New work opportunities appear daily, and, if you have the appropriate skills they may hold potential work pleasure for you. In this chapter we want to give you some ideas, and direct you to resources of information which will show you how to get additional education and training related to your work pleasure areas.

TRAINING FOR A NEW JOB

There are thousands of schools, courses, and training programs outside of colleges, which are used to train people in an unending variety of work-related subjects. Everything from cooking gourmet Chinese banquets to learning how to drive a tractor, or become a psychotherapist. Here are some major categories:

Community Colleges and Junior Colleges

These institutions can be public or private. They generally offer a variety of programs ranging from a two-year associate degree to a specific customized program which will teach you all you need to know to get a beginner's position in a particular field. These schools vary in size, location, cost, and courses offered. They often have good ties with the local business communities, and try to keep their curricula tied to actual employment needs.

To find out more about the specific community colleges in your area, you can write to your State Department of Education, or send for the Junior College Directory (cost $5.00) to *American Association of Community and Junior Colleges,* One Dupont Circle, N.W., Washington, D.C. 20036.

Trade, Technical and Business Schools

There are over 7000 private trade and technical schools, teaching close to 600 work related subjects. Courses last from a few weeks, to three years. Emphasis is on teaching those skills that can result in employment opportunities. The quality of training will vary from school to school, but the majority are well run, and give good value for their tuition fee.

But, remember, no school can *guarantee* you a job. It is your responsibility before starting a vocational school course, or any work-directed training, to determine whether or not it relates to your specific job targets, and, whether their are real openings available in the field once you obtain the skills.

The fact that jobs in a field are tight is not an automatic reason for not taking a course in the field if you really like it. With the techniques learned in this book you can probably do much better than average in digging jobs out of the hidden job market. Still, check it out, try to determine whether your investment of time and money is a sound one.

Make some inquiries about the school. Get an idea of the course material. Compare this with the material in other schools covering the same subject. If possible, find out from people in the field what they think of the school, and if they know of any better programs.

The *National Association of Trade and Technical Schools,* 2021 L Street, N.W., Washington, D.C. 20009 is the official accrediting agency for private vocational schools. Their free publication, *Directory of Accredited Private Trade Schools,* lists thousands of schools and courses which they have approved. To be doubly sure of the reputation of a vocational school, you could check with your local Consumer Affairs Agency, and the Better Business Bureau.

Home Study Courses

Home study requires strong self-motivation, a solid desire to learn, and putting in the effort required, often after a hard day's work. There are over five million individuals enrolled in mail-order correspondence courses for vocational training, including one million students of the armed services courses. Some trade and technical associations offer members their own correspondence courses. The placement services advertised by the correspondence schools often are inadequate, or nonexistent.

The National Home Study Council, 1601 18th Street, N.W., Washington, D.C. 20009, has been selected by the U.S. Office of Education as the accrediting organization for home study courses. They publish a free directory which you can write for: *Directory of Accredited Private Home Study Schools.* From your local Better Business Bureau you should also get a copy of the free booklet: *Tips on Home Study Schools.*

Apprenticeship Programs

Apprenticeship training is a system of learning while you earn. It combines classroom training with on-the-job instruction and a paycheck.

There are about 300 different apprenticeship trades, including such diverse occupations as photographer, rigger, roofer, painter, brewer, barber, tile setter, jeweler, upholsterer, leather worker, carpenter, etc. Apprenticeship programs are conducted through the cooperation of government, unions, schools, and corporations. The Bureau of Apprenticeship and Training in the Department of Labor, and various state agencies coordinate apprenticeship training through a network of field offices.

The requirements for apprenticeship training vary from place to place. Generally, however, you must be between the ages of 17 and 26. Veterans may add the years of service to the upper limit. To find out more about apprenticeship programs contact your local state employment office, or the Department of Labor.

Cooperative Work Study Programs

There are a growing number of schools which operate work study programs which allow you to support yourself and pay school expenses by combining work and education. Work and school attendance may be on an alternate day, alternate week, or other time periods. The training is work oriented, and normally well-coordinated with specific job openings.

For more information write: *Cooperative Education Association*, Drexel University, Philadelphia, Pa. 19104. Ask for the *Directory of Cooperative Education* which costs $6.00.

Adult Education Programs

Almost every community has developed programs of adult education—generally given at night and on weekends, where you can learn anything from crafts to cooking, film making, business administration, and hundreds of other subjects. These courses provide an ideal way for you to build up skills in a job target area, while still supporting yourself doing something less satisfying.

To find out what adult education courses are available, contact your local colleges and the board of education for your town or city.

Industry and Trade Association Programs

According to the *Guide to Career Education* something like $30 billion is spent every year by industry in the education and training of employees. Most of this training is done by the larger corporations, through in-plant training or tuition refund plans.

Regardless of the size of the organization you work for, you should check to see if they will help you pursue training in a field relating to your job targets. You will, of course, get more cooperation from an organization when the training you seek will improve your potential value to them.

Many trade associations and professional societies sponsor specific programs in their field which are available to members, and occasionally to nonmembers. Contact the associations or societies which are closely related to your job targets, and find out what training courses they have. These associations are also good sources of information about courses available in the field, and will often know what schools or courses are best for a specific subject.

How to Find Out About Training and Education Programs

Unfortunately, although much needed, there is no comprehensive directory of all work related education and training programs. To unearth the programs you are looking for, you will have to do your own research, similar to the research done in the Hidden Job Market chapter. Here is a brief recap of how to apply some of these techniques of job market research to locating training opportunities:

• *Third parties.* Contact people in the field, ask them to recommend programs they know about.
• *Yellow Pages.* Look up schools in the yellow pages. They are generally listed under types of instruction offered. (While looking in the Yellow Pages, you can also look up organizations in your job target area, call them, and see what training programs they know about.
• *Boards of Education.* Visit your local or state Board of Education. They generally have a list of courses and where they are offered.
• *Trade Journals.* Contact the editors or staff of trade and professional journals and publications for information. Look through back issues to see what courses might have been advertised.
• *Associations.* Be sure to check with the headquarters of the associations and professional societies in your job target field. They usually keep a list of approved courses in the field. You can obtain the names of the appropriate associations by consulting the *Directory of Associations,* published by Gale Research, Book Tower, Detroit, Mich. 48226 or the *National Trade and Professional Association Directory,* from Columbia Books, 917 15th Street, N.W., Washington, D.C.

Training References

The Guide To Career Education by Muriel Lederer, published by Quadrangle, 10 East 53rd Street, New York, N.Y. 10022. Comprehensive guide of schools and courses listed by subject area, giving names and addresses of sources of additional information on particular subjects of interest ($9.95; 395 pp.).

Directory of Accredited Private Trade and Technical Schools. Order this free publication from *National Association of Trade and Technical Schools,* 2021 L Street N.W., Washington, D.C. 20009.

Directory of Accredited Private Home Study Schools. Order this free publication from *National Home Study Council,* 1601 18th Street N.W., Washington, D.C. 20009.

Occupational Outlook Handbook. Covers over 800 different fields of work: qualifications needed, rates of pay, description of work, and sources of additional information ($6.85; 840 pp.). Order from: Superintendent of Documents, U.S. Government Printing Office, Washington, D.C. 20402.

Part Four

MORE TOOLS

22

JOBS FOR THE SEVENTIES AND EIGHTIES

No one can predict future labor market conditions in every industry and occupation with perfect accuracy. New inventions and technologies create some jobs while eliminating others. The ebb and flow of demand for a service or product will affect the number of workers needed to satisfy the demand. Changes in the size or age distribution of the population, their work attitudes, training programs and retirement programs—these and other forces affect the ratio of shortages or surpluses of candidates to openings in the job market.

The occupations listed below are a rough sampling of those fields that are expected to have a favorable outlook over the next years for an increase in available openings. But remember, this is *only* a *sampling*. There are many, many new burgeoning fields like mass transit, energy resources and conservation, parapsychology, nutrition, etc., about which not much is known, and statistics are short. But these fields may prove fertile for you, if you are interested and do the proper job market research.

For a more complete list of jobs in various industries and categories, write for the *Occupational Outlook Handbook*, Superintendent of Documents, U.S. Government Printing Office, Washington, D.C. 20402. The price is $6.85.

Accountants

Information about CPA's and aptitude tests given in many high schools, colleges, and public accounting firms may be obtained from:

American Institute of Certified Public Accountants
666 Fifth Avenue
New York, N.Y. 10019

Further information on specialized fields of accounting is available from:

National Association of
 Accountants
919 Third Ave.
New York, N.Y. 10022

National Society of Public
 Accountants
1717 Pennsylvania Ave., N.W.
Washington, D.C. 20006

Agricultural Engineers

For information write:

> American Society of Agricultural Engineers
> 2950 Niles Rd.
> St. Joseph, Mich. 49085

Automobile Service Advisors

Details on employment opportunities may be obtained from automobile dealers or repair shops, and locals of the unions (International Association of Machinists and Aerospace Workers; the Sheet Metal Workers' International Association; International Brotherhood of Teamsters, Chauffeurs, Warehousemen and Helpers of America). Information may also be obtained from:

Automotive Service Industry
 Association
230 North Michigan Ave.
Chicago, Ill. 60601

Automotive Service Councils of
 America, Inc.
4001 Warren Blvd.
Hillside, Ill. 60162

Banking Personnel

Local banks and state bankers' associations can furnish specific information about job opportunities in local banking institutions. General information about banking occupations and training opportunities is available from:

American Bankers Association
Bank Personnel Division
1120 Connecticut Ave., N.W.
Washington, D.C. 20036

National Association of Bank
 Women, Inc.
111 E. Wacker Dr.
Chicago, Ill. 60601

National Bankers Association
4310 Georgia Ave., N.W.
Washington, D.C. 20011

Information about career opportunities as a bank examiner can be obtained from:

Director of Personnel
Federal Deposit Insurance Corporation
550 17th St., N.W.
Washington, D.C. 20429

Ceramic Engineers

Information is available from:

American Ceramic Society
65 Ceramic Drive
Columbus, Ohio 43214

City Managers

Information is available from:

International City Management Association
1140 Connecticut Ave., N.W.
Washington, D.C. 20036

Commercial Artists

Information on employment opportunities in commercial art is available from:

National Art Education Association,
National Education Association
1201 16th St., N.W.
Washington, D.C. 20036

Computer Programmers

Details about the occupation of programmer are available from:

Data Processing Management
  Association
505 Busse Highway
Park Ridge, Ill. 60068

American Federation of
  Information Processing
  Societies
210 Summit Ave.
Montvale, N.J. 07645

For a list of reading materials on career opportunities in programming contact:

Association for Computing Machinery
1133 Avenue of the Americas
New York, N.Y. 10036

Construction Inspectors

Persons seeking information on a career as a state or local government construction inspector should contact their State Employment Service, their local building department, or:

National Conference of States
  on Building Codes
Building Research Division
National Bureau of Standards
Washington, D.C. 20234

International Conference of
  Building Officials
5360 Workman Mill Rd.
Whittier, Calif. 90601

Persons interested in a career as a construction inspector with the federal government can get information from:

Interagency Board of the U.S. Civil Service
  Examiners
1900 E. St., N.W.
Washington, D.C. 20415

Cosmetologists

For information about approved training schools and licensing requirements, write your State Board of Cosmetology. Additional facts about careers in beauty culture and state licensing requirements are available from:

National Beauty Career
  Center
3839 White Plains Rd.
Bronx, N.Y. 19467

National Hairdressers and
  Cosmetologists Association
3510 Olive St.
St. Louis, Mo. 63103

Journeymen Barbers International Union
4755 Kingsway Drive #320
Indianapolis, Ind. 46205

Credit Officials

General information about the field of consumer credit, including career opportunities, is available from:

The National Consumer Finance Association
1000 16th St., N.W.
Washington, D.C. 20036

Specific information about training programs available in consumer credit may be obtained from:

Society of Certified Consumer
   Credit Executives
7405 University Dr.
St. Louis, Mo. 63130

Credit Research Foundation
3000 Marcus Ave.
Lake Success, N.Y. 11040

Dental Hygienists

For information about approved schools and the educational requirements needed to enter this occupation, contact:

Division of Educational Services
American Dental Hygienists Association
211 East Chicago Ave.
Chicago, Ill. 60611

Other material on opportunities for dental hygienists is available from:

Division of Dental Health
Public Health Service
U.S. Department of Health, Education and Welfare
Washington, D.C. 20201

The Board of Dental Examiners in each state, or the National Board of Dental Examiners, 211 East Chicago Ave., Chicago, Ill. 60611, can supply information on licensing requirements.

Draftsmen

General information on careers for draftsmen may be obtained from:

American Institute for Design
   and Drafting
3119 Price Rd.
Bartlesville, Okla. 74003

American Federation of
   Technical Engineers
1126 16th St., N.W.
Washington, D.C. 20036

Electrical Engineers

Institute of Electrical and Electronic Engineers
345 East 47 St.
New York, N.Y. 10017

Exterminators

National Pest Control Association, Inc.
250 W. Jersey St.
Elizabeth, N.J. 07207

Floral Designers

Information about careers in floral design and addresses of schools offering courses in this field can be obtained from:

Society of American Florists
901 N. Washington St.
Alexandria, Va. 22314

Forestry Aides and Technicians

Information about a career in the federal government as a forestry aide is available from:

Forest Service
U.S. Department of Agriculture
Washington, D.C. 20250

For a list of schools recognized by the Society of American Foresters offering training in the field write to:

Society of American Foresters
1010 16th St., N.W.
Washington, D.C. 20036

Geologists

General information on career opportunities, training, and earnings for geologists is available from:

American Geological Institute
2201 M St., N.W.
Washington, D.C. 20037

For information on federal government careers contact:

Interagency Board of U.S. Civil Service
    Examiners
1900 E St., N.W.
Washington, D.C. 20415

Geophysicists

General information on career opportunities, training, and earnings for geophysicists is available from:

American Geophysical Union
1707 L St., N.W.
Washington, D.C. 20036

Society of Exploration
    Geophysicists
P.O. Box 3098
Tulsa, Okla. 74101

For information on federal government careers contact:

> Interagency Board of U.S. Civil Service Examiners
> 1900 E St., N.W.
> Washington, D.C. 20415

Health and Regulatory Inspectors

For facts about public administration inspector careers in the federal government, contact:

> Interagency Board of U.S. Civil Service Examiners
> 1900 E. St., N.W.
> Washington, D.C. 20415

Information about career opportunities as inspectors in state and local governments is available from the State Civil Service Commissions, usually located in each state capital, or from local government offices.

Home Economists

A list of schools granting degrees in home economics and additional information about home economics careers, the types of home economics majors offered in each school granting degrees in home economics, and graduate scholarships are available from:

> American Home Economics Association
> 2010 Massachusetts Ave., N.W.
> Washington, D.C. 20036

Hotel Managers and Assistants

Information on careers in hotel work may be obtained from:

> The Educational Institute of the American
>   Hotel and Motel Association
> 77 Kellogg Center
> Michigan State University
> East Lansing, Mich. 48823

For additional information on hotel training opportunities and a directory of schools and colleges offering courses and scholarships in the hotel field write:

> Council on Hotel, Restaurant,
>   and Institutional Education
> 1522 K St., N.W.
> Washington, D.C. 20005

Information on housekeeping in hotels is available from:

> National Executive Housekeepers Association, Inc.
> Business and Professional Building
> Callipolis, Ohio 45631

Instrument Repairmen

Instrument Society of
 America
400 Stanwix St.
Pittsburgh, Pa. 15222

Scientific Apparatus Makers
 Association
1140 Connecticut Ave., N.W.
Washington, D.C. 20036

Insurance Actuaries

For facts about actuarial opportunities and qualifications contact:

Casualty Actuarial Society
200 East 42 St.
New York, N.Y. 10017

Society of Actuaries
208 South LaSalle St.
Chicago, Ill. 60604

Landscape Architects

> American Society of Landscape Architecture, Inc.
> 1750 Old Meadow Rd.
> McLean, Va. 22101

For information on a career as a landscape architect in the Forest Service, write to:

> U.S. Department of Agriculture
> Forest Service
> Washington, D.C. 20250

Librarians

Information, particularly on accredited programs and scholarships or loans, may be obtained from:

> American Library Association
> 50 East Huron St.
> Chicago, Ill. 60611

For information on requirements of special librarians write to:

> Special Libraries Association
> 235 Park Ave. South
> New York, N.Y. 10003

Information on federal assistance for library training under the Higher Education Act of 1965 is available from:

Division of Library and Educational Facilities
Bureau of Libraries and Learning Resources
Office of Education
U.S. Department of Health, Education and Welfare
Washington, D.C. 20202

Those interested in a career in Federal Libraries should write to:

Secretariat Federal Library Committee
Room 310, Library of Congress
Washington, D.C. 20540

Facts about information science specialists may be obtained from:

American Society for Information Science
1140 Connecticut Ave., N.W.
Washington, D.C. 20036

Individual state library agencies can furnish information on scholarships available through their offices, on requirements for certification, and general information about career prospects in their regions. State boards of education can furnish information on certification requirements and job opportunities for school librarians.

Librarian Technical Assistants

For information on institutions offering programs for the training of library technical assistants, write:

Council of Library Technical Assistants
6800 South Wentworth Ave.
Chicago, Ill. 60621

Lithographic Operators

Details on apprenticeship and other training opportunities in lithographic occupations are available from local employers, such as newspapers and printing shops, local offices of the Graphic Arts International Union, or the local office of the State Employment Service. General information may be obtained from:

American Newspaper Publishers
Association
11600 Sunrise Valley Dr.
Reston, Va. 20041

The Graphic Arts International
Union
1900 L St., N.W.
Washington, D.C. 20036

Graphic Arts Technical
Foundation
4615 Forbes Ave.
Pittsburgh, Pa. 15213

International Printing Pressmen
and Assistants' Union of North
America
1730 Rhode Island Ave., N.W.
Washington, D.C. 20036

National Association of Photo-
  Lithographers
230 West 41 St.
New York, N.Y. 10036

Printing Industries of America
1730 North Lynn St.
Arlington, Va. 22201

Marketing Researchers

Information on careers in marketing research is available from:

American Marketing Association
230 North Michigan Ave.
Chicago, Ill. 60601

Mathematicians

There are several brochures that give facts about the field of mathematics, including career opportunities, professional training, and colleges and universities with degree programs. *Professional Training in Mathematics* is available for $0.25 from:

American Mathematical Society
P.O. Box 6248
Providence, R.I. 02904

Professional Opportunities in Mathematics ($0.35) and *Guide Book to Departments in the Mathematical Sciences* ($1.35) are provided by:

Mathematical Association of America
1225 Connecticut Ave., N.W.
Washington, D.C. 20036

For specific information on careers in applied mathematics and electronic computer work, contact:

Association for Computing
  Machinery
1133 Avenue of the Americas
New York, N.Y. 10036

Society for Industrial and
  Applied Mathematics
33 S. 17th St.
Philadelphia, Pa. 19103

Facts on careers in mathematical statistics are available from:

Institute of Mathematical Statistics
Department of Statistics
California State College at Hayward
Hayward, Calif. 94542

For federal government career information, contact any regional office of the U.S. Civil Service Commission, or:

> Interagency Board of U.S. Civil Service Examiners
> 1900 E St., N.W.
> Washington, D.C. 20415

Mechanics and Repairmen

Information about training in air-conditioning and refrigeration may be obtained from:

> Refrigeration Service Engineers Society
> 2720 DePlaines Ave.
> DePlaines, Ill. 60018

Information about training in oil heating systems may be obtained from:

> Education Department,
> National Oil Fuel Institute
> 60 East 42nd St.
> New York, N.Y. 10017

General information about gas burner mechanics may be obtained from:

> American Gas Association, Inc.
> 605 Third Ave.
> New York, N.Y. 10016.

Medical Assistants

General information on a career as a medical assistant and on the certification program is available from:

> American Association of Medical Assistants
> One East Wacker Drive, Suite 1510
> Chicago, Illinois 60601

> American Medical Technologists
> 710 Higgins Rd.
> Part Ridge, Ill. 60068

> Council on Medical Education
> American Medical Association
> 535 North Dearborn St.
> Chicago, Ill. 60610

Occupational Therapy Assistants

For information about work opportunities and programs offering training for occupational therapy assistants, contact:

> American Occupational Therapy Association
> 6000 Executive Blvd.
> Rockville, Md. 20852

Oceanographers

For information about careers in oceanography and about colleges and universities that offer training in marine science, contact:

> National Oceanic and Atmospheric Administration
> 6001 Executive Boulevard
> Rockville, Md. 20852
> Attention: AD 411

A booklet, *Training and Careers in Marine Science*, is available for $0.50 from:

> International Oceanographic Foundation
> 10 Rickenbacker Causeway
> Virginia Key, Miami, Fla. 33149

A booklet, *Oceanography Information Sources*, lists the names and addresses of industrial organizations involved in oceanography and publishers of oceanographic educational materials, journals, and periodicals. Copies may be purchased for $2.50 from:

> Printing and Publishing Office
> National Academy of Sciences
> 2101 Constitution Ave., N.W.
> Washington, D.C. 20418

Optical Mechanics

A list of schools offering courses for people who wish to become dispensing opticians or optical mechanics may be obtained from:

> Associated Opticians of America
> 1250 Connecticut Ave., N.W.
> Washington, D.C. 20036

General information about these occupations may be obtained from:

American Board of Opticianry
821 Eggert Rd
Buffalo, N.Y. 14226

Optical Wholesalers Association
6935 Wisconsin Ave.
Washington, D.C. 20015

Personnel Workers

General information on careers in personnel work may be obtained from:

American Society for Personnel Administration
19 Church St.
Berea, Ohio 44017

General information about government careers in personnel is available from:

International Personnel Management Association
1313 East 60th St.
Chicago, Ill. 60637

Psychologists

For general information on career opportunities, certification, or license requirements, and educational facilities and financial assistance for graduate students in psychology, contact:

American Psychological Association
1200 17th St., N.W.
Washington, D.C. 20036

Information on traineeships and fellowships is available from colleges and universities that have graduate psychology departments.

Radio and TV Announcers

General career information may be obtained from:

National Association of
Broadcasters
1771 N St., N.W.
Washington, D.C. 20036

Corporation for Public
Broadcasting
888 16th St., N.W.
Washington, D.C. 20006

Sanitarians

Information about careers as sanitarians is available from the following associations:

American Public Health
Association
1015 18th St., N.W.
Washington, D.C. 20036

International Association of
Milk, Food, and
Environmental Sanitarians
Blue Ridge Rd., P.O. Box 437
Shelbyville, Ind. 46176

National Environmental Health Association
1600 Pennsylvania St.
Denver, Colo. 80203

Secretaries

For information on careers in secretarial work write:

National Secretaries Association
616 East 63rd Street
Kansas City, Mo. 64110

Additional information on careers in secretarial work and a directory of business schools is available from:

United Business Schools Association
1730 M St., N.W.
Washington, D.C. 20036

For information about shorthand reporting contact:

National Shorthand Reporters Association
25 West Main St.
Madison, Wis. 53703

Soil Conservationists

Information on employment as a soil conservationist may be obtained from:

Employment Division
Office of Personnel
U.S. Department of Agriculture
Washington, D.C. 20250

Surveyors

Information about training and career opportunities in surveying is available from:

American Congress on Surveying and Mapping
Woodward Building
733 15th St., N.W.
Washington, D.C. 20005

General information on careers in photogrammetry is available from:

American Society of Photogrammetry
150 North Virginia Ave.
Falls Church, Va. 22046

Technical Writers

For information about careers in technical writing, contact:

Society for Technical Communications, Inc.
Suite 421, 1010 Vermont Ave., N.W.
Washington, D.C. 20005

Urban Planners

Facts about careers in planning and a list of schools offering training are available from:

American Institute of
Planners
917 15th St., N.W.
Washington, D.C. 20005

American Society of Planning
Officials
1313 East 60th St.
Chicago, Ill. 60637

Veterinarians

A pamphlet entitled *Today's Veterinarian* presents information on veterinary medicine as a career, as well as a list of colleges of veterinary medicine. A free copy may be obtained by submitting a request, together with a self-addressed stamped business size envelope, to:

American Veterinary Medical Association
600 South Michigan Ave.
Chicago, Ill. 60605

Information on opportunities for veterinarians in the U.S. Department of Agriculture is available from:

Agricultural Research Service
U.S. Department of Agriculture
Hyattsville, Md. 20782

Agricultural Marketing Service
Personnel Division
12th & Independence Ave., S.W.
Washington, D.C. 20250

Animal and Plant Health
  Inspection Service
Personnel Division
12th & Independence Ave., S.W.
Washington, D.C. 20250

U.S. Civil Service

For information about career opportunities working for the federal government in any of a variety of fields, contact your local office of the U.S. Civil Service Commission, or:

U.S. Civil Service Commission
Washington, D.C. 20415

23

DIRECTORY REFERENCES

The information explosion is as typically American as is our technological orientation. We have more information available on more subjects, including business information, than any other country in the world. As a result there are hundreds of different kinds of business directories that can help facilitate and ultimately make successful the outcome of your job campaign.

The Super Directories

Encyclopedia of Business Information Sources
Gale Research, Book Tower, Detroit, Mich., 48226
A detailed listing of business oriented source books, periodicals, organizations, directories, handbooks, bibliographies, and other sources of information on all major business topics.

Guide to American Directories
B. Klein & Company, 11 Third St., Rye, N.Y. 10050
This directory describes 3300 directories in approximately 400 topic categories.

The Standard Periodical Directory
Oxbridge Publishing Company, Inc., 150 East 52nd St. New York, N.Y. 10022
Describes 50,000 periodicals and directories in over 200 subjects.

Encyclopedia of Associations
Gale Research, Book Tower, Detroit, Mich. 48226
Lists over 1200 different associations in virtually every field.

Standard Rate and Data Business Publications Directory
Standard Rate and Data Service, 5201 Old Orchard Rd., Skokie, Ill. 60076
Names and addresses of the trade publications in thousands of fields listed by topic.

Geographical Index
National Register Publishing Co., 5201 Old Orchard Rd., Skokie, Ill. 60076.
Lists cities, towns, etc., and companies located within geographic areas.

General Directories:

American Men of Science
R. R. Bowker Company, 1180 Ave. of the Americas, New York, N.Y. 10036

Dun & Bradstreet Million Dollar Directory
Dun & Bradstreet, 99 Church St., New York, 10007
Lists 25,000 businesses with net worth over $1 million, classified by product and location, contains names of executives

Dun & Bradstreet Middle Market Directory
Dun & Bradstreet, 99 Church Street, New York, N.Y. 10007
Lists 18,000 companies with net worth of $500,000 to $1 million. Classified by industry & location with names of owners.

Poor's Register of Corporations Directors & Executives
Standard & Poors Subsidiary of McGraw-Hill, 345 Hudson St., New York, N.Y. 10014
Lists 260,000 key executives in 32,000 leading companies cross referenced by product and company location. Includes home address of executive plus title and duties.

Standard Directory of Advertisers
National Register Publishing Co., 5201 Old Orchard Rd., Skokie, Ill. 60076.
Contains a listing of 50 basic industries. Within each industry, companies are listed alphabetically. Also lists corporate officers from the top down to the purchasing agent, with name, address, and telephone number.

Thomas' Register
Thomas Publishing Co., 461 Eighth Avenue, New York, N.Y. 10001
Lists 100,000 manufacturers by product and location. All U.S. Chambers of Commerce.

Who's Who in Commerce & Industry
Marquis Who's Who, 210 E. Ohio St., Chicago, Ill. 60611

All occupational directories, such as those appropriate for advertising, electronics, drugs, apparel, etc., can be extrapolated from the super directories such as the *Guide to American Directories*.

Finally, each of the 50 states has a major state directory of trade and industry within its borders. You can usually purchase these for under $10.00. For your own state, contact your local Chamber of Commerce. For the Directory of another state, write to the State Chamber of Commerce Department, Chamber of Commerce of the U.S.A., 1615 H Street, N.W. Washington, D.C. 20006.

Most major cities have library networks with one or more branches that specialize in business. These branches, as well as the libraries of business schools, will often carry some of these directories. The library of your local Chamber of Commerce may also carry one or more of these directories. In addition, advertising agencies, trade associations and professional societies, brokerage houses, and government agencies may also provide these reference materials. Many libraries also have the *Directory of Special Libraries and Information Centers*. There you can find out information about 13,000 special libraries operated by businesses, government, educational institutions, etc. Your local librarian may be able to arrange permission for you to visit some not usually open to the public.

If ultimately, you decide to buy a directory, the price range can be anywhere from $20.00 to over $100.00. Write and ask.

A final word. One of the greatest, free directories of employers available is the Yellow Pages. It's a mine of information. And, if you are considering another city, the telephone company will gladly supply you with the Yellow Pages for that city.

24

A CAREER LIBRARY

The following suggested bibliography lists books and materials that might be found in branch libraries that specialize in business, as well as the libraries of any undergraduate or graduate school of business. One of the most valuable functions a library can perform is that of helping people find the jobs they want. Don't be shy about asking a library to order a particular book or directory. If a book or directory is requested often enough, a library may decide to purchase it.

General Career Information

SRA Occupational Briefs
Science Research Associates, Inc.
259 E. Erie Street
Chicago, Ill. ($0.60 each)
Individual briefs; Occupational Exploration Kit. These briefs are illustrated, four pages long, and contain information on the major job areas. Each brief includes a description of opportunities, future outlook, advantages, disadvantages, and selected references for further reading. Seventy briefs are revised each year.

Occupational Outlook Handbook
Superintendent of Documents
Government Printing Office
Washington, D.C. ($6.85)
Brief descriptions of 500 occupations and 25 major industries.

Occupational Outlook for College Graduates
Superintendent of Documents
U.S. Government Printing Office
Washington, D.C. ($2.95).

This book is a guide to employment opportunities in a broad range of professional and related occupations for which a college education is either required, becoming increasingly necessary, or is the usual educational background for employment.

B'nai B'rith Occupational Brief Series
B'nai B'rith Vocational Service
1640 Rhode Island Avenue, N.W.
Washington, D.C. ($0.35 each)
These briefs average four to seven pages in length. They are written for high school seniors and contain information on outlook, duties, preparation and entry qualifications, earnings and advancement, physical requirements, working conditions, advantages and disadvantages, and sources of further information. These briefs are frequently revised.

Vocational Guidance Manuals, Inc.
235 E. 45th Street
New York, N.Y. ($1.95 each)
Vocational Guidance Manuals—45 manuals. Average length: 113 pages. Presents a comprehensive picture of vocations covered. About half of the space in each manual is devoted to technical information of getting started and steps to advancement. The remaining half contains descriptions of the type of work, requirements, educational preparations, opportunities and qualifications for success.

Career Planning—General

Brown, Newell. *After College, Junior College, Military Service, What?*
Grosset & Dunlap, New York, N.Y. 1971.
A description of fields of work and a general discussion of career planning techniques. $2.95.

Denues, Celia. *Career Perspective: Your Choice of Work.*
Charles A. Jones Publishing Co., Worthington, Ohio, 1972. ($4.50)

Non-Technical Entry Jobs Open to the Liberal Arts College Graduate.
Published by Eastern College Personnel Officers. (Projects Committee)
A compendium of descriptions of jobs typically filled by liberal arts college graduates. To obtain copies, contact Miss Drue Matthews, Director, Vocational Planning & Placement, Mount Holyoke College, South Hadley, Mass. ($1.00)

Peterson, Clarence E. *Careers for College Graduates.*
Barnes & Noble, New York, N.Y. 1968.
A description of approximately 80 kinds of work with general information about obtaining a job. ($2.25)

Career Planning for Women

For information concerning a variety of career opportunities for women, write to CATALYST, 14 East 60th Street, New York, N.Y. 10022.

Miscellaneous Career Information

The College Placement Annual.
  College Placement Annual, P.O. Box 2263, Bethlehem, Pa. 18001 ($5.00)
    Lists thousands of employers seeking college graduates in all fields.
Lovejoy's Career and Vocational School Guide
  Simon & Schuster, 630 Fifth Avenue, New York, N.Y. ($7.50)
Over 2,000 Free Publications: Yours for the Asking. Frederick J. O'Hara (ed.)
  The New American Library, Inc., P.O. Box 999, Bergenfield, N.J. 07621. 1968. ($0.95)
    Free or inexpensive books selected from unclassified Federal Documents. They are listed under the department from which they are available. Helpful.
Psychology of Careers. Donald Super
  Harper & Row, 10 East 53rd Street, New York, N.Y.. 10022. 1957. ($5.75)
    Dynamics of vocational development, how this process is affected by aptitudes, interests, personality, family, economics, and chance.
Sources of Career Information in Scientific Fields
  Manufacturing Chemists' Association, 1825 Connecticut Avenue, N.W., Washington, D.C. 20009 (free).
    Resource list for occupational information in major scientific fields. Listings are limited to free or inexpensively priced materials.
Sources of Engineering Career Information.
  Engineering Manpower Commission of Engineers Joint Council, 345 E. 47th Street, New York, N.Y. 10017. (Free)
    Resource list of career data in the engineering field. General information about job opportunities and salary is included.
Sources of Occupational Information.
  Randolph Turner (ed.) Division of Guidance and Testing, State Dept. of Education, 751 Northwest Blvd., Columbus, Ohio, 43212. ($1.00)
    Listed are educational and career literature available from the

U.S. government, state governments, armed forces, commercial sources, and organizations concerned with careers in their specialty areas.

A *"Starter" File of Free Occupational Literature.*

Irving Eisen and Leonard H. Goodman, B'nai B'rith Vocational Service, 1640 Rhode Island Ave., N.W., Washington, D.C. 20036. 1970. ($1.25)

The materials listed here can be used to organize a cost-free, selective occupational library. The selection was based on the career interests and needs of counselees between the ages of 15–20 holding middle class values and oriented toward nonrural life. For each of the 103 careers, the *Dictionary of Occupational Titles'* code number, pamphlet title, year of publication, and name and address of publishing organization are included. These 103 pamphlets can be used to initially explore approximately 500 careers. In the index, the occupational titles of these related careers are cross-referenced with the 103 job titles listed in the main body of the paper.

25

EMPLOYMENT AGENCY REFERENCES

The *National Employment Association*, 2000 K Street, N.W., Washington, D.C. 20006, is the trade group representing about 2500 individual agencies, maintaining standards of ethical performance, and attempting to promote "professionalism." They will send you a free copy of their membership directory, listing agencies by location, name, and phone number. This directory includes the names of owners and managers, which will help you in reaching the top person in the agency.

There is no guarantee that the NEA member in a given area is the best qualified agency in your particular job field. This information can only be obtained through referral from employers, associations, and others with direct experience in the field. However, the fact that the agency is an NEA member indicates that they are concerned with their professional and ethical image.

If you experience unethical, or unfair treatment from any NEA member you may write to the national office, or to the head of your state association (the names and addresses of state association leaders are in the front of the NEA member directory).

Employment Agency Networks

There are several organizations of independent employment agencies which exist to provide a more effective level of applicant service and increase their own levels of productivity and profits.

Besides setting up standardized member operating and training procedures, their most important function is to provide a national and sometimes international exchange of applicant and job order information in a formal, mechanized way. This service is highly valuable to an applicant who is willing to consider opportunities in other parts of the country. It is also an additional source of income for the "corresponding" agency who finds the applicant. The placement fee (essentially paid by the employer) is split with the agency that makes the placement.

Three such agency networks are listed below:

1. *National Personnel Consultants*

   This organization has been in operation since 1932. They have 71 select offices in the United States and Canada, and handle all salaried occupational areas. To avail yourself of their service simply send a resume, with salary information to National Personnel Consultants, Inc., 1500 Chestnut Street, Philadelphia, Pa. 19102.

2. *Placement Services, Ltd.*

   This is a high quality interarea referral service, which uses a sophisticated computer retrieval system to coordinate applicant matching in major cities across the United States. They provide top quality professional service (all employer-paid fee) to job seekers in technical and administrative fields, with a strong emphasis in chemical, electronic, industrial, and power engineering.

   Send resume with salary requirements to Mr. George Sadek, Placement Services, Ltd., 635 Madison Avenue, New York, N.Y. 10022.

3. *National Personnel Associates*

   This is an extraordinarily fine service for applicants interested in relocating to any area of the United States, Canada, Europe and Asia.

   With its strong emphasis on attracting the most professional agencies in cities throughout the world (primarily in the United States), the NPA network has grown to 200 independent offices which exchange data on job orders and applicants in a fast, reliable manner. This gives the applicant the maximum exposure to potential job targets while retaining his or her confidentiality.

   NPA offices have a fine professional reputation, and applicants' complaints are closely reviewed. To use the services of NPA in your job search, simply look up the NPA listing in your local Yellow Pages. *You need only deal with one local office.* They will determine, with you, what other areas to investigate for job situations. If there is no office in your locality or you are in a highly specialized field or if you have questions concerning the service, you may call the NPA toll-free Job Line (800) 253-2578, and they will give you the name of the closest branch.

   These professionally run offices are highly recommended for both interarea referral, and for local area jobs. For additional information write to the Executive Director, National Personnel Associates, Suite 300D, Waters Building, Grand Rapids, Mich. 49502, tel. (616) 459-5861.